0607404

ZEV GOLAN

FREE JERUSALEM

T: E PALESTINE POLICE FORCE

REWARDS

REWARDS, as set out below, will be paid by the Government of Palestine for information leading to the apprehension of any of the persons named hereunder who are members of the organisation responsible for the explosion which occurred at No. 8 Yael Street, Tel Aviv, on Tuesday, January 20th, 1942.

Abrahami Ben Mordechai STERN, alias Yair.
Reward: £P.1,000

Yacov POLANI alias Poliyacof
Reward: £P.400

Nahman SHULMAN
Reward: £P.200

Zeroni BENYAMIN alias Ben Zvi, alias Yavniel, alias Avni, alias Kerner.
Reward: £P.200

Hanoch STRELITZ
Reward: £P.200

Aharon ZUKERMAN alias Asch, alias Bairvl
Reward: £P.100

and Abraham MAERI — Reward: £P.100

Information can be passed at any time to any Police Station

Heroes, Heroines and Rogues
Who Created the State of Israel

DEVORA
PUBLISHING

FREE JERUSALEM
Published by Devora Publishing Company

Text Copyright © 2003 by Zev Golan
Cover Illustration: Avi Katz
Book Design: Benjie Herskowitz

Photographs appearing on pages 282-283 are courtesy of the
Jabotinsky Institute.

ISBN: 1-930143-54-0

Email: pitspop@netvision.net.il
Web Site: www.devorapublishing.com

Printed in Israel

Esther stood at the table. By the candlelight she saw before her a Bible, a Jewish national flag and a gun. She raised her right hand and recited:

"I hereby swear to be a loyal soldier of the Irgun Zvai Leumi which protects our national honor, life and property, and assists in the revival of the whole nation in the land of its Fathers."

She was escorted from the room. Esther was only 17, but now she was a member of the Underground army fighting for Jewish independence...

In memory of my grandparents

Harry and Rose Herman
Philip and Josephine Perlmutter

Contents

"Niv Halochem" (Combatant's Voice) published by Herut

Sources

Dusty editions of memoirs with titles such as *Days Red With Blood*, *Four Paces from Death*, and *The Conquest of Acre Fortress* can still be found in used-book stores in Israel. In these volumes – many worm-eaten, some moldy, most unread – and in the yellowed newspapers of the National Library in Jerusalem, the archives of the Jabotinsky Institute, and the Bet Yair Museum in Tel Aviv, is the history of modern Israel. The events were news 60, 70, or 80 years ago and remain vivid on these pages, for those who search them out.

The English bibliography of the early days of modern Israel is not long. Menahem Begin in *The Revolt*, Itzhak Gurion in the long-out-of-print *Triumph on the Gallows*, Gerald Frank in *The Deed*, Samuel Katz in *Days of Fire* and J. Bowyer Bell in *Terror Out of Zion* tell of the fighting '40s. But little has been written of the first Hebrew underground movements of the 1920s and 1930s, the earliest battles in a war that in many respects has not yet ended.

Almost nothing that has been written of the early days of modern Canaan attains the force of the memories of the protagonists and the honesty of the day-by-day history recorded in the old newspapers. Most of the tales in this book have been drawn from interviews with the "soldiers without uniforms," those who swore allegiance to the Underground on Bibles and guns in dark rooms, the conspirators and pioneers who helped lay the foundation for a future Jewish army and state, supplemented by these old papers and books. Geula Cohen's *An Orange Between Hearts* was the source for some of the information regarding the last night of Barazani and Feinstein, Abraham Stern's prison dialogue about World War Two was taken from Haim Dviri's *Unforgettable Spring Day*, and the late Dr. Israel Eldad is to be thanked for permission to reprint his account of Warsaw on the brink of war, from *Maaser Rishon*. The secret British police dossiers on Abba Ahimeir, David Raziel and Joshua Cohen were left behind when the British left the country and are now in the Hagana Archive in Tel Aviv.

I am especially indebted to the late Rabbi Moshe Segal – Birion, Irgunist, Hasmonean and Fighter for the Freedom of Israel (in many respects, the quintessential revolutionary) – and the late constable and Betari Yehezkel Altman for their time and cooperation, as well as to the late Commanders Abraham Tehomi, Moshe Rosenberg and Nissim Cohen of the Irgun and Dr. Eldad and, wishing him good health, Yitzhak Shamir of the Stern Group. Also to Haim Dviri, Israel Haviv (brother of the hanged Avshalom), "Yoshke" Eliav, Moshe Svorai, David Begin, Shimon Barmatz, Defender of Jerusalem Ben Zion Homsky, Jacob Kotik, Joseph and Bat-Zion Kremin, Aharon Heichman and another dozen or so founders and members of the early underground armies that had the gall to declare war on the British Empire and defend Jewish lives against Arab marauders. These men and women, those of whom are still alive now in their eighties and nineties, living the length and breadth of the state they helped create, were the inspiration and source material for this book.

Thanks are also due Amira Stern, Irena Berdan, Batsheva Ortenberg, the late Pesach Gani and Tanya Gruss of the Jabotinsky Institute in Tel Aviv, and Orly Levy of the Hagana Archive.

I admiringly acknowledge the debt owed to Walter Noble Burns whose joy in history and linguistic playfulness provided the courage to begin this work. I have lovingly borrowed his approach and language and trust he would be flattered.

Introduction

WEST OF THE JORDAN

*The Lord your God will return and gather you from among
the nations...and bring you to the land of your fathers'
inheritance.*   Deut. 30:3-5

*How did I not board a boat headed for your shores, to be
brother to your suffering...I admit, you were stronger than I
was in Exile, you dreamt before I did the fiery dream that
burned: Eastward! and you went. Now I am among you, this
nation that dreams of seas, this kingdom of barefoot workers
on sand dunes and rocks...and the meaning of the dream is
both bitter and wondrous: ripped clothing, no socks, no roof,
blood on the sand...Hallelujah!*
Uri Zvi Greenberg, "The Earthly Jerusalem"

The infamous Mufti el Husseini and his gangs were in their heyday. Throughout the sparsely settled land of Israel, from Safed to
Hebron, the Arab attackers were harassing the mostly defenseless Jewish settlers in a war of ambush and pogrom. The yelping marauders
slipped through the hills and hid on the trails, they gathered in cities
and marched on murderous rampages. A Jewish car was ambushed on

a deserted road; a family was massacred in its home; watchmen were stabbed in the fields. Returning to their haunts, the "terrorists" and less glorious "killers" first took food, furniture, money. Often they proved themselves adept at raping or dismembering their victims. Such were the "battles" fought by Arab nationalists. The worst pogroms were those of 1920, 1921, 1929 and 1936-39. In 1920, the Arabs called it a "holiday"; in 1929, a "disturbance"; in 1936-39, an "uprising." To the dead Jews, it seemed more like cold-blooded murder.

And the law west of the Jordan River? The "law" was in the hands of the British, for England had captured Eretz Israel (the Land of Israel) from the Turks in 1917. The year 1948 was still distant future; not since the Jewish state of two thousand years earlier had the Land of Israel seen an independent state with its own government. Conquerors had come and gone but none had established self-government in this holy territory. In 1917, the British forces – aided by the Jewish NILI underground network and the Jewish Legion army – defeated the armies of Turkey and took control of the hills and deserts of the Land, promising to help the Jewish people return to its ancient home to re-create the Jewish state. But politics and anti-semitism soon took the upper hand, and the British proved perfidious in their promise to the Jews. They limited Jewish immigration in the years preceding World War Two when the Jews most desperately needed a haven; they arrested German Jews and deported them to Germany; they made the purchase of land by Jews illegal; they prohibited Jews from bearing arms though Arab killers lurked along the roads and in the markets; they even prohibited Jews from praying too loudly at the sacred Western Wall in Jerusalem. The official Jewish leaders could not believe, refused to believe, that England was turning its back and they continued for far too long to call England a friend.

The Arabs, on the other hand, had eyes and they saw. The proof? The slogan they chanted as they wiped out Jewish villages and homes was "The government is with us!" And indeed, the British soldiers stood by and watched the killing, afterwards arresting any Jews who dared defend themselves.

General Allenby reviewing an honor guard outside Jaffa Gate to Jerusalem's Old City, December 11, 1917 (Israel Government Press Office photo by Eric Matson)

Into this half-desolate wilderness country of frequent death came the then unknown future heroes Segal, Altman, Stern, Gruner. They came from Poland, Russia, Hungary, Yemen; some were born in the holy cities of Israel: Jerusalem, Hebron, Safed. They escaped massacres by Ukrainian nationalists and Russian pogromists. They traveled the seas in rickety boats and stole across borders in darkest nights. They lost family in encounters with border guards, left behind friends in European prisons, and found their way to the Promised Land with – or without – immigration papers issued by the British authorities. They burned with a desire to be free in a Jewish country. And they trained themselves and others to fight for independence.

These first pioneers of independence were Homsky, who went to jail for defending the Jews of Jerusalem in 1920; Rosenberg, who taught in a school training future Jewish soldiers; Segal, who was first to defy the laws of the British; Altman, who hit back at Arabs; Ahimeir, who organized the first Underground; Stern, who was shot by the British while planning the bombings of British installations. These were the people who dreamed of a Kingdom of Israel in Zion, and for future generations, their stories will be signals, their names passwords on the road to that Kingdom.

The Ingathering

Eastward across the dusty trail from Jaffa port, dolorous hills combined haphazardly to form a lackluster skyline. These hills had been deserted since the destruction of the Jewish state almost two thousand years earlier. Two or three way stations marked the path to holy Jerusalem. Hardly hostels, these stations were make-do shelter for the few weary travelers who had passed this way in centuries past. One or two of the hills revealed hints of concealed apertures, shadowy caves worthy of exploration, gorges once crossed – at least in the mind of an imaginative pilgrim – by Jewish rebels harassing the soldiers of the ancient Roman Empire. Sheep meandered across these hills, shepherds slept on them, nomads passed by, and British soldiers didn't give them a second thought. Few suspected that these hills were not only repositories of colorful memories but were also ready to burst with sacred dreams. For centuries these dreams lay dormant, undisturbed by men determined to wake a nation from its slumber. The clock had inched forward, calendar pages had peeled off, but these men had not yet arrived. When the hour was right, the hills knew – though shepherds and sheep and soldiers did not – the glance of one man would be enough to shake the hills and bring the dreams to life. One man whose heart carried these same dreams and whose arteries pulsed to their beat, the beat of the hills...

And now they were coming. Uri Zvi Greenberg saw the hills and sang of them in Hebrew verse unequalled since the days of the Biblical prophets. Jewish youth in Poland, Russia and America read Greenberg and even as they walked the streets of Warsaw and Odessa and New York they saw these hills on the road ahead. Altman saw them and volunteered to police them. Segal saw them and thought to himself as he wound his way to Jerusalem: They undoubtedly hear my heart beating, and it undoubtedly reminds them of the marching armies of Bar Kochba in revolt against the mighty Roman oppressors.

Segal's eyes caught the gleam of the precious treasure ensconced in the hills and valleys and dried riverbeds and thirsty trees and trodden paths; Segal's eyes took in the incongruity of British soldiers on Jewish land and roadblocks erected to disarm Jews while murderous Arabs slithered from one ambush to another, and in Segal's mind the dream already leapt from the mountains and danced before him. Two Hebrew words pulled Segal and so many others forward towards this unknown land of danger and opportunity, two words that Segal's blue eyes saw written across the wadis and foothills: *Medina Yehudit.* A Jewish state.

Segal climbed the winding road towards Jerusalem.

Chapter 1

The Roaring Twenties

From the pit of dust and decay...will arise a race proud, generous and fierce.　　　　　Zev Jabotinsky, "Shir Betar"

Jerusalem

Jerusalem is unique among the romantic cities of yore. According to legend, nine-tenths of the world's beauty rests in Jerusalem. Yet Jerusalem is a city peopled by humans, with an equal measure of human greatness and frailty. It has its saints but also its sinners, its builders and its would-be destroyers. It is a holy city on a mountaintop in the middle of desert country. It is the city of peace, whose streets are torn by strife.

It was in 1920 the Jerusalem of the Wailing Wall, the retaining wall of the sacred Biblical Mount Moriah, but also a city of Turkish brothels. It was home to the Jewish seminary of the mystic Chief Rabbi of Eretz Israel, Abraham Isaac Kook, but also to the Mufti el Husseini, who would one day become an ally of Hitler. It contained Nachmanides' thirteenth-century synagogue and Britain's torture dungeon in the Criminal Investigation Department (CID). It was once the site of a twenty-story Jewish Temple plated in gold, and now the site of the Moslem Dome of the Rock marking the Temple area. For two millennia it lay abandoned to poverty and filth but now glory was calling.

On February 27, 1920, one thousand excited Arabs marched through Jerusalem's streets, denouncing the city's Jewish population. On March 7, in Damascus, Feisal was crowned King of Syria and Eretz Israel. The British deputy governor of Jerusalem knew what was in store and took what he called "proper measures": Since he was unable or unwilling to challenge the Arabs, he ordered the city's Jews to remain docile. They were not to offend the Arabs, not to sing Jewish songs, not under any circumstances to raise Jewish flags or banners. The following day, three thousand Arabs led by Jerusalem's mayor Musa Kasim Pasha charged through the city chanting *Itbach el Yahud*, "Death to the Jews." One of the witnesses to these unruly "demonstrations" was Vladimir Zev Jabotinsky.

Jabotinsky was then almost forty years old. He was well known and respected, a gifted linguist, orator, poet and playwright, but also a decorated soldier and a master diplomat. Above all he was a Zionist, arguably the most charismatic Zionist leader since Theodor Herzl, the founder of modern political Zionism.

Jabotinsky had studied law in Rome, simultaneously serving as correspondent for Russian newspapers under the pen name "Altalena." In 1909 Constantinople, he was editing four publications in three languages – Ladino, French and Hebrew. Jabotinsky spoke eighteen languages, and when once challenged on a lark spent a night studying and by morning spoke nineteen. He translated the Hebrew national poet Haim Nahman Bialik into Russian, Edgar Alan Poe and Dante into Hebrew. When he was 21, the Odessa Municipal Theater produced a play he wrote. The next year they produced another.

He organized self-defense units in Odessa, he fought for and won British approval to establish the Jewish Legion of World War One – in which he enlisted, serving as a lieutenant in the 38th Battalion of Royal Fusiliers. He was in the first company to cross the Jordan River westward in the British conquest of the Holy Land.

15

Vladimir Jabotinsky in the Jewish Legion (Jabotinsky Institute photo)

In 1919, some thirty years before the creation of Israel, addressing members of the Jewish Legion as he was being demobilized, he said: "Far away, in your homes, you will one day read glorious news of a free Jewish life in a free Jewish country: of factories and universities, of farms and theaters, perhaps of M.P.s and ministers. Then you will lose yourself in thought – and then will come to your mind a picture of the Jordan Valley, of the desert at Rafa, of the hills of Ephraim, and of Abu

Ein. Then you shall stand up, walk to the mirror, and look at yourself proudly in the face. Jump to attention and salute yourself – for it is you who have made it."

Jabotinsky was an idealist, a dreamer. One of Jabotinsky's secretaries, Rachel Schechtman, remembers, "He was humble and would never impose on anyone. But anyone who heard him argue could only agree. People loved him or hated him. He acted like a statesman though he did not yet have a state."

Yet, Mrs. Schechtman recalls, though the incoming mail was voluminous, Jabotinsky insisted on responding by hand; he considered typewriters too "impersonal." Finally, after much argument, Jabotinsky was persuaded to dictate his correspondence. At night, he would often sneak into the office and discard the typed letters after writing them out by hand.

Jabotinsky was not a religiously observant man, but every year on the anniversary of his father's death, wherever he was, he found a synagogue, joined the prayer services and recited the memorial Kaddish prayer.

In Vilna once, a promoter sold more tickets to a Jabotinsky speech than his hall had seats. The members of Jabotinsky's youth organization, Betar, were left out in the cold. Jabotinsky asked them to wait. At 1:00 A.M., he finished his speech, cleared the auditorium, invited his young fans in and over the next two hours repeated the entire oration.

In 1925, he founded the World Union of Zionist-Revisionists. In 1935, he founded the New Zionist Organization – representing 713,000 members. He was Supreme Commander of the Irgun Underground till his death in 1940.

In 1931, the Seventeenth Zionist Congress refused to accept Jabotinsky's proposal to define the aim of Zionism as "the establishment of the Jewish state." In 1932, Jabotinsky endorsed and gave the impetus for mass illegal immigration to Eretz Israel, suggesting that the youth adopt stealing the borders of the homeland as the Jewish "national sport." To him, it was far more important to get Jews out of Europe than to obey British immigration quotas. In 1937, he was jeered by the socialist Zionist leadership when calling for the evacuation of millions of European Jews to Eretz Israel.

When Ychezkel Altman was sentenced to death, Jabotinsky intervened with the Queen of Holland who secured a pardon from the King of England. When Menahem Begin was arrested in Poland, Jabotinsky convinced Count Lubiensky to have him freed as a special favor.

In 1938, in Warsaw, on the Jewish memorial day marking the anniversary of the destruction of both the First and Second Temples, Jabotinsky solemnly intoned, in the spirit of the Old Testament Jeremiah: "I continue to warn you incessantly that a catastrophe is coming closer. I have become gray and old in these years, my heart bleeds that you, dear brothers and sisters, do not see the volcano which will soon begin to spit its all-consuming lava...If you do believe me, then listen to me in this eleventh hour: In the name of God, let any one of you save himself as long as there is still time. And time there is very little of.

"Whoever of you will escape from the catastrophe, he or she will live to see the exalted moment of...the rebirth and rise of a Jewish state. I don't know if I will be privileged to see it; my son will. I believe in this as I am sure that tomorrow morning the sun will rise."

But these events still lay in Jabotinsky's future. Now, in the spring of 1920, Jabotinsky stood and watched thousands of Arabs chanting *Itbach el Yahud*.

* * *

Every spring, Jewish communities celebrate Purim. Purim commemorates a victory of Persian Jews, led by Queen Esther and her cousin Mordechai, over the evil Haman some twenty-five hundred years ago. Children don colorful costumes, Jewish neighborhoods assume the air of Rio de Janeiro at carnival time, and so many gifts of food are sent back and forth between families and friends that only the most stalwart succeed in consuming the cakes, pastries, wine and preserves before the holiday of Passover arrives a month later. The Purim holiday of 1920 was celebrated in mourning and trepidation.

Three days earlier, on March 1, in the verdant mountains of the Galilee, Fort Tel Hai had fallen.

Tel Hai may well be called a Jewish Alamo; in which case, Joseph Trumpeldor was the Jewish Davy Crockett. Tel Hai held on for two and a half months though surrounded by Arabs bent on razing it to the ground. Urgent messages were sent to Jerusalem in the days and hours before communications were severed, begging for reinforcements but boldly declaring that they would under no circumstances surrender. If reinforcements, ammunition and moral support failed to arrive, they swore, they would know how to fight to the last man's last breath.

Trumpeldor had established the Jewish Legion of World War One together with Jabotinsky and was no stranger to battle. He completed dental school in 1902, but was immediately drafted into his native Russian army. When war broke out with the Japanese, he was dispatched to an East Siberian front – at his own request. The amputation of his left arm in the Battle of Port Arthur failed to dampen Trumpeldor's ardor. He successfully sought to remain with his unit in combat, spent a year in a Japanese prisoner of war camp, and was awarded his officer's stripes upon his release. The Tsar awarded Trumpeldor the Cross of St. George. Trumpeldor wore four of the medals. He was so decorated for heroism that his anti-semitic commanding officer refused to believe he was Jewish, noting that "no Jew could be so brave."

In 1912, aged 32, he arrived in Israel with dreams of a farm; but the guns of August were already darkening the European horizon. When his and Jabotinsky's agitation for a Jewish Legion bore fruit he enlisted in the Zion Mule Corps and served in Gallipoli. In December 1919, back in the Upper Galilee with all this military experience under his belt, he assumed command of the defense of Tel Hai.

Within the month, nearby Metulla and Hamara were abandoned by haggard Jewish settlers far outnumbered by the Arabs. The three dozen defenders of Tel Hai stood fast, hoping against all hope that reinforcements would indeed arrive, ever conscious that should even

Joseph Trumpeldor during World War I (Jabotinsky Institute photo)

hundreds of Jews buttress the fort, they would not yet be enough to ward off the thousands arrayed against Tel Hai.

At a meeting of the Zionist leadership in Jerusalem, Jabotinsky was the sole speaker to plead that the precariousness of the fort's situation made urgent evacuation of its defenders the only plausible solution. The establishment leaders countered that national honor required remaining in position and that one never knows when an admittedly unknown element will tilt the military balance in one's favor, even if it be at the very last moment. The leadership voted to send reinforcements, supplies and a commission of inquiry to determine the surest mode of defense. This was one week before the dreadful final battle. Jabotinsky remarked, "Any hopes for energetic action on the part of the Zionist leadership are groundless."

Fort Tel Hai (Israel Government Press Office photo)

Indeed, that last week, no one was drafted, no one was sent – only a few independent irregulars, men and women, made their way north – and the commission of inquiry was safely garrisoned nearly 15 miles away in Ayalet Hashachar when the fort fell. Perhaps the militarily aware Trumpeldor was alert to the eerie similarities between the sad fate of his fort and that of the long-remembered Texas stronghold. He could not, of course, have had any notion that the name of Fort Tel Hai would soon be as impassioned a slogan in Judea as "Remember the Alamo!" had been in its time in America.

Now this pioneer of Jewish defense, this hero of the Russian military theater, cheered his beleaguered colleagues as they listened, day and night, to the petrifying war cries of their besiegers. The assault began at dawn; seven of the thirty-five defenders fell in the battle. Trumpeldor was shot twice in the stomach, once in his right arm. As he lay mortally wounded, he uttered words which became the unofficial anthem of Jewish youth around the globe: "It does not matter, it is good to die for our country." Fort Tel Hai was overrun and set aflame.

Jabotinsky swore Tel Hai would not fall again. Eight hundred Jewish youths were quickly recruited. At night they learned the science that had long ago swept every nation, somehow overlooking the Jewish nation: the science of weaponry. For the first time since Bar Kochba had organized a Jewish army in the year 132 to fight the Romans, Jews in Jerusalem were organizing into independent armed units to fight for Jewish lives. Before dawn, the young cadres practiced the art that had so long eluded the Jewish people: the art of military discipline. Marches, salutes, presentations of arms, trumpet calls and flag hoisting. On vacation days when they were free from educational obligations, the young troops went on nature hikes and camping trips – to gain experience in navigation and the tossing of grenades. Training also included boxing practice, running, jumping, and lots of crawling on bellies. "A tragedy may occur," said Jabotinsky, "but not an embarrassment. We won't allow them to treat us in our own country as they do in Exile."

Jabotinsky enlisted Yirmiyahu Halperin as one of his commanders. Halperin had completed maritime school in Italy and London. Now he was all of 18 years old and obviously ripe for military command. As Halperin entered his home one afternoon, his mother informed him: "A Mr. Jabotinsky visited, he wants to see you urgently." Halperin found Jabotinsky in an apartment the older soldier-statesman shared with his own mother – and sister, wife and son. Jabotinsky didn't waste any time: He suggested Halperin assume coordination of the self-defense forces in Jerusalem. The Hebrew word for self-defense is *Hagana*. Thus Jabotinsky offered Halperin charge of the forces of the Hagana, and a future army was born.

Yirmiyahu ("Irma") Halperin, aged 19, 1920 (Jabotinsky Institute photo)

Jabotinsky then suggested that should Halperin refuse the mission, he would do well to forget his part in this conversation, which, as the cliché goes, "never took place."

Jabotinsky told Halperin he wanted him to become his aide-de-camp, and explained his duties. Jabotinsky added, "You will of course receive a salary for your services."

Halperin felt as though he had been slapped in the face. He snapped back: "I doubt if you will find anyone willing to undertake such a task even for a salary but I, in any event, will not accept payment for my services."

Not to be swayed, Jabotinsky insisted: "I don't want amateurs. I need soldiers and officers, on full duty – an army. I'll need you at all hours of the day and night. You will be paid – and not out of my own pocket – for service in the Hebrew army." Halperin did indeed receive a regular salary check, the first one arriving exactly one month later; it would be posted by Jabotinsky himself – from a prison cell in the coastal fortress of Acre.

Halperin's first mission was to arm the fledgling force. Jabotinsky asked Colonel Ronald Storrs, the military governor of Jerusalem and Judea, to arm the defenseless Jews. Storrs replied by demanding to know: "Is it true you are arming Jews?" Jabotinsky readily admitted doing so, to prevent, he said, "the slaughter of Jews in Jerusalem." Both Storrs and his superior, General Louis Bols, refused to allow the Jews to arm, and refused to supply the Hagana with arms. Storrs promised Jabotinsky that there was nothing to fear; not even a windowpane would break in Jerusalem during the dangerous days of the upcoming Moslem festival of Nebi Musa.

Halperin was therefore left to his own wits. He and Zvi Nadav entered a gun store just outside the Jaffa Gate to the Old City. The large Armenian who owned the store looked, they decided, like the legendary Ali Baba, and so thus they nicknamed him, for conspiratorial purposes. Hiding behind piles of packages, so that they were unseen from the street and any eavesdropping British eyes, they passed Ali Baba the money and he gave them the guns, which they stuffed under their belts and under their shirts. This was the first arms purchase by the Hagana, which by 1948 would be adept at smuggling even entire airplanes to the Holy Land.

The first two arms caches of the future army were located in Jabotinsky's and Halperin's homes. The cache in Halperin's fit snugly under his mother's bed, where it remained unnoticed during a surprise British search. His mother, de facto quartermaster for the Hagana, nonetheless lowered the guns into a well before the next search.

Chief Rabbi Shabtai Djajin of Rumania visited Jerusalem during those turbulent days and naturally sought out the famous Jabotinsky. After a friendly introduction, Jabotinsky asked his distinguished guest if he had ever seen the sun rise in Jerusalem. The Chief Rabbi agreed to meet Jabotinsky at 5:00 A.M. the following morning in the center of the city.

They walked and walked; Jabotinsky seemed to be always choosing the path less traveled, taking unpaved trails and climbing rough crags. Finally they reached a plateau where Jabotinsky's youth were practicing military drills. The darkness had not yet dispersed; clouds in fact blotted out even the possibility of sunlight this particular morning. "Look. And see," Jabotinsky said to the rabbi, extending an arm towards the young men and women ahead, on these flatlands just outside the city. "Here, this is the sunrise of Jerusalem."

Tension between Arab and Jew built for a month. On Friday, April 2, the eve of the Passover holiday, the troops of the Hagana waited in a courtyard in the Nahalat Zion neighborhood of Jerusalem. They had so few guns that the men collected stones to keep in reserve; as the day wore on, some found cloth and created makeshift slingshots. If it worked for King David against Goliath, they must have thought, it could work for us.

The tenuous calm was shattered on the second day of the Passover holiday. The Arabs celebrated their own holiday of Nebi Musa on this same day, April 4. In an ironic twist no doubt lost on the rampaging Arabs, their leaders had chosen this holiday, created hundreds of years earlier in honor of Nebi Musa – the Prophet Moses – as a day to murder the children of Moses.

Jabotinsky put all his forces on alert. The officers gathered in the early morning hours at the Lemel School building, about a 15-minute walk to Jerusalem's Old City. Ten to thirteen-year-old children served as scouts and signalmen. Jabotinsky positioned them on strategically located rooftops throughout the city, from which they could relay important information from outlying areas, not yet serviced by telephone, to the central command.

Six hundred angry Arabs arrived from the nearby city of Hebron, coalescing into a mob at the sixteenth-century Jaffa Gate to the old, walled, section of Jerusalem. As Hebron's Arabs mixed with Jerusalem's, Jerusalem's mayor Kasim Pasha whipped the crowd into a frenzy. He was followed by the Sheik of Hebron, who railed briefly before making his deadly point: *Itbach el Yahud*!

The other sheiks responded: "Death to the cowards! Death to the palefaced! Death to the Jews!"

At 11:00, the Arabs commenced throwing stones, assaulting Jews and plundering Jewish stores near Jaffa Gate. Then they moved through the gate into the Old City. The British army was, conveniently, nowhere to be seen.

Jabotinsky ordered his forces to Jaffa Gate; the young would-be defenders of Jerusalem moved as one in a desperate attempt to head off the attackers before they reached their intended prey. As two hundred of the Hagana's troops ran towards their helpless brethren, the British army suddenly appeared. And as the Arab pogromists inside the Old City began their labor of destruction, the British marshaled all possible strength – to keep Jabotinsky outside the city walls. Rifles were pointed not at the Arabs who were at that very moment hacking Jews to death, but at those who had come to protect the defenseless. The British, now stationed outside Jaffa Gate, effectively allowed the pogromist mobs to lay the Old City waste while bayonets kept the defenders at bay.

A second company of Jabotinsky's men was joined by many of those who had just been locked out of Jaffa Gate. They attempted to enter the Old City through the Damascus Gate, slightly to the north and east of the Jaffa Gate. By the time they reached Damascus Gate, they had mustered over six hundred of their own forces. A British machine gun nestled on top of the Gate, however, convinced them of the folly of trying to force their way in. Most of them were armed only with sticks. Several members of this company later managed to steal their way inside the walls, dressed as doctors or accompanying some of the Hadassah Hospital ambulances that were plying back and forth between the scene of the pillage and the medical center. By the time these individuals arrived inside, they afforded only a minimal amount of protection, though they did raise the morale of the besieged Jews.

The rest of the company meanwhile encountered an Arab gang charging from the Old City towards the new Jewish neighborhood of Mea Shearim; the defenders stood their ground and eventually forced the Arabs to retreat, chasing them as far as the ancient Tomb of the High Priest Shimon Hazaddik before the British intervened. The English troops arrested 30 of the young Jews.

When Jabotinsky saw Colonel Storrs that afternoon he demanded that action be taken to defend the city's Jews. The military governor answered that he was a very busy man, perhaps Jabotinsky could return in an hour or so?

By the chaotic day's end, hundreds of Jews and Arabs had been detained by the British, the Jews during the pogrom, the Arabs afterwards. At 6:00 P.M., a curfew was imposed.

The remnants of the Jewish Legion, about four hundred troops, were stationed at Sarafand, some 15 miles from Jerusalem. Two Legionnaires, Captain Joe Katz and Moses Nelson, were dispatched to Jerusalem with orders for local units of the British army, probably having nothing to do with the disturbances. Once in the Holy City, however, they were not unmoved by the events witnessed and appeared at the Hagana headquarters to offer their services. Their British uniforms gave them a distinct advantage – they could move at night despite the curfew. Jabotinsky used them to maintain lines of communication between the various Hagana companies stationed in different neighborhoods. They also escorted Jabotinsky himself, along with Pinhas Rutenberg (who would one day establish the first electrical plant in Eretz Israel), as they surveyed the Hagana's outposts. Afterwards, Jabotinsky asked Nelson to return to the Bukharan neighborhood to stand guard. Nelson did as he was asked, and was finally relieved two days later.

Early the next morning, April 5, the British jailers took all the

Arabs for morning prayers, after which they let them go. At dawn, the British troops stationed in the Old City left. When the newly released pillagers of yesterday, joined by those of Hebron's Arabs who had spent the night in Jerusalem and a number of locals, began marching up Patriarch Road towards the Temple Mount, the Old City was effectively in their hands. They initiated another pogrom while Jabotinsky tried, largely unsuccessfully, to evade the British who again kept his soldiers out of the endangered Old City. The future second president of Israel, Itzhak Ben-Zvi, reported in a newspaper column how he personally came upon the body of a murdered Jew left in the shuk and carried the corpse to the Tower of David, near the inner section of the Jaffa Gate.

All told, six Jews were killed, two hundred and eleven injured.

The British spent the following days and nights searching Jewish institutions and homes for weapons. Eliahu Ginsburg was one of many Hagana members living in a house called the "Bachelor Pad," in what would one day be the center of modern Jerusalem's business district; but he was nervous about living in what was then an isolated building. He therefore took several guns from their hiding place in the Bezalel Art School, which was a five-minute walk up a nearby hill, and stashed them in the Bachelor Pad itself. Late one night the Military Police entered the Pad. Three British officers and twenty soldiers conducted a search, which uncovered the three rifles, two pistols and three hundred bullets hidden under the basement stairway. A British officer demanded to know to whom the arms belonged. Eliahu Ginsburg replied: "To the armies of the Defenders of Jerusalem."

"Who are these armies?" barked the officer.

"Any Jew capable of defending himself," was the answer.

The British arrested 19 defenders in that house.

Shortly after midnight, the British lined up their arrestees and marched them towards the police station where they would be detained. The route took them past Jabotinsky's house; the 19 began to sing, hoping to wake their leader and thereby let him know they were on their way to jail (Jabotinsky was not at home). The police station, known as the Turkish *kishleh*, was located in an Old City fortress just inside of Jaffa Gate. At the gate the march halted. The British guard gave the password and they were allowed through, to be imprisoned on the second floor of the *kishleh*. Ironically, that morning they would have given their right arms to be allowed to enter Jaffa Gate – and now they were being led through, but it was too late to save their brothers and sisters inside the Old City.

Captain Joe Katz found Jabotinsky at headquarters at 3:00 A.M. and delivered the news. When Jabotinsky protested to the police, declaring himself, as official Commander of the Hagana, solely responsible and demanding, therefore, the release of the19, he became number 20.

They were interned for five days. When the interrogation began, Jabotinsky insisted on being questioned in Hebrew and the 19 others followed suite. The British acquiesced.

Their trial for possession of arms and inciting some segments of the local population against others – those were the official charges – was set for Saturday, April 10, the Jewish Sabbath. The great rabbi Abraham Isaac Kook issued a ruling of Jewish law permitting Jews to violate the ancient ban on writing on the Sabbath, in order to submit a petition on Jabotinsky's behalf. Twenty-five hundred of Jerusalem's Jews signed this petition. Several hundred members of the Hagana asked to be put on trial along with the twenty defendants.

The 19 Hagana men received three years of hard labor each. Jabotinsky was sentenced to fifteen years to be followed by deportation. After a week in the Jerusalem Central Prison, they were put on a train to Egypt. Apparently someone had decided to add immediate deportation as an additional punishment. All along the route crowds mobbed the train to cheer them. They never reached their intended Egyptian prison, however; by the time they reached the Suez Canal, British General Edmund Allenby had decided he did not want any more "criminals" in Egypt. He ordered them returned and they were trans-

ferred to Acre Prison, north of Haifa. There, Jabotinsky composed, with
the help of his cellmates, one of his most popular songs:

> *From Beersheba all the way to Dan*
> *From Gilead to the Mediterranean*
> *There's not one inch of our land*
> *Where blood's not claimed the sand.*
> *Hebrew blood flows and fills*
> *Fields, valleys and hills.*
> *But from age to age, each with its dead*

*Jabotinsky (center, without hat, seated on stone) and
fellow Hagana prisoners in Acre prison, 1920. Ben
Zion Homsky is standing with boxing gloves.*
(Jabotinsky Institute photo)

No purer blood has ever been shed
Than the blood of the tillers of Tel Hai.

Between Ayalet and Metulla lies a field
Within its lonely soil lies concealed
A one-armed man with iron will
He guards our border, though silent and still.
We are, yes, behind bars
But Tel Hai in the north draws our hearts
And we know that Mt. Hermon, summit and all
Will one day be ours, all ours.

General Allenby quickly reduced the defenders' sentences to six months, and Jabotinsky's to one year. That July, Britain's first High Commissioner for Palestine, Herbert Samuel, pardoned and released all the prisoners – Jews and Arabs – being held for crimes relating to the Jerusalem attacks. Jabotinsky refused to accept the moral and legal implications of such a pardon, which put rapists and raped in the same category, and he did not rest until, under orders from the War Office in London in March 1921, the original verdict against the Defenders of Jerusalem was quashed.

The British, nonetheless, did not quite forgive Jabotinsky, and he was considered an undesirable in British-controlled Palestine. The authorities finally rid themselves of Jabotinsky when he traveled abroad at the end of 1929; they simply refused to allow him back in.

1929

As Moshe Segal stood immobile on the steps of the Lemel School, British detectives rushing towards him from the right and furious officials of the established Jewish leadership coming at him from the left, he was perhaps pondering practical matters.

Where is the blue-and-white flag concealed? How many people from how many cities have responded to our primitive posters? Will the youth follow when we lead?

Or perhaps the taut Segal, back straight and fists clenched, was inclined to wonder how he had come to be on these tumultuous steps, and where his steps would lead this fateful day, the Ninth of Av 5689, August 15, 1929 – the 1859th anniversary of the burning of the Second Temple.

Moshe Segal was born on the sixth of Shevat 5664 (1904) in the Ukrainian city of Poltava. At seven, he happened to read in the Biblical book of Deuteronomy the injunction: "Thou shalt set a king over thee from among thy brethren, thou shalt not set a foreigner as king over thee." At Sabbath prayer services the following Saturday morning, little Moshe was for the first time astonished as the cantor led the synagogue choir in a melodious blessing for the beneficent Czar Nicholas. Segal instinctively staged an ad-hoc "sit-in" of one, sitting demonstratively amid an entire congregation on its feet in honor of the "foreign" Czar. Segal adamantly refused to budge, then as throughout his entire life. On future Sabbaths, to spare his father embarrassment, young Moshe left the synagogue for the duration of the homage to the Czar, which he saw as sacrilegious.

At around the same time, in an unrelated incident, soldiers one day appeared at the Segal household – killers in army garb who were making the rounds of local houses, arresting and summarily shooting men whose bodies were usually left in roadside ditches. One of the armed militiamen announced that they had come to arrest Mr. Segal and his son Moshe. The father deliberately and patiently turned towards his children and bade them repeat everything he would say, word for word. The old man then began reciting the verses of the first Psalm: "Blessed is he who has not walked in evil paths..." The soldiers, come to commit cold-blooded murder, habitualized to pleas for mercy and shrieks of terror, seemed shocked by the sedate recitation, in the traditional Hebrew singsong manner, of this half-prayer, half-proclamation.

The baffled soldiers had not noticed that Mrs. Segal had meanwhile exited via a secret door behind a closet; she alerted her neighbor's eldest son Nahum, officially a member of the Communist Party – though a loyal and diligent Jew at heart – who was resting in his apartment. Nahum self-assuredly opened the Segal's door and arrogantly demanded, rather than asked, of the soldiers: "What are you doing here?" His voice rose in volume and in authority as he demanded their written orders, which he knew never existed in such cases. The bewildered soldiers were treated to a chewing-out and ordered to leave.

As the beset-upon Segal stood in the Jerusalem sun almost two decades later, he remembered how he had seen one Jew with courage enough to command seven armed soldiers – and how those soldiers had meekly obeyed.

The man who was about to make his mark on history stood firm, sturdy and determined. Segal's friends from all periods of his life, teachers from his past as well as future students, comrades in arms and those who would farm by his side, today recall different aspects of his appearance, depending on the period of their acquaintance. Some recall his firm chin, others speak of his long, white beard. Some can picture his watchman's uniform, others his pioneer's shorts, still others his dark rabbinical suit. But all who ever met Segal remember as his most distinguishing mark the soft, blue eyes.

The eyes remained ever calm, ever sure. Even when peripherally faced with charging secret policemen and furious Jewish leaders, even when years later he would speak of expelling enemies – or shed tears over Christians murdered by Moslems in various Mideast countries. The calmness was undoubtedly rooted in the knowledge that his eyes would never see his hands do anything that was not in the service of his people and his God. Segal's eyes expressed his inner fibre, the placid acceptance of any hardship in the unshaken faith that all would eventually be overcome, that Israel's God would eventually triumph.

When, a few short years before Tel Hai, the heroic one-armed Joseph Trumpeldor – already famous for his exploits in battle and his World War One role in establishing the Jewish Legion – struck out on the Russian and Ukrainian roads, thousands of local Jewish youth were swept with desire to join Hehalutz, the organization he was promoting. He promised practical training for eventual relocation to Eretz Israel. In Poltava, any Jewish teenagers not members of the Communist Komsomol youth league were already members of the Zeiri Zion Youth. And now they all tied their fortunes to Hehalutz. Segal and his friends were sent for agricultural training to Nikolayev. From there the treacherous but inevitable road included years of starvation, last-minute evasions of Soviet agents, stow-away train excursions and hazardous sea-routes in unseaworthy boats. Once in the land of Israel, Segal and others of his ilk drained swamps, stood lonely guard at night in orchards and fields (nomadic Arabs were burning Jewish fields or stealing produce—if not murdering guards or families even without a profit motive) and sweated in the intense desert sun as construction workers.

Segal was one of fifteen thousand people who heard the fiery Jabotinsky speak in 1927 in Tel Aviv's sports stadium. Jabo, as he was affectionately called by some of his followers, had only recently established the Betar youth movement in memory of his by then legendary friend Trumpeldor. Segal wasted no time and ran to the unofficial headquarters of Jabo's movement in Tel Aviv, the Altschuler Cafe on Allenby Street, where he enrolled as the seventh Betari in the land of Israel. The first was Shmuel Halevi.

Allenby was old Tel Aviv's main thoroughfare, and Altschuler's was two storefronts in from Star of David Square, a raucous intersection of six of Tel Aviv's most teeming streets. Allenby's broad width was lined with two- and three-story businesses, with many of the proprietors inhabiting the upper levels of their establishments. Above Altschuler's were the offices of the Revisionist and Betar Workers Association, a sort of employment agency for stubborn workers denied regular jobs for refusing to carry the red cards which would prove their membership in one of the omnipotent socialist unions or political parties. Below, old-man Altschuler and his one-eared son – no one seemed to know precisely where the junior partner had lost his left ear – presided over a medium-sized café famous for its *kneidlach* (dumpling) soup. This was an eatery where one could sit for six hours over one cup of coffee, where management never begrudged a hungry revolutionary the cost of nourishment. And Altschuler's buzzed perpetually with revolutionary activity. Segal prophesied that one day a monument would be erected on the site, a bronze notation that "Here the nationalist movement was founded."

In the course of a short meal at Altschuler's on a pleasant afternoon, one would most likely see most of the men and women who would soon be sharing battlefield and prison cell in the struggle for a Jewish state. The "Poet of Redemption," Uri Zvi Greenberg – a red-haired Isaiah incarnate – might be sipping tea with history teacher and student of national revolutions Abba Ahimeir; at another table Dr. Yehoshua Yevin, a chain-smoking, wild-haired journalist and author, might be sitting alone writing his monumental *Jerusalem Awaits*, or perhaps the notes he is scribbling are for his 35-page essay on Ataturk, father of the modern Turkish state, which will soon be published as the first in the "Birion Library Series." *Birion* means thug, tough, extremist, zealot. Soon the troika – Ahimeir, Greenberg and Yevin – will brazenly found a Brit Habirionim, Union of the Tough Thugs, to teach atrophied Jewish youth that the way to redemption necessarily passes through prison cells, and a land is redeemed, in Greenberg's words, not by money but by blood. ("Your teachers taught that land is purchased with money...but I say land is conquered with blood.")

Over the next few years, whenever Altschuler's door opens, shouts of "*Hazit Ha'am*! *Hazit Ha'am*! Get your *Hazit Ha'am*!" will waft in. One or two members of the Brit Habirionim will almost certainly be peddling this newspaper, edited by Yevin, which is the sole source of

35

income for many of the young Birionim. Yevin himself often lays down his pen and picks up a bundle of papers to hawk on the street. Any division of labor in the Brit is purely arbitrary and hunger proves the great equalizer. Yevin is on occasion so overcome by hunger pains that he is unable to write.

But now it is the Ninth of Av, 1929, and Altschuler's is quiet, for on this day commemorating ancient tragedy Jews the world over are abstaining from food and entertainment. The day is traditionally spent sitting on bare ground in mournful, dour prayer, lamentations being wailed for Jerusalem's lost glory. But Segal, Ahimeir's right-hand man, remembered that the wooden shack in which, as a child, he received his religious education – served also as headquarters for the local Cossacks. Occasionally, he would look into the yard and see the big-mustached Cossacks being drilled by their officers. The gleam of their sabres held at attention reflected the unfettered sunlight and also the honor and might of the Great Russian Empire. Segal was offered two worlds and rejected neither. Some wise rabbi stated ages ago that "the book and the sword descended together from heaven." Segal chose as his underground motto in the 1940s a verse from Psalms: "Words of God in their mouths and a double-edged sword in their hands."

Now Segal transformed the prayers of the Ninth of Av into deeds. A week earlier, he had heard of the draconian oppression perpetrated by the British regime: Jewish prayer was to be curtailed at the holy Western Wall, no benches would be allowed for even the elderly worshippers, no divider could be placed between men and women. Segal requested leave from his watchman's position in Rehovot, where he was fending off Arab thieves attracted by the almonds and grapes, and began delivering speeches in Tel Aviv. "Either we have blood in our veins or water!" he exhorted the youth he met. He, Shmuel Halevi and one or two others penned a call to Jewish youth to rally on the Ninth of Av in Jerusalem, to march to the Western Wall with a Jewish flag held high. At 2:00 in the morning they woke Uri Zvi Greenberg in his seaside hut and submitted the call for his approval. He crossed out, added and reworded and that very night, on a single stencil machine somewhere in Tel Aviv, the first wall poster of the Zionist Revolution was printed. Thousands responded.

"Yes," Segal thought as he surveyed the assembled crowd and those on their way, "they've come from all over. Members of Maccabee and Betar, Yemenite kids from Shearayim and Kurdish youth from Jerusalem, Soviet Georgians and Persians as well. Even socialist members of Ahdut Haovada (United Workers) and members of the Histadrut union. And so many yeshiva students, too. And the entire student body and staff – 30 in all – of a Betar Officers Training School headed by Yirmiyahu Halperin – the women carrying concealed pistols, just in case..."

Segal called upon the crowd to fight a war for Jewish rights at the Wall. Mounted police under the direction of Jerusalem Commander Harrington surrounded Segal and ordered him to the basement where they "suggested" he conduct the demonstration more in the spirit of the Ninth of Av, without any flags and without singing provocative Jewish songs. The Jewish leadership took another tack: "You are the advocates of Jewish military discipline. We are the official leadership

Moshe Segal (center; the flag is being carried by the man on Segal's left) leading the march to the Western Wall, Ninth of Av, 1929 (IDF archive)

of the Jewish community and we are ordering you not to proceed. Will you disobey our decisions and set that kind of example for our youth?"

Segal answered, "We see things differently. The nationalist Jewish youth will decide for itself what must be done." Forcing his way back upstairs, Segal weaved through the crowd towards the corner.

Out of the coffeehouse on Yellin Street came the flag; Segal, Shmuel Halevi and Eliezer Friedberg held the wooden pole high. Irma Halperin's Betarim were the vanguard, followed by the flag and then the thousands, marching towards Jaffa Road singing "Oh, Homeland" and

Marching to the Wall in 1929 (Jabotinsky Institute photo)

chanting "The Western Wall is ours!" and "Long live the Hebrew state!" British police blocked the way – and were shunted aside without a second thought. Sporadic fistfights and blows from the police were barely noticed by the mass of marching Jews. Again, the British formed a human chain to block the road; again, the marchers broke through and brushed them aside.

They marched up Neviim Street, through the Damascus Gate and into the walled Old City. Perhaps some of the older ralliers remembered how they had been locked out of these same walls ten years before, as Arab mobs were murdering their brothers inside. Now the Jewish youth were pushing aside British policemen. The defenders of Jerusalem had already sat in prison; now Greenberg was writing odes to the gallows and Ahimeir was preaching prison as a goal. Freedom lay ahead; the march, once begun, would be unstoppable.

Deputy Jerusalem Police Commander Kingsley Heath lunged for the flag and felt the fury of Jewish fists. Inside the Old City, Arab shopkeepers quickly bolted their doors and hid inside. Reaching the Wall, the throngs pledged allegiance to the Temple site and sang *Hatikva*. In a slip into uncharacteristic hyperbole, Segal noted that this "is the first time in two thousand years that *Hatikva* has been sung at the Wall!" Of course, even as he spoke these words, Segal himself realized that the *Hatikva* anthem had only been written fifty years earlier. But, indeed, songs of Jewish independence truly had returned to the Wall after two millennia.

On the return march, Segal was lifted onto the demonstrators' shoulders at Zion Square, as the British governor of Jerusalem watched from a balcony. Segal urged his listeners to fight "against the plots of perfidious Albion." Turning to the British dignitaries, Segal exclaimed, in a balcony scene still awaiting a Jewish Shakespeare to immortalize it in myth, "We will chase you from this land and establish a free Hebrew state!"

Upon his return to Tel Aviv, Segal was warned by friends on the police force that he was a wanted man. It was time to go into hiding.

Tel Aviv, 1929

Haim Dviri was tall, slim, but well muscled. His name can still be spotted today, engraved on the floor of one of the long-vacant solitary-confinement cells in the former Jerusalem Central Prison. His name may or may not be chiseled into the cement floors of the Jaffa Prison cells he frequented, or those where he rested his head in Acre Fortress, or the stone quarries where he shattered rocks in the sweltering Samarian sun that shone over occasional periods of hard labor in Nur Chams.

Wanted, arrested for or actually guilty of hooliganism, trespassing, bank robbery, assault and countless other offenses against the British in Eretz Israel, Dviri was and remains one of the most avuncular and generous men hosted by the British Empire in its prison hostelries. He was a veritable knight of the Hebrew Revolution. His first three weeks in prison were spent in the Jerusalem solitary cell because he maintained silence during his interrogation. Abba Ahimeir, in his *Prison Reportage*, tells of an Arab who had received 15 years for murder. While doing hard labor at the Nur Chams quarry, he had fallen from the rocks and was now almost fully paralyzed. "What pain he suffered when pulling his body to the bathroom...stooped over...his face scarlet...I, embarrassed, never did – but Dviri frequently carried him on his shoulders to the bathroom..."

Haim Dviri walked along the Tel Aviv seashore on a Friday morning in late August 1929. He had passed the First World War in Minsk, then a city whose government and occupying forces were changed as often as most people change shirts. His thoughts wandered from the thick, acrid artillery smoke above Minsk to the immaculate skies above the Tel Aviv beach, from the days spent under fire hiding in basements to the sun-drenched shores of the Mediterranean. Up ahead he spied the beachside photographer, a boisterous chap, pant legs extending just past his knees, positioned daily with his huge camera-box, ready to offer black and white immortality to the couples who usually passed by hand in hand.

Noise, at first nebulous but soon clearly indicative of the clatter of knives and the pounding of wood, the cocking of guns and the whooping of bloodthirsty scourges. Dviri was still observing the photographer when the first salvo erupted from the Arab side of Jaffa. The pogroms of 1929 had begun. Sixty Jews would die in Hebron, twenty-five in Safed. All told: 133 in Eretz Israel, and another 329 injured.

The photographer grabbed a knife and ran towards Tel Aviv's Ezra Street, the border with the Arab neighborhoods behind the Hassan Bek mosque. Dviri grabbed whatever was handy and followed. "It was quite ridiculous," he'll say today. "The photographer shouted in Hebrew, 'Forward, towards them!' and I ran after him; I was 17, he brandished a knife and I – an old dagger."

In one of the last buildings of the besieged Jewish area stood a member of the Hagana holding a grenade. Dviri noticed the grenade was "no larger than a pigeon's egg." In the midst of the attack, Dviri remained silent. But he thought: "Here, I have lived through a World War, with Russian and Polish and German and White and pogromist bullets whistling all around me. And now the Hagana expects to defend the Tel Aviv beach with one hand grenade, and the city with men riding in horsedrawn wagons clasping wooden boards?" Fortunately, the Arabs behind the Hassan Bek mosque were under the illusion that the Jews beyond Ezra St. were armed to the teeth, and an attack from the beach never materialized.

Joseph Kremin lay prone on a southern Tel Aviv rooftop for three nights, exchanging fusillades of gunfire with the would-be Arab destroyers of his city. The 60 feet which separated the two parties to the gunfight were no man's land. In an optimistic mood, Kremin interpreted a prolonged silent spell to mean that the assailants had fled; just to be sure, he set his hat on the tip of his gun barrel and slowly raised it above the roof's wall. "Just like in the movies, but this was in 1929 and we had not yet seen the movies," Kremin recalled years later. In any event, the hat was promptly shot through with "more holes than a beehive."

Kremin's route to the rooftop was roundabout. He was patrolling the city of Bat Yam even before the eruption of the pogroms, on the hunch that trouble was brewing. The 20 callow fighters in his unit left one step ahead of the law – just as an Arab police force, privately hired by local residents, took the neighborhood under its protection. Kremin, his outfit and another dozen volunteers boarded buses for Hebron where the condition was already beyond critical. The buses never reached the city, for the overly cautious Jewish leadership concluded that three dozen fighters arriving in Hebron might give the appearance of a deliberate provocation. The buses were ordered to turn back. Kremin marvelled at the ironies of history: In 1920 he'd been sent from Jerusalem to guard Hebron. "I'm 12, but I have a gun," he had said. Kremin had inherited the pistol from his late brother, killed in a World War One bombing which also took the life of his father. "This will be yours," his dying brother had whispered. At 12, untried Kremin had been sent to help protect Hebron; at 21, accompanied by three dozen armed and able-bodied troops, he was prevented from protecting the 60 Jews who were about to be butchered.

The Hagana, originally founded by Jabotinsky in 1920 in Jerusalem, had over the years slowly drifted from Jabo's determined insistence on military preparedness. By 1929 the Hagana was stubbornly insistent on executing only defensive actions, and even these often too little, too late.

Segal and a few friends had actually been expelled from the Hagana in 1927 for insubordination. At a standard roll call, they had been asked the purpose of the Hagana; a cadet was expected to recite: "To defend lives and property." Segal answered: "To become a Jewish army for a Jewish state." Asked again, he answered again. Given a third opportunity to reform, he stuck to his insolence. He and like-minded fellows soon found themselves outside the Hagana. Most gravitated to the Betar School run by Yirmiyahu Halperin, who had also left the Hagana he helped found.

Halperin now offered his services, again, to the Hagana, whose leaders replied that they would allow his men to enlist only if they did so as individuals. Halperin's group intended to remain a unit and therefore decided to operate independently.

By Sunday, Tel Aviv's deputy mayor Israel Rokach asked Halperin to move his forces to the Shapiro and Oved neighborhoods which were under fire and cut off from the center of the city. Halperin's 30 men were based on Allenby Street, opposite the Great Synagogue. Halperin and his second-in-command, Moshe Rosenberg, ordered them to arms and to the field. They crossed from Allenby into the surrounding orchards. When they reached the last Hagana outpost, the Hagana men begged them not to proceed. "Are you crazy?" they were asked. "They'll shoot you, kill you. Where are you heading? Going in there will mean your death!"

Halperin turned to his men: "Are we going in?" Over two dozen voices responded as one: "We're going in!" As they plunged into the narrow path the Arab guns thundered from three sides. Bullets crashed into Somolinsky, whose arm would later have to be amputated. Two others were also immediately hit and evacuated. The rest pushed tenaciously forward on their bellies and reached the beleaguered

The Betar Officers School in 1929. Front row, seated: (left to right) Nissim Cohen, Abba Zelivansky, Joseph Paamoni, Yirmiyahu Halperin, Moshe Kagen, Moshe Rosenberg (Jabotinsky Institute photo)

neighborhoods. They provided an escort for the women and children back to Tel Aviv. One mother refused to move, until Segal pointed his gun at her and threatened to shoot. She grabbed her children and ran. Armed Betarim remained in Shapiro to check any attempts by the Arab pogromists to cross into the city.

When all the unarmed citizenry had been evacuated for their own safety, the panic-inspired commotion calmed and the shrieks and weeping ceased. The Betarim, short of ammunition after a full day in the fray, crawled out into the orchards, 50 feet between each man, and there they lay in position. Segal saw Irma Halperin "walk between the bullets, giving us orders to shoot. He and Bayevsky, a Russian officer who had converted to Judaism and was now a clerk in some office, but also one of our group leaders, told us exactly where to shoot. Bullets were a precious commodity, we knew, and we could not afford to be wasteful. Every bullet must strike its target."

Joseph Kremin laughed at Bayevsky's novel method of goading his gunners to open fire. His orders were issued in the form of Russian curses. *Dai yemu pochornay jopye!* shouted Bayevsky and rifles flared. "This guy's good," Kremin spat. "He curses and an Arab falls!" Such was the defense of Tel Aviv – a former gentile dispatching Arabs with Russian curses shouted at presumptive soldiers.

They remained in position until nightfall, when word reached them that the British, who had called up reinforcements from Egypt in order to crush the pogrom, were on their way. The Betarim knew that the first move of any British troops would be to disarm and arrest them; as the British approached, they made their exit.

Segal remarked to a comrade: "This story is important because it won't be included in any history book, because it doesn't make the Hagana look good. It's important because 30 young men without an organizational name, 30 Betarim with weapons, saved two Tel Aviv neighborhoods which would have shared the fate of Hebron or Safed or any Jewish city abroad in a pogrom, when Jews are killed without knowing how to defend themselves."

Deputy Mayor Rokach again sought Halperin's commandos. The new northern neighborhood of Kiryat Shaul was cut off, in imminent danger of destruction. Rokach wanted the residents evacuated. The lads, battle weary but ever eager for action, set forth in the black of night. Wandering through orchards and fields, woods and swamps, no one was particularly sure where they were or where they were headed. They knew only that potentially, every tree concealed a sniper, every bifurcation an encounter with death. And then in an instant they found themselves in a clearing – facing a hundred or more Arabs. Nissim Cohen drew his gun – 20 others levelled theirs as they wondered if they would be forced to open fire, and how many could they kill how quickly, and weren't they outnumbered five to one, and where in heck were they anyway?

The Arab mukhtar wasted no time explaining: "We called this meeting to tell our people we have no intention of involving ourselves in what's going on. We do not favor the wars being waged." The mukhtar

Yirmiyahu Halperin (left) watches Nissim Cohen (second from left) and another Betari learn how to box while at the Betar Officers School (Jabotinsky Institute photo)

could not help but add: "But where are you going, out here in the middle of the night in the middle of nowhere?" When the fighters explained that they were on their way to defend Kiryat Shaul, the mukhtar provided two scouts to show the way. The helpful Arabs turned back just before the village.

Up ahead, Halperin's men were ordered to halt – by children with guns. "This is impressive!" Cohen joyfully exclaimed. The veteran fighters announced they had come to evacuate the town's residents, but only the women with their youngest children agreed to go. The armed 14 year olds refused to budge. "What fearless youth!" Cohen said. "What self-respect, refusing to run. Every kid who knows how to use a weapon is staying!" Three of Halperin's troops remained in Kiryat Shaul as reinforcements, the rest accompanied the women and infants to central Tel Aviv.

This group – Rosenberg, Kremin, Segal, Cohen and their comrades, 30 soldiers lacking even a banner to fly, units in an unformed army – was the kernel from which grew the Irgun Zvai Leumi (IZL, or Irgun) and the Lohamei Herut Israel (Lehi, or Stern Group).

Yirmiyahu Halperin (far right) teaching swordsmanship at the Betar Officers Training School (Jabotinsky Institute photo)

Chapter 2
Dawn

My brother, do you know where the Messiah will be born?
He'll be born in a prison, on the floor...   Yair, "The Messiah"

I see how they ascend the gallows, and the dawn of Jerusalem
in the lustre of their faces...
U.Z. Greenberg, "Judah Today, Judah Tomorrow"

The brave boys of the Hagana Leumit, or "Nationalist Hagana," as they were referred to by the awed residents of the Tel Aviv environs – those who had been in the front ranks of the Hagana and those who had grown with Betar, those who had been training in the Betar Officers School and those who had simply been walking along the beach – this eclectic group whose hearts beat to the same drummer, temporarily split into as many directions as there were endangered settlements in Eretz Israel.

Dviri, anxious for action, had first met up with his like-minded colleagues defending Shapiro and Oved after he'd pursued Arabs in the south. Now he headed north to Mahanayim and Yesod Hamaale where he and others fended off midnight Beduin attacks. "In Yesod we have two Canadian rifles and a few Turkish ones made to hold only one bullet," Dviri wrote to a friend. "We have to order trespassers to halt in three languages, and by that time who knows what will have happened." After they'd fired, before the British came to investigate, the cautious guards often hid their few guns, clasping only wooden planks by the time the hostile British arrived. Sometimes the investigators did not fully believe that the bursts of deadly gunfire had originated in these wooden boards. But the Galilee has known its share of miracles...

When Dviri read an article by Ahimeir, he hunted the man down and insisted on joining his ranks.

Nissim Cohen, short, dark haired, his easy-going speech punctuated with the guttural *a*s and *h*s of his Yemenite heritage, remained on duty in Tel Aviv for two months until the last embers of the murderous Arab violence had been extinguished. He attempted to attend to as many of his private affairs as possible, continuing to serve as Moshe Rosenberg's deputy, in charge of accepting new members into the nationalist resistance.

Rosenberg, a man Segal described as "a soldier, through and through," was heir to a typically tragic Jewish family history. His father had been kidnapped by the Czar's soldiers and forced to serve in the Russian army. Moshe Rosenberg somehow preserved his Jewishness, but willingly suckled his military inheritance as well. Rosenberg taught military tactics at the Officers School and assumed command when Irma Halperin left for Paris.

Halperin journeyed to Paris at Jabotinsky's request. Jabo had himself been exiled by the British in 1929, destined to wander from Jewish community to Jewish community for the last 11 years of his life, warning all that a holocaust of unknowable proportions was darkening the imminent horizon. Since he and Aharon Propes had founded the Betar movement in Riga in 1923, Jabo had put more and more of his hopes into it. "The political parties we found will come and go, but Betar – will be forever." Jabo handpicked Halperin to coordinate the worldwide Betar organization from France, and Halperin reluctantly left his troubled homeland as ordered. Betar would soon enough number well over one hundred thousand adherents, with ninety thousand in Poland alone – the largest youth movement in that desperate country on the eve of World War Two.

Segal hiked northwards into a stint as watchman in the Jordan Valley and Galilee. A knife in his belt and a rifle in his hands, Segal found farmers short of labor and arranged for Betarim from Tel Aviv to man the jobs. Segal went from kibbutz to kibbutz, his inner calm and open honesty winning him friends everywhere, despite heated ideological differences. Eventually Segal signed up for the British-sponsored Border Army, a sort of forerunner to the Jordanian Legion (the state called Jordan did not come into existence until 1946). At the time, a tightly knit group of Galilee watchmen enlisted in this all-Arab British army in order to "keep an eye on the enemy."

"Besides," Segal wrote in his diary, "I've always wanted to see those regions on the way to Amman which my people conquered on their way from Egyptian slavery to the Promised Land." Segal and his determined associates crossed the Jordan River eastward, wandered the hills and valleys of Eastern Eretz Israel, the land given by Moses to the tribes of Reuben, Gad and Menashe, and at a desert army camp volunteered for service; they were not accepted. During their stay at the base, they noticed that most of the conversation concerned scorpions and mosquitoes, salaries or transfers to desert areas where gold is worth its weight in water. One man remarked that "the climate in Eretz Israel is excellent; in winter you go to Egypt and in summer to Europe." On Yom Kippur in 1930, Segal was back in Jerusalem.

* * *

Some events seem simple in hindsight. Some news takes years to travel, some is heard round the world even as it occurs. Some events, taken out of context, cannot be understood.

After decades of Jewish independence in Israel, with an army the U.S. Marines admit to admiring, with heroes of the Soviet Jewry movement like Sharansky, Zalmanson, Kosharovsky and Mendelevich living freely in a Jewish state, and the return of tens of thousands of Jews to their roots, some events such as blowing the shofar ram's horn on the Day of Atonement are easily taken for granted.

But in 1930, no Jewish army patrolled the cities of Eretz Israel. No Jews knew the meaning of Hebrew independence. After the catastrophic Arab pogroms of August 1929, Jews stayed or were kept away from the holy Western Wall on the Day of Atonement. This year, 1930, they would worship there, within the restraints imposed by the "enlightened" British Empire: no benches, no curtained separations, no singing too loudly, and no shofar.

Sometimes one solitary man must be so impatient with oppression, must be so hungry for redemption that he will take the first step into the churning waters of the sea.

Moshe Segal worshipped in the Etz Chaim Synagogue on Yom Kippur morning. Then he walked into walled Old Jerusalem towards the ancient Western Wall of Temple Mount. His steps were alternately hesitant and belligerent. Each was an as yet unpronounced challenge to British imperialism.

The Western Wall as it appeared in the past, with a six-foot-wide corridor for worshippers. This photograph is from the 1880s.

"On that day a great shofar will be sounded," prophesied Isaiah. Perhaps these words popped unexpectedly into Segal's thoughts as he walked.

On Yom Kippur, prayer is an all-day endeavor. A short break is afforded the fasting, fervent worshippers just before the afternoon service. Segal is now at the Wall; he notices the wavering indecision of the congregants, the crestfallen air in the prayer-filled alley alongside the Wall. A number of prayer-shawled Jews are whispering in a corner, and Segal eavesdrops on the Yiddish: "What about the shofar blast? Where should we go?" The number of British policemen is about as great as that of the Jewish devotees. And the British have but a single concern: to prevent the sounding of the shofar.

Segal thinks excitedly to himself, half arguing and half expounding: Will we forego the shofar blast, which expresses the kingship of God embodied in its accompanying verses: "Hear O Israel, the Lord is God, the Lord is one," and "The Lord is God!"? Can we skip the blast, symbolizing the redemption of Israel? True, in itself it's only a tradition...but here, at this holiest of all spots, at this holiest of all moments...

Segal steps towards Rabbi Itzhak Orenstein, the rabbi in charge of the Wall area, and speaks quietly but insistently:

"Give me, please, a shofar."

"What do you need a shofar for?"

"I will sound it."

"What are you talking about? Don't you see the police watching?"

"Nonetheless, I will sound it."

The old rabbi turns to leave, but not before nodding in the direction of a prayer-stand in the left corner. Segal leans against the stand and as dusk descends, his fingers rummage through its drawer until they rest upon a shofar. He slips the ram's horn into his shirt and determines that whatever is about to happen, the British will not discover the shofar before he blows it. He asks an elderly gentleman to lend him his large, white prayer shawl. Segal wraps himself in the shawl, and underneath its warm folds feels an emotional charge.

"I've created, for one moment, a bit of private property. Inside this space I can do as I please, despite the foreign ruler outside which prevents my brothers from freely worshipping God. Under this shawl there is no foreign ruler, there is a free Jewish state, and here I am free to do God's will."

As the worshippers raise their voices reciting "Hear O Israel the Lord is God, the Lord is one," Segal draws the shofar and sounds a deep, bass blast that shakes those who hear it – and those faraway who will hear of it. Segal is himself shaken by the many British police who grab him.

He is arrested, denied food to break his Yom Kippur fast, and held on the second floor of the police station adjacent to David's Tower, just inside Jaffa Gate.

Segal asks the Arab left guarding him for a drink of water. The guard says no, he cannot leave him even for a minute. But in an attempt to soften his refusal and seem friendly, the Arab lets forth a barrage of blustery curses aimed at the despicable British. "What brotherhood there is between us," Segal laughs to himself.

The Chief Rabbi of Eretz Israel, the revered Rabbi Abraham Isaac Kook, is informed of events by his students who had heard the blast at the Wall. Rabbi Kook phones the British authorities and flings a threat: Either you let the lad go, or I do not end my fast. Not much time passes before the British decision makers realize that world-wide headlines reading "Chief Rabbi of the Holy Land Declares Hunger Fast" will do more damage than Segal is worth. The Arab guard is called downstairs and once there he is told to leave. No one bothers to inform Segal that he has been released.

At midnight, Segal realizes he is unguarded and on his own initiative rises and leaves the police station. He is greeted outside by Rabbi Kook's students who explain that he is expected at the home of the Chief Rabbi's assistant to break the fast.

Jewish newspapers all over the world carried the story of the young Jew who had dared defy the British Empire in Eretz Israel. Eldad, Shamir, Begin – the future leaders of the Jewish Revolution – were in Poland in 1930 while Ahimeir and Rosenberg were laying the foundations of an underground army. But ask Yitzhak Shamir today what he remembers about Yom Kippur 1930, and he'll tell you: We remember being electrified at the courage of a man we had never met, Moshe Segal. "A wonderful man," remarked the future prime minister. "A courageous fighter, a commander...leading the way...we will learn from him."

Segal's shofar blast was a luminous beacon of light to the restless Jewish youth in Eretz Israel, a North Star beckoning to directionless rebels depressed in the night of oppression. A Yom Kippur tradition was born: Every year afterwards, Jewish youth followed Segal's path to the Wall, smuggling shofars to be sounded at sunset. Abba Ahimeir's Brit Habirionim provided the shofar blowers and their back-up teams for the first several years. Haim Dviri was a regular, forming part of a perennial Brit circle around each year's herald of redemption.

Two weeks before Yom Kippur in 1937, Betar officer Eliahu Meridor asked a new 16-year-old recruit, Jacob "Sicka" Aharoni, if he were prepared to sound the shofar at the Wall. "You will be arrested and you will sit in prison," Meridor warned. Aharoni eagerly accepted the mission and was ordered to report to his neighbor, Moshe Segal, and to Baruch Duvdevani, for instruction in the art of shofar blowing. The youthful and even now new-to-the-movement Aharoni did not know that Segal had initiated the tradition. Segal, who impressed Aharoni as "humble and modest," did not tell him. "You are about to do a great deed," Segal said. After teaching him how to sound the horn, Segal taught him the religious laws and devotions involved in the act, too.

Aharoni approached the Western Wall that Yom Kippur afternoon with the shofar tucked under his belt, covered by his shirt. The entrance to the prayer area was blocked by British and Arab police sitting behind a table. Waiting on line to enter, Aharoni passed the shofar to a devoutly religious Jewish woman who happened to be nearby. When his turn came, the Arab policeman asked him if he had anything dangerous. "Be careful, I've got a cannon," the boy replied in Arabic. Inside, the woman returned the shofar, and Aharoni, a cantorial school graduate, organized his own prayer group in the far right corner. His prayers were melodious if somewhat modernized: "Our Father, our King," he recited from the prayer book, "raise the strength of Israel Thy people and," he ad-libbed, "break the strength of the British kingdom." His prayers aroused great enthusiasm. When he discerned a Jewish detective watching him a bit too closely, he improvised again: "Our God and God of our fathers...Please notice the guy with the cap, he's on the enemy's side; surround me, surround me so he won't stop me." Aharoni's makeshift congregation formed a solid wall around him till the shofar was sounded. The detective pointed him out, the British and Arabs arrested him, and he spent two weeks in the police station near David's Tower. His lawyer got him off with time served, but his accomplice that night, Israel Tevua, was sentenced to six months.

Betar and eventually the Irgun adopted the activity as their own. Yedida Feiglevich, née Mizrahi, recalls that "in those days there was no television, only radio. The first thing after the conclusion of the fast, people turned on their radios to hear whether the shofar had been blown at the Western Wall. On my street not many people had radios, and our neighbors would ask us to turn the volume up on ours so they could listen to the news. It was a national event, something in the souls of the Jews. It wasn't a question of whether you were in the Underground. If you were Jewish, you wanted to know whether the shofar had been blown at the Wall."

One Yom Kippur, Yedida saw her brother, Rahamim Mizrahi, leave the synagogue earlier than usual. Rahamim walked home and donned his father's policeman's jacket. Yedida had begun to suspect something was up the week before, when she caught snippets of her brother's conversations with his friends. Now she was sure. She and her friends followed Rahamim and his friends as they headed for the Old City and the Wall. The young women planned to help protect this year's shofar blower from the police. Yedida did not see her brother blow the shofar because the crowd was too thick, but she and her friends did their bit. They locked arms and interfered with the efforts of the police to move through the crowd towards the sound of the shofar. A second sister, Geula, describes the siblings' return home that night: "We were waiting to eat. I was standing on the porch looking for Yedida and Rahamim. When they came home they were so happy. Father asked Rahamim why he had left the synagogue and Rahamim mumbled something about the heat. Mother had been very anxious, and I saw Rahamim and Yedida with Mother when he told her the truth. He said, 'I did something holier to me than being in synagogue with Father. I blew the shofar at the Wall.' Mother hugged him and hugged him, and she cried."

Yedida and Rahamim never exchanged a word about the event, as

Rahamim Mizrahi, early 1940s

they were not supposed to openly discuss such a secret mission. But Geula says their eyes spoke more than they ever could have said in words, and six decades later she still remembers the look of joy in those eyes.

Two years later, Rahamim did it again. "This time," Geula says, "we didn't wait for them to return before we ate. We assumed Rahamim and Yedida were at the Wall. When they came in, Rahamim told Mother, as his fist pounded the table, 'I succeeded a second time. You'll see, we will yet have a state...and I'll be prime minister.'" Geula says their mother was proud as can be.

Most of those who sounded shofars were beaten, their blood further sanctifying the site Josephus writes once "flowed with rivers of Zealots' blood." And most were arrested and sentenced to between three and six months.

Menahem Begin had other ideas. In 1944 the Irgun, recently come under his leadership, plastered the walls of Jerusalem with ominous warnings to the British. Begin felt the time had come to tell the British that the Jews were adamant about their religious rights. "ANY BRITISH OFFICER INTERFERING...WILL BE TREATED AS A CRIMINAL AND PUNISHED ACCORDINGLY."

The ironic truth was that the Irgun was bluffing. Begin had not yet built it up to its future strength and the British were free to do as they pleased in Jerusalem. But of this truth the British were blissfully unaware and when the shofar was blown that year, the Wall, which for two thousand years had been a symbol of Hebrew wailing, and which had already been recast by Segal as a symbol of resistance and Jewish pride, now became a symbol of victory, the first battle won – even if only a psychological win – by the Irgun in its war against the British.

In 1948, the Old City fell to the troops of the Jordanian Legion and the stones of the captive Western Wall became once again hard symbols of the harsh Jewish reality. And then in 1967, six wonder-filled June days restored the majesty to the stones. An entire nation sang of these "stones with hearts of men," thousands flocked – and thousands left following their prayers. Only one man, one still-solitary man, remained, unable to tear himself from the gravitational force that had been pulling him all his life to Old Jerusalem. One man remained within the city walls when all others departed, one man cleaned out a ruined synagogue complex and built himself a home, one man labored day and night to reconstruct the synagogue so others could worship there. That man was Moshe Segal.

★ ★ ★

On Yom Kippur in 1967, thousands of Jews worshipped in dozens of prayer quorums at the newly liberated Western Wall, and as dusk fell tens of shofars were prepared to signal the conclusion of the holy 25-hour fast, but even as the voices rose from the many quorums, declarations of "Hear O Israel" blending with shouts of "The Lord is God," the shofars were held in abeyance, the rush to finish the prayers was slowed, the shouts and the murmurs were silenced and everybody stood expectantly and waited. And the Yom Kippur prayers were concluded when one man, no longer a young revolutionary but now a dark-suited, elderly, obviously pious Jew with a black yarmulke and a graying beard, sounded the shofar blast. And that man, too, was Moshe Segal.

The Burning Bush

"Dear Burning Bush," the great Expressionist poet Elsa Lasker-Shuler opened a 1925 letter she was writing to her friend in Eretz Israel, Uri Zvi Greenberg.

The appearance in the songs of Uri Zvi Greenberg of the 1940s underground armies, the war for the independence of Israel, the European Holocaust and the 1967 Six Day War may not astonish many readers today – unless they read the fine-print dates at songs' end. Each of these events was recorded by Greenberg twenty or more years before its historical occurrence.

Hebrew poet Haim Nachman Bialik once asked Greenberg how he

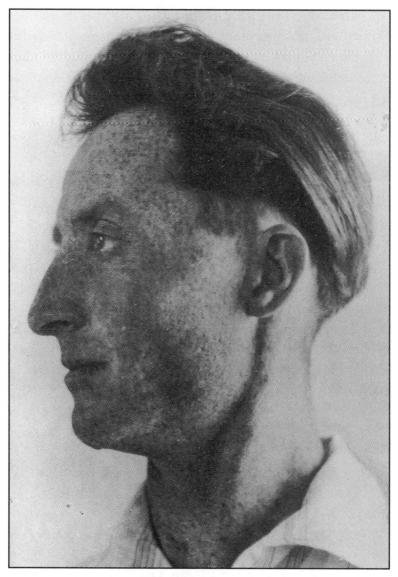

Poet Uri Zvi Greenberg, ca. 1930

was able to write of the Holocaust and describe the murder of millions of Jews in 1922 ("We had to leave. The ground screamed under our feet, the beds shook...we had to leave the towns sadly and look back through burning tears, one last time, at the homes – knowing they would one day burn"). To Bialik, Greenberg replied: "But I see it." Uri Zvi's widow, poet Aliza Tur-Malka, recalls the startling fact that "many of the poems in *Rehovot Hanahar*, a 1951 volume detailing the atrocities of the Holocaust, were written the previous decade, before Uri Zvi had read the grim news reports from Europe. Yet all the facts we know today correspond to the poems." "Holy of Holies" describes the murder of the poet's mother. He wrote it before the event, from a nighttime dream. He "simply" recorded that which he torturously saw with his mind's eye.

Philosopher Dr. Israel Eldad, foremost student of UZG's poetry as well as a friend of the poet and one of the Stern Group's three commanders in the 1940s, noted that "Greenberg does more than prophesy and more than mourn. His poetry commands." Thus in "Holy of Holies" he imagines he has carried his mortally wounded mother to the Land of Israel where she speaks: "Let me touch your body... / your garments are rough, my son, soldiers' clothes / and a rifle on your shoulder...Good for you my son / Once I wished to see you robed only in silk. / No longer..." While other Hebrew poets accompanied the Jewish people on its way and gave expression to the struggle for statehood, explained Dr. Eldad, Greenberg predated it and commanded it. "His books forged history." Eldad's theory is that "Three songs created the IZL and Sternist Undergrounds: Greenberg's 'One Truth and Not Two,' Stern's 'Soldiers without Names,' and Jabotinsky's 'Betar Song.'" And of this last, UZG once confided to Eldad that he was jealous he had not written it himself...

The Jewish youth of the '30s and '40s read Greenberg and understood that their lot was not silken robes but rather readiness for deprivation and battle. Abraham Tehomi, 1920s Hagana commander in Jerusalem and later Commander in Chief of the Irgun Zvai Leumi, granted that "It is a given that Uri Zvi Greenberg influenced the Irgunists, but he had tremendous influence on members of the Hagana, too." Menahem Begin, attending Greenberg's funeral in 1981 as prime minister, confided to Eldad as they, President Navon, Moshe Segal and half the cabinet followed the poet's prayer-shawled body that he, too, arrived at his political outlook when he read UZG's "I'll Tell It to a Child."

Earlier, in his first work, young Uri Zvi factually describes how he came to write. Perched on a rock with his feet dangling in the river below, he was suddenly unable to breathe. Throwing his head back, he felt a warmth engulfing his body. Years later, in another poem, he reflects: "My God surely cursed me / for he caused me to see the charred and slaughtered of my tribe / the old and young, and the infants, too, like sheep in a butcher shop / He commanded my eyes to see and my nostrils to smell / and my hand to hold the paper, to record it all in a book. / This is no blessing. My God has greatly cursed me." Eldad said every event in the poet's hectic life was transformed into metaphor, much as with the Biblical prophets of yore. Greenberg liked to point to the lines which creased his forehead in the shape of the Hebrew letter "shin" which also adorns doorpost mezuzahs. And he had an eye for tragedy. "He would read a paper," recalled Eldad, "and find a two-line disaster everyone else had missed." "He sat with his fists clenched, all the time," remembers Aliza.

Greenberg fought in the First World War and was moved by the determination of the Serbs to be free. "And I even reached, far from the mountains of Bosnia and Montenegro, that faraway site in Albania where lies the body of Shabtai Zvi. There I stood, a young Jewish soldier in the unkosher *shaatnez* uniform of Emperor Franz Joseph's army, alone in a distant world...I lowered the rifle from my shoulder and struck the unkempt mound marked by a stone on which the name of the banished Shabtai is not inscribed, and I declared: I, Uri Zvi the son of Batsheva of Lvov, serving in the foreign army of Franz Joseph, stand by your grave, Shabtai Zvi, you-whose-sufferings-after-the-con-version-cannot-even-be-imagined, Mahmoud Effendi..."

After the Serbian battles, Greenberg, rather than return to the

Hasidic garb of his youth, turned to the Expressionist Yiddish poetry which won him fame. In Warsaw he teamed with Peretz Markesh and Melekh Ravitch to proclaim with explosive emotion the end of the old order. They called themselves, these three Yiddish giants, the "Gang," which was perhaps symptomatic of Greenberg's proclivity for tantalizingly offensive names. When Ahimeir, Dviri, Segal, Yevin and their colleagues gather a few years hence in Eretz Israel to formally incorporate their activist organization, the youth will choose the name Brit Zionim Mahapachaniim, the "Covenant of Revolutionary Zionists." Greenberg will request the floor and tell them they are wrong, the name will be Brit Habirionim, harking back to the extremist Zealots of old. And so it will be. Eldad's 1950s journal *Ladder to the Freedom of Israel* will be renamed by Uri Zvi *Ladder to the Kingdom of Israel.*

UZG consolidated his position as a poet with two ouvres: *Mephisto*, a retelling of the Faust legend in which Mephistopheles, not the forces of good, wins and rules the world; and "In the Kingdom of the Cross," the work prophesying a Holocaust, published in July 1923.

Ravitch will eventually sail for North America where he will come to represent Western Yiddishism, Markesh will return to Soviet Russia where he will be murdered by Stalin, and Greenberg – who had written a "Salute to Lenin" upon the revolutionary's death – will sail for Eretz Israel and the Hebrew language.

Aliza Greenberg says her husband was influenced by Heine, enjoyed Whitman and Blake, but drew first and foremost upon Jewish midrash and prayer. "What springs from the 365 joints of our body today and expresses them in Rising Judea – roars like a chapter of Hebrew Psalms from the great sovereign past," he wrote.

Uri Zvi reached the shores of Eretz Israel in December 1923 and spent three days walking, as a true pilgrim, to Jerusalem. His early poems in Eretz Israel glorify the pioneers and kibbutzim ("We are the army of the barefoot..."; "Sing of how our stomachs shrivel in the Land of Israel..."; and "This is the Land in which fever is glory and tuberculosis a Vision...") but Greenberg quickly grew disillusioned with the local political establishment. The rebel had alienated the Jews of Berlin by warning that time was running out; he had alienated the Yiddishists by switching, at his mother's urging, to Hebrew; and now he alienated the Labor movement by criticizing the complacency of its leaders in the face of Arab attacks.

From *Sdan* (Anvil), an opinionistic journal he edited in late 1924:

"I raise *Sdan*, to give expression to what is new on the ground of Israel. The hour is most deep. I know the holiness of the spot: I stand on the flesh of a new Jerusalem. The terrible prophecies have all come to pass. With my eyes I see the hurled curse of God. I have in mind the awe, the great responsibility that rests in writing Hebrew after Ezekiel, also the great joy in being a Hebrew troubadour, born in Europe and denying his birth there, for the voice of the race has overcome Latin rhythm. The first Hebrew voice! And I am poor but joyful in a torn Israeli prayer shawl, longingly belonging to this land..."

And: "The time has come for the Hebrew artist to break with the established limits of art, to join with the collective Israel, to ponder with it the complex of problems which the nation is experiencing. Poetry can no longer be recited in classic rhythm. The situation is terrible. Dispersed Judaism, after every atrocity imaginable, is atrophying on Slavic land and sinking. The Diaspora, a sort of world-wide territory, has disintegrated. There is no longer a monolithic Israel-in-trouble, rather masses upon masses in various countries, speeding on every train and every boat in the world, ready to go in an insane direction: Anydamnplace. We have not risen to these awful times, not the artists and not the nation's leaders. We are perhaps confused, or maybe degenerates. Everyone is concerned with his own worries and pleasures. Everyone has a passport ready for visas...

"God is missing from Hebrew literature. Infinite shock is missing. A desire to overcome is missing...

"We need a radical cure here...We must declare that Hebrew literature has rotted away, as has our Zionist leadership. We must proclaim with disdain the idiocy and meanspiritedness of our literary critics...

"I do not fear the various party newspapers, nor the literary mosquitoes. It is a good sign that all the dogs in the yards are barking. The new will come without asking an elder's permission and without literary legitimacy. Let it come!"

After the Arab pogroms of 1929 the poet went to see the bodies of the murdered Jews. "He did things like that," says Aliza. "In one body he counted 80 wounds. Imagine, to stand there and count!" The sensitive poet felt this was his obligation.

In the seventies, he told a reporter how he came to write "I'll Tell It to a Child": "I dreamt one night...I saw the Temple Mount, above it an eagle, and around it circles and circles of Jews, and from the Mount a slope inclined straight to the sea. On either side were lines of soldiers from all the world's armies. In the dream I felt that the Divine Presence, *She-chinat Israel*, was leaving the Mount. I woke up weeping; my cries woke everyone in the house. They asked: 'What happened, what happened?' That morning I went to (Chief) Rabbi Kook and found him wrapped in his prayer shawl. I told him the dream. He didn't say a word, just took my hand in his and wept. I went home and wrote 'I'll Tell It to a Child.'"

This song about "the good Messiah who didn't come," who was in fact chased out of Jerusalem as he offered it glory, electrified Jewish youth and eventually brought more members to the Jewish Underground to fight for redemption than any other single speech, article or personality of the time – perhaps more than all others put together.

"UZG's writing often reads like Old Testament prose," remarked Bialik, "occasionally like intensely personal romantic lyrics. The reader is taken on a demanding journey through Jewish history and pushed pell-mell into the history-yet-to-be-made...The lines are sometimes a bit long, but what strong expressions, pathos, meaning, and the main thing – a fabulous central theme: the redemption of Israel."

Despite Uri Zvi's great love for Jerusalem – he spent many nights sleeping on its ancient walls and he usually entered the city on foot – he could not live there for long: "I cannot bear it – the destroyed Jerusalem all around me." Greenberg spent the 1930s travelling back and forth to Poland, renting auditoriums at his own expense to warn Jews of the impending disaster. At first he warned; later he was to develop what he once called "a science of mourning." The destruction of European Jewry left the poet racked and ever restless. In *Rehovot Hanahar*, Dr. Eldad postulated, he settles accounts: the account of a prophet with his people, who mostly ignored or even hated him; and the account of a people with its God who stood by during the Destruction. And then Greenberg goes a step further, making his Holocaust poetry unique: He formulates the demands incumbent on God and the Jews in the wake of the Holocaust.

"After the despair there is no more despair / and all descents are also ascents."

Greenberg made demands on the healthy Jews of the Land of Israel, calling them to majesty and vision. His greatest honor, he thought, was that the Jewish fighters hanged by the British government in pre-1948 Eretz Israel went to the gallows quoting his poetry. Indeed, many years earlier he had written of martyrs "ascending the gallows, and the dawn of Jerusalem in the lustre of their faces."

In one poem, Greenberg writes of the Patriarch Abraham who walked along the Euphrates River – interestingly, Eldad noted, against the current – to Israel, thereby beginning Jewish history. Eldad explained: "Now, after its long history of suffering, Greenberg is telling us that the Jewish people has returned to the land of the Euphrates. Jewish history thus begins anew."

But the writer was not overly optimistic on Jewish relations with Arabs: "We could not live with the nation of Kant," he wrote (in 1936!), "how will we be able to live with Arab *fellahin*?"

Greenberg seemed to live simultaneously in the time of Abraham,

King David, Titus, the present and the future. Nor did he distinguish between the imagination and the rational. "Everything is possible, for the mind grasps what the imagination grasps." He united feeling and thought, all aspects of the Jewish people, and all aspects of Jewish culture. He referred to the partisans of the Holocaust as "lamed vavniks,"

Uri Zvi Greenberg in tallit (prayer shawl) and tefillin at the Western Wall after its liberation, June 9, 1967

the 36 righteous men, and called bloody shirts "holy prayer shawls." Greenberg's poetry is full of cities that are altars drenched in Jewish blood, full of placid snow with red drops, full of Messiahs who come to the very threshold before stopping. If Greenberg perfected mourning to such a degree that it became a science, his widow Aliza remarks, his religion was one of longing and of desire, for God and for greatness.

"Tomorrow you will not be able to want what today you can do...Tomorrow God will not hear your prayers...Tomorrow you will not have a man of Vision calling to you..."

In 1930, Uri Zvi Greenberg could be found in Altschuler's cafe.

Prison

Abba Ahimeir was in many respects the professor of the Hebrew revolution, a bifoculed instructor whose seminars were held in his book-crammed bedroom, a teacher whose students volunteered for classes which often lasted all night, a lecturer who led his wards out of school and into the streets and who urged his serious students to enroll in the unavoidable universities of the unborn Jewish state: the British prisons which blighted the Eretz Israel landscape. He exhorted the Jewish youth without mincing words:

"We are speaking clearly: *Fight*. Really fight, as all oppressed nations have fought for the freedom of their homelands. No propagandistic speeches, no rattling of fund-boxes, no wars of words, but real war against the enemy's regime and the [Jewish] leadership serving as its agent. A war that leads its fighters to prison and torture...that is how you will fight, young Hebrew residents of Eretz Israel, for your people and land."

A secret British police profile assessed Ahimeir and his influence in 1931 and 1932:

"In his speeches he would attack any policy of conciliation or co-

Abba Ahimeir (Jabotinsky Institute photo)

operation and would often include gross insults against the characters of private persons.

"During this time he succeeded in gathering around him the enthusiastic youths ready for any sacrifice in the liberation of [Eretz Israel] and the creation of a Zionist State."

Up in Altschuler's Cafe, a few days after Segal's partisan action at the Wall (a future generation of activists might call it "civil disobedience," or in Martin Luther King, Jr.'s phrase: "creative confrontation") serving as alarum to the cadres of anxious youth, Ahimeir and a few of his comrades sat chewing over recent events and the little food they could afford to order. Ahimeir had taken the unusual step of sending for them, of calling an actual meeting. Dviri would often ponder, as he headed towards Abba's Jerusalem apartment, the strange nature of this pseudo-army. "We've got no commanders or soldiers," Dviri thought, "we just cooperate. Decisions are simply that which everyone agrees upon. Our relationship with the leaders is one of friendship, a feeling of brotherhood. None of us have anything to eat. Ahimeir and Yevin go without bread. They aren't even leaders, the term is too bombastic, they're thinkers – and we've latched on to their thoughts. Whoever is in the room, decides on our activity..." And now Ahimeir had called them to Altschuler's.

The London government had recently further restricted Jewish rights to purchase land in Eretz Israel and even to immigrate into the land. Now Dr. Drummond Shiels, deputy minister for the colonies, was on his way. Ahimeir explained that the official Jewish leadership would invariably toady up to him, and suggested as an alternative an anti-British demonstration to highlight the different approach of the nationalist youth. To sharpen the contrast, the demonstration should be held at the Palatin Hotel, Tel Aviv's swankiest, where Shiels is to be wined and dined by the establishment "leaders."

On the first day of *Hol Hamoed Succot* (the first intermediate day of the Festival of Tabernacles, which is the second day of the holiday in Eretz Israel) the festivities began. As planned, five of Ahimeir's group, including Ahimeir himself and Segal, sallied forth into Tel Aviv's jammed rush-hour streets with a banner protesting Shiels' presence in Jewish Tel Aviv. Before they began the march to the hotel, they swore that if stopped they would move forward, if pushed they would continue, if beaten they would rise. Under no circumstances would they flee. "We will sing *Hatikva* and move forward." Thus, their decision to march was in effect a decision to be the first to enter prison as Zionists since Jabotinsky's 1920 arrest and the first to knowingly choose that path.

As they headed for the hotel, Ahimeir's Hebrew pipers collected under their simple banner hundreds of supporters from among the pedestrian onlookers. Naive Jewish officials informed Shiels a crowd had gathered to welcome him; the deputy minister decided to put in an appearance. At first he mistook the whistles and hoots for a local form of greeting, but the boos and catcalls were soon obvious even to him. Shiels, Meir Dizengoff and the establishment leadership looked out upon the sea of screaming protesters and chose to be evacuated via a rear exit, incidentally leaving half their banquet uneaten.

With the dignitaries safely out of the way, the club-swinging Tel Aviv police swarmed to the scene from Rothschild Boulevard. A pitched battle ensued, with the protesters attempting to locate and follow Shiels. One rather tall, corpulent member of Tel Aviv's finest reared back to throw a very hefty punch at Segal. Segal, coincidentally standing adjacent to an equally sturdy tree, stepped aside – and the poor fool mangled his hand with one powerful blow to the seemingly unperturbed tree. The cop barked at Segal: "I'll swear in court that you sliced me with a knife!" to which the evidently unfazed Segal replied: "Then you'll be a liar."

Ahimeir, meanwhile, was repeatedly knocked to the ground, only to rise again, each time a bit more battered but not yet down for the count, and through it all ever singing *Kol od balevav...*; *Hatikva* had perhaps been sung in more respectable circumstances, but never more earnestly. By this time the mass of spontaneous demonstrators had fled the melee, and the police soon overcame and arrested most of the instigators.

A Jewish officer took Ahimeir, as the oldest of the arrestees, to an inner room of the police station for more intensive questioning. The sounds emanating from the chamber indicated the physical nature of the questions, leading Segal to raise himself to a window to investigate. He witnessed the interrogator breaking Abba's glasses, drawing blood from his face and beating him. Segal looked lovingly at Abba: his long, pale face; his curly, chestnut-colored hair falling ever so slightly over his high forehead; his wire-thin body (Dviri had once said he looked like a professional hunger striker – which, considering his income, he probably was). Segal's only thoughts were of how to alleviate Abba's pain – and then the rabid officer noticed the witness to his crime.

"What?! You want to tell people what I do with Abba Ahimeir?" yelled the furious guardian of the law, grabbing Segal by the ears and repeatedly pounding his head against the wall. Despite the thudding pain, Segal was satisfied: "I'm glad that I'm absorbing the blows otherwise intended for Abba."

The Birionim were locked up and officially charged with organizing an illegal demonstration, inciting to rebellion, disturbing the peace and insulting a member of the government.

Ahimeir pleaded innocent, declaring the guilty to be those who "close the gates of immigration to Jews." Ahimeir further demanded that the police be made to pay the medical bills resulting from their beatings.

The judge: Have you had previous encounters with the police?

Ahimeir: Only with the Russian secret police.

Judge: And since then you haven't had any contact with the police.

Ahimeir: I haven't had the honor.

Judge: Did you honor Dr. Shiels with cries of "boo"?

Ahimeir: Yes, and cries of "[Remember] Hebron" and "Pogromchik!" as well.

Judge: Were you the only one shouting?

Ahimeir: I don't think so.

Judge: Were you trying to express anything in particular?

Ahimeir: The sympathy I feel for the Colonial Office...I've seen their police watch Arabs stab Jews; they disperse the Jews and not the Arabs...and I believe Shiels is directly responsible for preventing aliya.

Judge: And you don't think he should be received in Tel Aviv with tea?

Ahimeir: I don't think he should be received with tea.

Judge: You saw Shiels leave the Palatin?

Ahimeir: And I heard scattered applause.

Judge: You felt the applause was staged?

Ahimeir: I felt disgusted.

Judge: You heard the order to disperse?

Ahimeir: No, I felt as if a bear had run into a tree, had gotten excited, attacked me and knocked me down.

Judge: You sang?

Ahimeir: *Hatikva*.

Judge: Did others sing?

Ahimeir: I think everyone sang.

Judge: Do you regret booing?

Ahimeir: I do not.

Judge: Do you regret singing *Hatikva*?

Ahimeir: A Zionist will never regret singing *Hatikva*.

The judge asked Segal why he had stabbed the policeman. Segal answered, "Not only is he stupid for striking a tree, but he's a liar to boot."

As the judge was about ready to issue his ruling, a messenger arrived with word that the British authorities in Jerusalem had decided to drop the charges. The judge read this message aloud to extended and enthusiastic applause from the spectator's section.

On the Ninth of Av, 1929, one thousand young Jews had asserted their national pride and their determination to reach their goal despite British opposition. On Yom Kippur, 1930, one young Jew had openly defied the British regime and willingly been arrested. Now, on Succot, a group of young Jews and their mentor had marched, battled, been arrested and stood trial, and had been transformed in the docket from defendants to accusers.

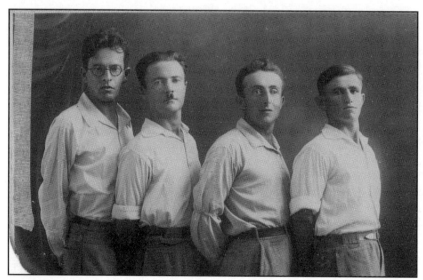

Arrested for demonstrating against Shiels: (left to right) Abba Ahimeir, Moshe Segal, Ephraim Ben David, Shmuel Tagansky

.. THE NE

THOMAS LOSES POST IN THE LABOR PARTY

British Dominions Minister Is Punished for Failure to Solve Unemployment Problem.

MOSLEY PLACED ON BOARD

Election of Radical Who Was Put Out of Government Is an Added Rebuke to Laborite.

By CHARLES A. SELDEN.

Special Cable to THE NEW YORK TIMES.

LLANDUDNO, Wales, Oct. 9.—Arthur Henderson, British Foreign Minister, saved the Labor Government from future embarrassment today by staving off a resolution at the party conference at Llandudno instructing the MacDonald Cabinet to disarm this country, regardless of what other countries might do.

The resolution, which originated with the rebellious group of radicals led by James Maxton, denounced the London Naval Conference as a failure so far as effective disarmament was concerned and demanded that Great Britain's next step toward peace should be to promote disarmament by setting an example to the world without waiting any longer for the rest of the world to co-operate.

The Maxton resolution also would have pledged the government against any further preparations for war. This would have meant, of course, a refusal to provide in the next budget for any appropriations for the army, navy and air forces.

Mr. Henderson had no difficulty in convincing the conference that any such omission from the estimates of government expenditures would mean immediate defeat in the House of Commons and downfall of the government. Mr. Henderson also declared that if the party forced the Cabinet to adopt such a peace policy it would invalidate everything Great Britain had already accomplished at Geneva for peace and render its future program for disarmament useless. So the resolution was allowed to die by the parliamentary process of moving the previous question.

The sensation of today's session was the defeat of J. H. Thomas, Minister of Dominions, for re-election to the National Executive Committee of the Labor party. There were fourteen candidates from the trades union division, of whom the conference had to select twelve. Mr. Thomas was at the bottom of the list of voting results and so for the first time in many years he dropped from the executive group which manages the party.

This was due chiefly to Mr. Thomas's failure as Lord Privy Seal to render any adequate service in solving the unemployment problem. But the defeat also reflects the resentment of the rank and file at Mr.

Thomas's "putting on airs" and dining out too often in evening clothes with capitalists.

For the first time in Mr. Thomas's long political career many of his old associates and fellow workers in the railway union voted agianst him. To make the rebuke more pointed, the conference elected to the executive committee Sir Oswald Mosley, who was forced out of the government because of his controversy with Mr. Thomas over unemployment.

The defeat of Mr. Thomas and the election of Sir Oswald, together with the significant absence from the conference of Miss Margaret Bondfield, Minister of Labor, shows more emphatically than much oratory the bitter disappointment of the rank and file of the party with the government's failure to relieve unemployment.

The radicals had their way in passing a resolution favoring 60 insteady of 65 years as the age for eligibility for old-age pensions, and also in the adoption of a resolution urging the government "to take from the Bank of England the privileges of exploiting national credit and to use that credit itself for national needs and social purposes."

REICH ACCUSES LITHUANIA.

Germans Say She Has Not Kept Faith in Memel Agreements.

Wireless to THE NEW YORK TIMES.

BERLIN, Oct. 9.—The resignation of Lithuania's Foreign Minister, Dr. David Zaunium, is taken here as an indication that the Lithuanian Government does not intend to keep the promises which Dr. Zaunius gave to Foreign Minister Curtius of Germany at Geneva in regard to Lithuania's policy toward the Memel population, although Dr. Zaunius was in constant contact with his Cabinet colleagues during the Geneva negotiations.

Three of the most pressing points under discussion were the lifting of the censorship within the Memel territory, replacement of two Lithuanian members of the Memel directorate by two Memel citizens and permission for the electoral committee to prepare elections. Lithuania has not complied with these points, despite her promises.

The German Foreign Office has repeatedly tried to have a direct understanding with Lithuania before and since the Geneva session without result, although Wilhelmstrasse has asserted German-Lithuanian relations might be troubled if Lithuania did not keep her promises.

CROWD HOOTS AT SHIELS.

Young Revisionist Zionists Conduct Demonstration at Tel Aviv.

Wireless to THE NEW YORK TIMES.

TEL AVIV, Palestine, Oct. 9.—A hostile demonstration today greeted Dr. Drummond Shiels, British Under Secretary for Dominions, who is here on an unofficial visit. As Dr. Shiels was leaving his hotel a crowd of young men and women shouted, "Away with a Parliament which does not do justice to Jews," "Shame to the British Government," "Remember Hebron, Safed and Motza."

The demonstrators consisted mostly of young revisionist Zionists. The Zionist flag was unfurled and the crowd surrounded Dr. Shiels, singing the Zionist anthem. Finally Dr. Shiels sped away in an automobile under police guard.

The demonstration was caused by a report from London that Dr. Shiels had promised an Arab delegation the establishment of a parliament for Palestine.

ADOPTS PRINCIPLE FOR BALKAN UNION

Conference at Athens Supports Plan Which Would Outlaw War and Aid Solidarity.

ECONOMIC MOVE INCLUDED

Cooperation Set as Aim In Proposal, Which Does Not, However, Have Any Official Support Now.

Wireless to THE NEW YORK TIMES.

ATHENS, Oct. 9.—The plan for a union of the Balkan States, prepared by former Premier Papanastasiu of Greece, was adopted in principle at a full sitting of the Balkan conference today. It is an ambitious proposal, the adoption of which would have more significance if the delegates to the conference were official representatives of their governments.

Explaining his scheme, M. Papanastasiu said the form of the Balkan union would approximate that of the German Confederation before 1870, but that the Balkan organization would be an alliance of separate sovereign States within the League of Nations. The principle of the confederation is unconditional exclusion of the possibility of war among the Balkan States, and in this respect it would hold fast to the spirit of the League of Nations.

The proposed Balkan union would develop economic cooperation and solidarity and would promote a cultural union. Minorities would enjoy satisfactory protection, as otherwise the Balkan union would be built only on sand.

M. Topalovitch, Yugoslavian delegate, deplored the fact that the conference was aiming at such a distant goal instead of showing itself more concrete in details, but M. Kyroff, Bulgarian representative, expressed pleasure that the conference had displayed such ambition and he commented that its deliberation had turned out to be much more important than he had expected.

The conference adopted a resolution requesting the Foreign Ministers of Balkan States to meet regularly every year to exchange opinions on Balkan affairs and discuss means of bringing about solidarity among the Balkan peoples. The resolution also urged Balkan States to study the proposed pact based on the following principles: First, outlawry of war; second, peaceful settlement of all disputes that arise among them, and, third, mutual assistance in case of violation of the obligation to abstain from war.

The resolution provided that the council of the conference should appoint a special committee to examine the project of the Balkan pact and report at the next conference.

Danes Plan to Slash Defense Budget

COPENHAGEN, Oct. 9 (AP).—The proposed reduction of Denmark's annual military budget from $15,000,000 to $5,000,000 was the principal feature of a new defense bill introduced today in Parliament by the Minister of Defense. The bill proposes to abolish the ranks of General and Colonel and replace them with Chief Inspector and Inspector.

New York Times report of the Shiels demonstration, October 10, 1930

A year earlier, the surprised British had not known how to respond to the crowd which pushed them aside; on Yom Kippur, the British at first arrested and on second thought released the shofar blower. After the Shiels demonstration, the British arrested the ralliers and brought them to trial, releasing the defendants only at literally the last moment.

Ahimeir's boys were learning and so were the British usurpers of Eretz Israel. The British were learning how to deal harshly with freedom fighters. They were not learning that the cause of Hebrew freedom was just and unstoppable. The Betarim, Hagana veterans and Jewish youth were learning not to fear police clubs or prisons or, further on, even gallows. The first steps towards Hebrew revolution were being taken by independence-minded fighters. At this juncture, four fighters had entered prison's steel gates and stood in the court docket.

In 1931, when British cabinet minister Lord Passfield announced a census which would prove a low number of Jews in Eretz Israel (therefore deserving of fewer rights), Ahimeir's Brit Habirionim wreaked havoc with harried census takers' attempts to verify and retain records of local populations. Jabotinsky had written from exile: "The purpose of the census is to prove the Jews are a small minority in the land. Why such a small minority? Because they will not let Jews in! Now the government plots to have Jews help prove the superb success of their locked-gate policy....Nothing should be easier than to break this census...True, punishment will follow, but every Jew will pay a higher price if the census succeeds." The Brit took up the cudgels.

The British themselves eventually admitted the failure of the census; but for inciting citizens not to cooperate in the doomed census (Dviri and a friend once exhausted their transportation budget in Afula while carrying sacks of anti-census pamphlets for their Rosh Pina branch. Dviri tossed the stuffed sack over his shoulder. "We're young, we can walk," he laughed. And so they did, 30 miles to Tiberias), destroying evidence of pollsters' visits and daubing walls with anti-British slogans – 120 members of Brit Habirionim were arrested.

Soon enough, thousands more would follow.

A Brit Habirionim demonstration at Hebrew University in Jerusalem was organized with the aid of two students. One was David Raziel. The other was Abraham Stern.

The Flag

Lag B'Omer is one of those anomalies of Jewish life, a bright spot on a dark calendar, a lone white spot enveloped in blackness which has been the yin and yang of Jewish existence ever since Abraham tragically bound Isaac one moment only to joyously receive his son into his arms the next. Lag B'Omer is the conclusion of 33 days of mourning observed each year in memory of the twenty-four thousand students of Rabbi Akiva who perished in a second-century plague. Lag B'Omer is also the anniversary of the death of the great mystic Rabbi Shimon Bar Yochai, author of the holy Zohar.

In Israel, the day and especially the preceding evening are celebrated with boundless fun. Families and youth groups gather in woods, parks and vacant lots to light bonfires, picnic and sing campfire songs into the early morning hours. Men, women and children carting firewood and cans of kerosene would hardly be noticed on Lag B'Omer, much less rouse any suspicion.

On Lag B'Omer of 1933, a group of Birionim strolled Jerusalem's Neviim Street carrying a stretcher packed with firewood and several bottles of kerosene. The German consulate burned that night.

Not long afterwards, Abba suggested to some of his children – that is how he referred to the Jerusalem Birionim, "my children," and they, in calling him by his first name, Abba, were very much aware that *Abba* is Hebrew for "father" (Moshe Svorai, who joined the Brit in 1932 and who was on his way to becoming the Stern Group's Tel Aviv commander, purposely signed a newspaper article "Abba's son" to display the filial emotions of Ahimeir's followers) – Abba suggested that the accursed swastika flying high above the German consulate had no place in Jerusalem. He later gave the Tel Aviv organization the same hint about a similar flag in that city.

By now, following the Lag B'Omer flames, two guards were posted at the consulate. An alley was discovered leading from Jaffa Road to the consulate's back fence. A photographer whose house fronted that alley agreed to lend the spirited youth a ladder, without being told the hardly reputable or legal intentions of the apparently industrious students. The operation lasted 15 minutes and took place in broad daylight.

Svorai, the thinnest, shortest and most gymnastically talented of the group, climbed first to the intermediate roof and from there jumped to the consulate's higher roof. Earlier, not owning a pair of sneakers, and the entire party being too poor to afford such a luxury, Svorai had borrowed the gym shoes of an American classmate. Yaacov Orenstein mounted the first roof, Dviri positioned himself behind Orenstein and below were Penina Horn, Rachel Mark (later Mrs. Dviri) and Yaacov Broshi. The Birionim, inexplicably inexperienced at flag cutting, had assumed the flag was fastened with easily sliced rope, and only by chance had they brought a huge pair of shears capable of splitting the steel cable which actually ran through the flag.

Nor had the group correctly estimated the size of the faraway German flag, and Svorai gasped in astonishment as he held the tremendous swastika. He tossed the odious cloth to Orenstein, who passed it to Dviri, who flipped it to Penina and Rachel, who with great exertion stuffed it, or most of it, into the small schoolbag they had brought. Svorai had to hurry down with his shears to chop away at pieces of the cable entwined in the flag, finally enabling the women to walk away with a well-packed if overfull schoolbag. An elderly Yemenite employee of the adjoining Bikur Holim Hospital recognized Rachel. "Ruchelle!" (Little Rachel) he exclaimed, "In here!" He opened a side door to the hospital to allow the flagnappers to escape and quickly wrapped in newspapers those parts of the flag that were still visible. Then he glared grandfather-like at Little Rachel: "Whatever will your father say?" Rachel walked briskly to Mahane Yehuda, caught a bus for Tel Aviv and delivered the flag to an apartment on Rehov Shlush.

Ahimeir sent an article to the *Hazit Ha'am* newspaper from his jail cell later that year, in which he describes the moment his Jerusalem "children" made him a gift of the flag in his Tel Aviv hideout. "One of the happiest moments of my life, a Nazi flag plummeting from its pole into the hands of a Birion...I think of the removal of that flag as a first flickering of redemption."

Where the Money Is

Brit Habirionim's largest demonstration brought five thousand angry Jews to Tel Aviv's streets to protest the British policy of deporting – back to the poisoned soil of Germany – Jewish tourists who had overstayed their visas.

The five thousand ralliers were proceeding up Ben Yehuda Street towards Allenby when British police, waiting in ambush at Star of David Square, attacked. The demonstration turned violent and the Brit boys were no louts. Dviri divided his time between exchanging blows with the British and doling out orders to urchins from the nearby Yemenite Quarter who were streaming in asking: "What can we do?" When Avner Ehrlich yanked a mounted Englishman from his horse, Dviri stood transfixed: "The first time blue blood has been spilled here!"

When two Arabs murdered Labor Zionist leader Haim Arlosorov on a Tel Aviv beach one Friday night in June of 1933, Labor leaders orchestrated a blood libel against their political rivals, the Zionist-Revisionists. Betar was the Revisionist youth movement; Brit Habirionim its activist wing. The witch hunt which followed saw thirty members of the Brit arrested; two were framed for the actual murder (acquitted on appeal) and Ahimeir was charged with inciting the crime. Ahimeir was found innocent the following May, but less than a month later the

British dragged him back to court, along with five other Birionim, to face the more generic charges of conspiracy and incitement to illegal activity.

Haim Dviri spent the first three weeks of the pretrial investigation in the final solitary cell in a row of tick-infested, perpetually darkened stone cells on a lower level of the Jerusalem Central Prison. For days he

Under arrest for initiating the Hebrew revolution: (right to left) Elhanan Halperin, Yossi Haglili, unidentified, policeman, Abba Ahimeir, Haim Dviri (in white shirt), "Grandpa" Judah Leb Schneerson, and unidentified (Jabotinsky Institute photo)

was alone, singing aloud in the almost forlorn hope someone, some-where would respond. Finally, one morning, as he half shouted, half sang "She Has Gentle Hands," Moshe Svorai picked up the refrain from the prison courtyard where he was exercising, exclaiming to a friend: "Dviri's here, Dviri's here."

Among the exhibits submitted to the court to bolster the charges against the Birionim were a proclamation in Ahimeir's handwriting signed the "Organization of Revolutionary Zionists"; a document writ-ten by Dviri postulating a day when the youth will flock to the battalions of Brit Habirionim; and the rough draft of a letter which Dviri readily admitted was his: "I am writing on behalf of the movement 'Brit Habirionim,' which is the organization of extremist nationalist youth, which does not care for parliamentary niceties... We must fight merci-lessly in every way against the British imperialism which prevents us from establishing our home... Revolutionary youth must prepare to sacrifice themselves on the gallows or on the guillotine if necessary...[The Brit] intends to take and will take this country from the British..." Dviri had closed his letter "With the blessings of the Zionist Revolution."

The court found Moshe Svorai innocent of all charges, the others innocent of incitement but guilty of possession of dangerous literature and membership in an illegal organization. "I don't think I will do you an injustice," the judge told Ahimeir before sentencing him to 21 months of hard labor, "if I say you are head and shoulders above the other defen-dants in ability, knowledge and education. I can only express my sorrow that you have not chosen to exert your unquestionable talents in a more worthwhile direction." Dviri received 15 months of hard labor, "because I view you as Ahimeir's able deputy and I do believe you are clearly a dangerous man." For technical reasons Yevin was tried separately and sentenced to four months. Yevin was therefore freed in late 1934; fol-lowing reductions in their sentences Dviri and Ahimeir left prison in early and late 1935, respectively.

While Ahimeir sat in jail, the British High Commissioner himself struggled over the question of whether to revoke Ahimeir's citizenship. The High Commissioner was sure he had the legal justification and necessary evidence to do so, but based on Ahimeir's exemplary behavior behind bars, he decided not to – a decision he undoubtedly soon regretted, given Ahimeir's Promethean talent for rabble-rousing.

As Ahimeir stepped through the prison's gate to freedom, a young woman in a Betar uniform handed him a bouquet of flowers. Trying to be both grateful and tutorial, Ahimeir took the flowers, then looked her in the eye and whispered: "Guns, not flowers."

As an organization, the Brit was effectively terminated. But its ideology – Ahimeir's stencilled wall posters were the first to refer to the British as a "foreign regime" destined to be chased from Eretz Israel by the armed forces of a Hebrew uprising – continued to win adherents, especially among the youthful Betarim in Eretz Israel and Europe now enlisting in the swaddling Irgun.

The Birionim, however, did not depart without one final, typically blazing flourish. After all, Dviri and friends were eventually freed...and you can't keep a truly resilient revolutionary down.

The Arabs were busy in the years 1936-39. They talked of an "uprising." The Jewish establishment, evidently inured to death, referred to "disturbances." Actually, the Arabs were perpetrating massacres, pure and simple. The men and women they murdered were often raped or tortured, more often than not hacked to pieces after or before their grisly, untimely deaths. The first year, 89 Jews were killed, hundreds injured. Statistics are drily unsentimental; among the thousand and one assaults on Jews, however, were three attacks on old-age homes, nine on nurseries and orphanages, nineteen on schools, and twenty-six on hospitals or ambulances. By 1939, 380 Jewish buses had been ambushed. The number of dead had passed five hundred.

Within the Nationalist Hagana, the nascent Irgun Zvai Leumi, pressure grew for a response to the almost daily murder of Jews. The dissatisfaction was greatest among the rank and file, which felt betrayed by a leadership perceived as lackadaisical. Since 1931 they had been drilling and navigating and shooting at targets – mainly to free Eretz Israel from British rule, but also to prevent a repeat of the awful 1929 massacres. Now warmongering Arabs were once again spilling rivers of Jewish blood, and the Jewish commanders were hesitating.

Individual members of the Irgun perpetrated so many partisan reprisals against Arab targets that the flustered Irgun Commander Abraham Tehomi, pining for military discipline, returned to the establishment Hagana he'd left six years earlier. Jabotinsky appointed Robert Bitker, a Betar leader from Shanghai who held the rank of colonel in the Russian army, as military commander of the Nationalist Hagana/Irgun. Portly, rotund and double-chinned, Bitker's figure suggested an epicurean who rubbed his hands unctuously at the prospect of partaking of the pleasures of the here and now. His demeanor, however, was 100 percent martial and it was this solid military bearing which lent Bitker an air of eminence.

History dealt Bitker a poor hand, for it was to him a restless group of Birionim came with a grand plan.

The organization's coffers were empty. Arms had to be purchased, major operations devised and executed and the general public informed as to the activities and revolutionary aims of the new combat-spirited enterprise. So...why not rob a bank?

Haim Dviri, Abraham Selman and other like-minded activists published a provocative brochure entitled "Sdan" critical of the organization's inaction. While the Revisionist movement took disciplinary measures, one sympathetic party official mentioned to Selman that many Revisionists thought as he did, "including Bitker. Why don't you meet?"

Selman was soon introduced to the Irgun Commander in a Tel Aviv casino. "What do you want?!" barked Bitker. Selman launched into an explanation of his political ideology.

"I'm not interested in your relationship with the movement's Board of Directors!" snapped Bitker. "Are you loyal to Jabotinsky?"

"Yes," Selman replied. "And we'd like to talk matters over with him..."

"You should act," said Bitker peremptorily. "That will be the best conversation."

Bitker suggested Selman immediately enter the IZL with an officer's rank, saying he would be part of an "avant-garde" group acting with the knowledge only of the Commander in Chief and a few top men. Bitker then asked Selman if he was ready to "expropriate" funds and Selman responded that he was "ready for anything." When Selman's preparations dragged on and repeatedly stalled, Bitker sent word: Hurry up, the organization is almost bankrupt.

Bitker had approved the operation without consulting his inner circle. The five members of the bank-robbing cabal were all Irgunists but also all "former" members of the theoretically defunct Brit Habirionim. For an added measure of poetic justice they chose to "expropriate" funds from Bank Hapoalim – the bourgeois-socialist bank which represented those most vociferously opposed to Birion endeavors.

At 9:30 A.M. on September 12, 1937 – a dreary and prosaic morning even by Tel Aviv's hot and humid standards – a messenger left the Anglo-Palestine Bank's Herzl Street branch, headed north and turned right to Montefiore. He paused to wipe the first beads of sweat from his brow, afterwards surrendering complacently to the slow soak of his shirt. As usual he carried a satchel of money bound for Bank Hapoalim. The listless sidewalk crowds paid him no attention. Perhaps the crowds would have taken only slightly more interest had they known that thousands of lira were in the sack. It was a lot of money, but this was Tel Aviv's banking district and such transfers were commonplace. So the messenger plodded onto Nahalat Benjamin Street almost unnoticed.

But the slow steps of this bank messenger led to one of the most momentous events in early Irgun history, not to mention in the lives of Haim Dviri and his cohort Haim Buchko.

"Freeze!"

Zion Gabai, the driver, wheeled the car towards the messenger, but perhaps just a second too soon. Abraham Selman stepped from the languid crowd, filched the money pouch and made for the car, which, unfortunately, was one short second ahead of schedule. As Selman chased the speeding vehicle, the newly invigorated crowd chased Selman. With the agitated vigilantes following close behind, Gabai went tearing through the narrow streets where peddlers were jostling with horse-drawn buggies for room. The car veered left on Rambam Street instead of the preplanned right and plowed into a fruit stand in the Carmel Bazaar. The heretofore sleepy Carmel shoppers were unaware of the robbery but now had a cause of their own: They pursued the fleeing driver and passengers, shouting: "Hit and run!!"

A Jewish policeman coincidentally stationed on the nearby corner choreographed the arrest of the fugitives: Dviri, Buchko, Selman, Gabai and Avigdor Kipnis. By the time they came to trial, the charge was not hit and run but armed bank robbery, and the political motive was an open secret. Buchko played a diversionary role in the theft but was nonetheless convicted of snatching the sack. Selman, who actually grabbed the sack, was released with Kipnis for lack of evidence. Dviri and Buchko each received three years of hard labor.

Joseph Kremin was asked by a friend if he ever cooperated with Dviri and the Birionim. Kremin: "Well, Dviri is a great guy, very active, he's done important things, but we keep our distance. If you follow Dviri, you are sure to be arrested..."

Dviri's own view: "Brit Habirionim was the first underground in Eretz Israel and we lacked experience. Despite all the revolutionary literature in the world, one always begins with the basic alphabet. You must travel the whole road and develop through your own experiences."

In any case, the failed heist brought Robert Bitker's Irgun career to an untimely demise. Bitker's High Command had until then comprised

Abraham Stern, David Raziel, Aharon Heichman and Moshe Rosenberg. Rosenberg had been Halperin's deputy in the Betar Officers Training School and later Tehomi's deputy on the first Command of the Irgun organization. When Tehomi had double-backed to the Hagana, Rosenberg had held together the ailing Irgun by tightening the reigns on the Betar coterie, most of which was unflinchingly loyal to him. Joseph Kremin, Nissim Cohen and most of the Irgun commanders had remained with Rosenberg, after which Jabotinsky had appointed Bitker.

Rosenberg considered the freshly transplanted Bitker "an excellent chap...but a commander who doesn't speak Hebrew, a pure goy." Following the foiled "expropriation," Bitker spoke to Rosenberg honestly and selflessly: "Look, I don't know Hebrew, I can't read it or write it, and I'm not convinced that I completely grasp what's going on in this country. So why don't you run things around here...and I'll ask to be relieved." Rosenberg took over.

Rosenberg had one year earlier journeyed to Egypt to help update Jabotinsky on events in Eretz Israel. He had requested Jabotinsky's authorization to order reprisals against Arabs after attacks on Jews. Jabotinsky was already a seven-year exile and probably did not fully comprehend the desperation of the Jews' plight or the extent of the Irgunists' alienation. He refused to approve reprisals, telling Rosenberg that if ever he reconsidered he would send a coded telegram signed "Mendelson."

In July, Rosenberg and Abraham Stern had accompanied Bitker to a tête-à-tête with Jabotinsky in Alexandria. Again the matter of reprisals was discussed. "We must avenge!" declared Rosenberg, and Stern pressed even more forcefully. According to Stern's biographer Ada Yevin, "Jabotinsky had difficulty approving counterterror...though he considered reprisals politically justified, the moral problem continued tormenting him. Jabotinsky insisted that in the event of reprisals, women and children should not be hurt and...the condition still stood: no actions until they receive a telegram signed 'Mendelson.'"

But the roadways and trails of Eretz Israel were smoldering with the charred frames of vehicles torched by roving Arab killers. Blackened bones were frequently the only remains of Jewish passengers. Ambush was the fear with which many innocent Jews set out on interurban travel, and travel after dark was unsafe, undesirable and when unavoidable – by convoy. The official Jewish establishment stuck to its declared policy of *havlaga* (self-restraint), a pathetic attempt to offer the other cheek – of course, not their own well-protected cheeks, but the vulnerable cheeks of young Jewish girls and boys or old men and women – in order to proffer a superior moral position to a world which could not have cared less. "Our weapons are pure, they have been used only in defense," the established and anachronistic leaders proudly stammered as Jews were murdered in Eretz Israel, as the British locked the gates of the Jewish homeland to the desperate Jews of Europe, as the Germans moved troops into the Rhineland.

Altman

By November of 1937 David Raziel was in Jerusalem commanding the city's branch of the Irgun. Moshe Segal had founded his own underground, Brit Hashmonaim (the Hasmoneans), and he served on the Irgun's Jerusalem Command as well. Now he and Raziel temporarily turned their attention from the British to the unimpeded Arab gangs. "It's about time we changed *havlaga* to *hagava*," Segal quipped, using the Hebrew word for "response" as he planned retaliatory bombings in areas used as rendezvous by the Arab gangs.

> *Segal:* We can stop using the name Nationalist Defense Hagana) and refer to ourselves as the National Military Organization (Irgun Zvai Leumi).
> *Kremin:* We've been using that name since 1931 amongst ourselves...

Segal: But now that is what we shall be called.

Moshe Svorai was out of jail, crisscrossing Poland establishing Irgun units for combat training and eventual aliya. Abraham Stern of the Irgun High Command was there, too, coordinating the units, procuring arms for shipment to the Irgun in Eretz Israel and, later, attempting to organize forty thousand Jews for an armed invasion of Eretz Israel. Uri Zvi Greenberg had published his greatest work to date, the watershed *Sefer Hakitrug Vehaemunah*, which warned of a Europe about to burst into flames and an Eretz Israel already burning while Jewish leaders played politics as usual. Greenberg sailed for Poland to warn Jews to flee while time remained. Jabotinsky, too, spoke to thousands in Poland – where he was the most admired of all Zionist leaders – urging an immediate evacuation before the tolling of the bells. "It is the eleventh hour," he pleaded, "a terrible holocaust is on the horizon..."

One inspired youth was Yehezkel Altman. Soft-spoken and jovial, he had been organizing Betar chapters throughout Rumania since 1929. The socialist Labor Zionists on the boat to Eretz Israel at first laughed at his Betar uniform, then threatened him, changing their tune only when they were all overcome by seasickness, and Altman tended to their comfort as they writhed and groaned.

Altman served in Herzliya's Betar chapter under Abraham Stern's brother David. "I'll volunteer" became his password, and he was soon guarding orchards, then farming in Zichron. He joined an early Irgun chapter commanded by Eliahu Lankin, farming by day and gathering and concealing firearms by night. When Arab shepherds in Jewish employ fled the area after some disturbances, Altman assumed the shepherd's mantle. On one ramble with his flocks, two armed and stern Arabs accosted the herder and asked for a cigarette.

Altman understood the precariousness of his situation: "If I refuse they will use my inhospitability as an excuse to pick a fight; if I give them what they want and appear obsequious, they will assume they can take advantage of me." Altman's creative solution was to calmly place the cigarette in the barrel of his rifle, which he then extended to them. "Please," he said politely.

The Arab riots and pogroms of 1936 brought Altman to Jerusalem's once-again beleaguered Old City, where he helped found a Betar chapter while guarding Jews on their way to prayers at the Western Wall. A year later, he provided labor during a shortage of workers in Rehovot.

Altman had been molded by innumerable attempts to immigrate illegally from prewar Rumania to British-blockaded Eretz Israel, and by years of working the barren rocky soil of his new homeland, simultaneously protecting the crops from Arab pilferers. He was 5'4", thin, brown eyed, a sparse moustache occasionally gracing his upper lip. He was straightforward, unaffectedly honest, and completely genuine in his attempts to offer assistance wherever needed. He had no illusions about living a comfortable life in those early days of modern Israel; he was no saber-rattling hero, but neither was he afraid of anything. And anything that might be wept over was also capable, Altman believed, of being laughed at.

Recent news from Jerusalem's Old City was not good. "The territory is shrinking," wrote Moshe Stein in a bulletin from the Old City's Betar chapter, "because of the bloody events: After 1929, the last Jews left Hebron Street in the northern part of the city. Now the business district is being gradually abandoned – King David Street was once all Jewish, and now a Jew cannot even cross it. Since the outbreaks of 1937 – Medan and Habad Streets stand almost abandoned...and the Western Wall, the relic of our glory, inherited from the ancient Hebrew state, is alone and forsaken by almost everyone. Sometimes a prayer quorum cannot be assembled, and were it not for Betar's Plugat Hakotel (Western Wall Force) the prayer service would not be held. And those who hate us want so much to see that there will not be services on the Sabbath, they wait impatiently for this 'evidence.'"

The second night of Rosh Hashana, shortly after 6:00 P.M., the New Year holiday prayers concluded, Jewish worshippers made their way up a street with many Arabs, and no police, present. Two Betar members led the way, followed by three Jewish old-timers and, several yards behind them, the rest of the Jews. More Betarim formed a protective cordon around the Jewish pedestrians. A suspicious-looking Arab loitered at the corner of Hebron Street. The two front-running Betarim kept their eyes on him; from up ahead, an Arab approached, leading a donkey with packages strapped to both its sides. The packages were so bulky that no room was left for passing. As the Betarim pressed up against the wall, they heard a gunshot and turned to see Eliezer Hacohen Gerstein fall to his knees, both hands clutching his right side. The 70-year-old rabbi was mortally wounded.

A Friday night. Same hour, same place. Four Betarim up front. The religious Jews behind them. An Arab sprang from the dark and fired eight shots. The Betari Aharon Alkabetz died immediately. Rosenzweig took two bullets to the stomach. Rabinowitz, hit in the leg, crawled to the safety of a nearby store.

Another evening, the Betar members were just sitting down to dinner in their local headquarters. A bomb thrown into their courtyard exploded, fortunately, near the office and not the dining hall.

And so, Yehezkel Altman stood guard in the hills above the Motza-Jerusalem road. He saw the promise in the ravines, felt the mother lode of Jewish redemption under his feet in the sandy, stony, rolling mountains of the homeland. But at night, he saw only Arab vehicles, for Jews lived in fear. And by day he saw Jews travelling four or five cars in a row for protection, and he saw British police disarming forsaken Jews.

"Like this," he said to his fellow guards, "things cannot continue." One night five Jews were murdered by Arabs; three days later Altman was riding shotgun for a Sephardic bride and groom on their way to be blessed by Chief Rabbi Uziel in Jerusalem, when shots fired from an ambush forced the white-gowned bride and finely suited groom onto the muddy car floor. On the evening of December 27, 1937, Altman set out with fellow constable David Niv. Niv at some point in their patrol hitchhiked a ride back to base. Altman wandered the hills outside of Nahalat Itzhak, near the Castel, and came to his decision.

As an Arab bus moved slowly through the canyon, up the rough road, around corners hidden by cliffs firmly set at 90-degree angles to the road, Altman stood in the coolness of the hills and fired. The metallic whine of bullets disturbed the stillness of the hills as the Arab vehicle ground to a halt. Psychologically unprepared for the concept of being attacked by Jews, the Arabs naturally assumed this was another standard ambush by Arabs who had mistaken them for the proverbial Jewish victim. The Arabs cheerfully waved their traditional kaffiyas from the window and shouted, "We are Arabs!" But as the flames continued spouting from Altman's rifle, the idea that a Jew might be angry enough to give Arabs a taste of their own medicine finally dawned upon the bus driver, who revved his engine and sped away.

A second bus came by and spurts of dust began dancing around its wheels, as Altman again filled the echoing hills with the popping sounds of his rifle bullets. Then a third vehicle, and more shots. "I didn't intend to kill anyone," Altman later told confidants, "just to stop and frighten them."

The thick darkness was again still, if only for a few eery seconds, and Altman made quickly for the summit, from which he surveyed the area below which was by now brimming with lights. The third vehicle was clearly visible in the light, and Altman saw that he had been shooting at an armored British police car with mounted gun.

Altman recognized the irony of his situation: Shots had been fired – albeit by himself – in an area that he was ostensibly guarding. In the morning, therefore, he made a beeline for the police station to report that he had heard noises, quite similar, in fact, to shots, that night. Altman learned that the bullets had killed a man in the first bus, wedged in the food and provisions of the second, and entered the very barrel of the mounted gun on the third, a fortuitous shot which explained why the British had not been able to return fire.

Altman was questioned by two investigators, one Jewish and one British. After offering his testimony, he overheard the two in conversation:

The Jewish major: You know, he is a Betari.
British investigator: What's that?
Major: A Revisionist.
Investigator: I still don't understand.
Major: He's part of the group sitting in Acre Prison for fighting the British.

Altman found himself in jail and under continued interrogation. He was advised by his Irgun commander not to attempt an escape as there might not be sufficient evidence to hold him. Altman nonetheless realized he was in trouble when he was transferred to a police unit in Jerusalem. Exploiting a card game which seemed to occupy a guard more than he did, Altman spent quite some time in a bathroom attempting to pry off a window. Peering through, he realized that even if he were to remove the window grating an impenetrable amount of barbed wire would still stand between him and freedom. The time for anything he could possibly be doing in a lavatory long over, Altman returned and, finding his guard as engrossed in the cards as ever, proceeded to the front gate. "Got a cigarette?" he demanded of the sentry, assuming the air of an overworked cop. "Sorry," apologized the sentry, "why not try a kiosk on Jaffa Road?" Altman acknowledged the helpful suggestion and walked on. He managed only about 50 feet on Jaffa Road when a screeching police car careened in front of him. Inside was the major handling his interrogation, who poked his head out the window, looked Altman in the eyes, and was just a bit suspicious of Altman's persistent insistence that he simply wished to purchase some cigarettes.

Again, in court, Altman's Irgun commanders refused his request: Altman longed to speak his mind, to proclaim openly that "I want to make the roads such that if Jews cannot travel at night, neither will Arabs." He craved to respond to the judge's inquiries by decreeing: "Long live the Jewish state on both banks of the Jordan River." But his commanders ordered him to play it safe on the off chance that he might yet be found innocent. A week into his trial, Altman was instead found guilty and sentenced to death by hanging.

"How do you feel?!" shouted a *Times* reporter above the courtroom din. "No different than before," answered an Altman finally free to speak his mind. "If you know where you're going and that every moment may lead to a hangman's noose or some such form of death – well, an underground fighter makes an agreement with Fate: She will never be in your hands..."

Altman was taken to death row in the Jerusalem Central Prison. The warden magnanimously offered to grant a final request, already planning the lavish meal he would soon share. Altman asked only for a Bible. He tore a raggedy strip from his "mattress" and, twisting it through the grated wire ceiling, created a hammock for the holy book. A livid Arab guard shook Altman as he slept that night and ripped the hammock from the ceiling, accusing Altman of attempting to hang himself (Altman to the guard: "You've got it all wrong. You're the people who want to hang me, remember?"). The knotted remains of the shredded cloth can still be seen in that death row cell today.

Rabbi Arye Levin, the saintly Jerusalem rabbi who showered decades of prison inmates with love, and whose gentle heart professed an extra measure of warmth for caged fighters, encountered an Altman lounging informally with a towel wrapped around his neck. "It's the only part of my body with any value today," Altman told the inquiring rabbi. "I must keep it in good condition."

Four days passed on death row. Altman was finally summoned to

Altman was here: Yehezkel Altman waiting for visitors at the Jerusalem Central Prison (Jabotinsky Institute photo)

the prison office. "You must thank the King of England," he was told, "for giving you your life."

"My parents gave me my life," sneered Altman, "and no one else."

His sentence reduced to many years in jail, Altman never felt alone. "Lots of kids came to see me," he recalled after his release. "Lots of Hasidic kids, too, even five year olds. They expected to find a big guy, a giant of sorts, some kind of hero. The joke was on them, it was only me..."

Altman was also visited by members of the Irgun. As the months passed, more and more Irgunists ended up on his side of the bars as activity escalated against Arab and British targets on the "outside."

Altman attempted one more escape. He feigned appendicitis in order to be transferred to an outside hospital where he would be op- erated on and recuperate. The plan was for his Irgun comrades to arrange an escape on the seventh day when, according to procedure, he would be returned to prison. Altman actually had his appendix removed, but suspicious guards had him returned to prison on the fourth day.

Six years later, when the British granted clemency to the Arab killers and rioters of 1936-39, a hardened but still convivial Altman was also pardoned, on the condition that he report twice daily to the Jerusalem police. Altman unsuspectingly searched for the proper address that first morning out but found a half-ruined shell of a building. The newly freed felon crossed his arms and leaned against a tree to consider mat- ters. A distraught policeman passed by, unaware of Altman's identity, and correctly remarked: "Your boys did this!" informing him that the Irgun had blown up the building the previous night. Altman eventu- ally resumed his underground activities, participating in the demolition of the railway to Egypt and the Irgun's successful battle to conquer Jaffa in 1948.

Altman was the first Betari sentenced to death. On one of the spe- cial holiday visits allowed at the Jerusalem Central Prison, a young

Betari dropped in. Shalom Zurabin had been a charge of Altman's in the Jerusalem Betar chapter, and now he told his former boss: "Soon you will hear from my friends and me, there will be an action similar to yours, but much bigger..." Two and a half months later Shlomo Ben Yosef, Shalom Zurabin and Abraham Shein of Rosh Pina attempted an operation reminiscent of Altman's. In response to the Arab ambush of a Jewish taxi in which two female acquaintances of Ben Yosef had been violated and three men hacked to death, the three Betarim shot at an Arab bus. A gun misfired and a grenade failed to explode; no one suffered the slightest injury. The British chose to make an example of Ben Yosef, to use gallows to frighten hot-headed Jewish youth. To the shock and consternation of even the Jewish establishment, on June 29, 1938, Ben Yosef became the first Jew to be hanged by the British in the struggle for a Jewish state.

His final words were "Long live Jabotinsky, long live the Jewish state on both banks of the Jordan River!" He ascended the gallows singing. The British had sought an example and they had gotten one. Jabotinsky declared, "Ben Yosef has taught me the meaning of Zionism." Segal led an anti-British riot in Jerusalem, leaving the city's main thoroughfares looking like a battle zone, littered with bloodied police clubs and helmets strewn where they had fallen. A teenager named Yehiel Dresner wrote in his diary: "The blood of Ben Yosef screams for revenge!" Dov Gruner wrote to his girlfriend: "It is a shame that Ben Yosef had to go to the gallows to create a Jewish state, and it is more of a shame that others will have to follow him. But it is on the necks of the Ben Yosefs that a free Jewish state will one day rise."

Little did Dresner and Gruner know that nine years later, as soldiers in the Irgun, they would share the same prison cell in Jerusalem. And little did they know that, spirited in the middle of a spring night to Acre, they would be hanged one-half hour apart on the same gallows that had taken Ben Yosef's life.

They, too, ascended the gallows singing.

* * *

David Raziel took the telegram Benjamin Zeroni extended towards him. "Invest heavily," it read. It was signed: "Mendelson."

Death notice signed by "a nation in mourning" for "Shlomo Ben Yosef: Hero of the nation, the first official martyr in Eretz Israel since the days of Rabbi Akiva and his friends, a pillar of fire to the nation fighting for its freedom, hanged today at 8:00 A.M. in Acre Fortress."

Memorial booklet for Shlomo Ben Yosef

Chapter 3
My Name Is Death

The wolf shall lie down with the lamb, is how the Bible escribes the Messianic Age, meaning that until then, we'll have to fight. And even then, who says the Jews always have to be the lamb?　　　　　　　　　　　**Israel Eldad**

Esther Halevy approached the six-foot-high rock alongside Jerusalem's Jaffa Road. She was seventeen. Two years ago she had joined the nationalist Betar youth movement and now she was on her way underground.

Maybe the rock was not six feet high; it was taller than her, that much she knew. Atop the stone platform was a kiosk. At that moment she could not remember what was sold there or whether it was usually open at this late hour. All she knew was that she was told to present herself there, and now she was walking along the road that she knew would not end, but only begin, at that kiosk.

Esther stood beneath the kiosk, looked up at what and whom she could not see, and said, "I've come to..."

"I know why you have come," a voice responded from above. "Follow me."

Esther walked several paces behind the man. In the dark, all she could ascertain was that he was heavy and sported a box-shaped Bukharan yarmulke on his head. She identified him as the owner of the kiosk. They reached a local school building, seemingly shut tight for the night. At the instructions of the man she was following, she ascended the steps to the locked door of the school. At his instructions, she knocked. At his instructions, she recited a password. The man in the Bukharan skullcap disappeared into the darkness and Esther stood alone.

The school door opened and Esther was led inside. Not a bulb was lit, no light penetrated the windows. In the blackness, Esther was taken down hallways, through classrooms and back again. She was walked through a door and soon found herself sitting in one of the classrooms. Through a different doorway, from behind a curtain, another young woman entered the room, approached a table Esther had not noticed till then, recited an oath, and was led out via yet another door. Now it was Esther's turn.

She stood at the table. By the candlelight she saw before her a Bible, a Jewish national flag and a gun. She raised her right hand and recited:

"I hereby swear to be a loyal soldier of the Irgun Zvai Leumi in Eretz Israel, which protects our national honor, life and property, and assists in the revival of the whole nation in the land of its Fathers."

Esther was escorted from the room and back into the street. Esther was still 17, but now she was a member of the Underground army fighting for Jewish independence.

In the years that followed, Esther herself swore in other members of the army. Some people were inducted in vacant rooms, others in caves outside Jerusalem. Sometimes the room was lit by candles, sometimes by a lantern, sometimes the room was completely dark. Sometimes a flag stood on the table, sometimes a large one was draped over the table. Sometimes, there was no Bible.

There was always a gun.

* * *

"'Do not hurt the innocent'...this is superficial and hypocritical chatter," wrote Jabotinsky in "The Lesson of Ben Yosef." "In war, any war, each side is innocent. What crime has the enemy soldier done me – he is as poor as I, as blind as I, a slave like me drafted against his will...After the first air attack on London and Paris expect a reprisal by aircraft over Stuttgart and Milan which will be just as full of people and children. All war is against innocents as all war is of brothers against brothers. Therefore cursed be all war...and if you do not want to touch the innocent – Die. And if you do not want to die – shoot and stop chattering."

The sinister villainy of the Arabs continued. Every day helpless Jews were stabbed, shot, or if fortunate, merely bereft of crops, farms or produce. The established leaders continued to preach nonresistance but by this time even members of the proudly defensive Hagana were itching for action. Within the Irgun the impatience was tenfold. The organization was transformed into a pressure cooker with commanders trying to keep the lid on the wrath and energy of the rank and file.

Even prior to "Mendelson's" terse telegram and Jabotinsky's "Amen" and the published "Ben Yosef Lesson," the steaming exasperation of Irgun youth forced to witness the daily and wholesale slaughter of their people demanded a release. When this pent-up anger finally flared it blazed its own merciless trail of annihilation and vengeance among the Arabs of Eretz Israel.

The boys and girls of the Irgun were not trying to be heroes. Some had to become cool, hard killers, experts in elimination and destruction. "What we are doing is not heroic," remarked former Birion Moshe Svorai, "and we know it is dirty work. Unfortunately it must be done." The first vindictive Jewish avengers in two millennia consciously chose to immerse themselves in the grimy business of murder in order to save their less violent brethren. Their assumption was that if Arabs had chosen to open fire, no logic in the world dictated that only Arab communities be immune from the bloodletting, or that this be the first war ever fought in which one side was allowed to shoot while the other was not.

At 8:30 P.M. on August 13, 1936, Alter Ungar, a thirty-six-year-old American, and his three children – nine-year-old Yaffa, seven-year-old Eva and six-year-old Abraham – were murdered by Arabs who had broken into their home on Rehov Hasepharadim in the Jewish Quarter of Safed. Alter heard rifles being cocked in the children's room. He ran in, in time to see the three youngsters shot to death as they lay together in bed. The intruders then threw a hand grenade at the father, killing him on the spot. At the same hour, Tuvia Rabinowitz was gunned down as he guarded the orchards of Zofit. He left a wife and a six-year-old daughter. On August 14, a car was ambushed outside Haifa and its four passengers massacred: Haim Shulrer, an ambulance driver with six children; Joseph Hammerman, a 23-year old policeman; Michael Wiser, a 24-year-old factory worker and member of Betar; and Bronia Collin, a 25-year-old member of Hashomer Hatzair. On the sixteenth, Jewish crowds waited patiently and unsuspectingly at a crossing as the morning train passed through Tel Aviv. Suddenly shots flared from the train's windows and tranquil Herzl Street turned pandemonious. The Arab killers had wounded ten and taken the life of eight-year-old David Albalah as he walked to school. The same day, electrician Julius Washgal was killed as he repaired some high wires, and 23-year-old Haya Freund was shot to death while on guard duty at her kibbutz. The next day, two Jewish nurses were butchered in the Jaffa hospital: golden-haired Martha (Miriam) Fink, whom sister Dina eulogized: "You cared for poor and destitute Arabs with so much love and so much dedication. You were but a tender girl and yet already a serious nurse...and now you have been taken from us, so young and tender. Why have they murdered you, my sister, my little sister...?" and 19-year-old Nehama Zedek who, as she lay dying, called to her colleagues a warning to "Get out of this dangerous place." She cried, "Where's Martha!? I know they shot her and I want to die, too," and finally she gasped, "Momma, Poppa! Just don't tell them about this, don't tell my parents!" But by the time of the nurses' deaths the newspapers were less interested in the already routine, "understand-able," murder of Jews and more enthused about a strikingly novel phenomenon which seemed to astound the pundits: revenge as a means of deterrence.

cording to Curtis C. Shears, who has just returned from a speaking tour as a representative of the club in the Roosevelt First Voters League.

The Young Democratic Club is sponsoring the work of the Roosevelt First Voters League, particularly in . Manhattan and the ' Bronx. It also is working for Governor Lehman's re-election.

TEL AVIV JEW KILLED
BY BOMB FROM TRAIN

Boy of 8 Loses Life and 19 Are Injured When Arab Hurls Explosive Into Street.

Wireless to THE NEW YORK TIMES.

JERUSALEM, Aug. 16.—A Jewish boy, 8 years old, was killed and nineteen Jews were injured by the explosion of a bomb thrown by an Arab from a train window into one of the principal streets of Tel Aviv today, as the train was passing through that city en route to Jaffa.

This attack in Palestine's largest Jewish city, following other recent outrages at Safed, Haifa and on the Jerusalem-Tel Aviv road which took a death toll of ten Jews, including three children within three days, served to raise tension to the highest pitch among Jews tonight.

Although during the four months of the Palestine disturbances the Jews have not retaliated for the numerous murders and wide destruction, many observers here fear that the provocation of the last three or four days has become so great that some Jewish youths may become uncontrollable and resort to reprisals.

By The Associated Press.

JERUSALEM, Aug. 16.—Violent death to two more Jews tonight, it was reported by Palcor News

Special to THE NEW YORK TIMES.

MONTREAL, Que., Aug. 16.—Nationalism, an old factor in French Canadian politics, and fascism, a new one, will have their appeal tested tomorrow in Quebec's second general election within twelve months. The broad issue which the voters will be asked to decide is whether the Liberal government under its new Premier, Adelard Godbout, has purged itself of the scandals which drove its former head, Alexander Taschereau, and his Cabinet to resign or whether the sins laid to his predecessors shall be visited upon him.

Premier Godbout's rival, Maurice Duplessis, asserts that the Godbout government is only the Taschereau government under another name, and asks that his National Union party be elected "to clean up the government." Mr. Godbout replies that "things were never so bad as they were painted," and that in any case he will have them thoroughly investigated. He has framed a platform containing nearly every social reform plank promised by Mr. Duplessis.

Scandals are not new in Quebec, but the Fascist and separatist views cherished by a large section of Mr. Duplessis's followers are novel. The idea of a separate French Canadian State on the shores of the St. Lawrence was first ascribed some years ago to no less a personage than Cardinal Villeneuve, The Cardinal repudiated the construction generally put upon a statement by him, but the idea took root among a section of French Canadian youths and was encouraged by some of the Roman Catholic clergymen in Quebec. Of late it has been associated with attacks on parliamentarism, on international finance and industry and with that hatred of foreigners which have marked the rise of fascism in other countries.

A fortnight ago Mr. Duplessis's campaign was embarrassed by the issue from National Union headquarters of a pamphlet bitterly attacking "British imperialism, which seeks to keep our country under the eternal tutelage of England," and urging Canada "to strive with its might to achieve complete independ-

It w
Cori
surv
sigh:
by,
port'
Tw
were
who
a sn
ferre
was
Mc
then
arriv
and
less.
skirt
Pa

in—t
tingt
engit
Th
In
Raot
pass
were
abou
liftec
Cat
Corit
the
he s
plain
thick

WC

Film
ly

Gif
prod'
tel I
Stree
unsu
renc
ican
Gern
anti-:
aboa
Sin
July
pone'
charg
been
place
Mr.
went
to al'
had '
also
natio

New York Times, August 17, 1936

101

Azriel Bensenberg happened by Herzl Street minutes after the attack there, an attack distinguished from umpteen others at the same
spot only by the addition of the long-inevitable if delayed fatality.
Bensenberg was shaken and angry but without direction; he went home,
where he reported the news to his mother. Mrs. Bensenberg thus became the impctus for the first official major operation of the IZL. She
scolded her son: "You are always teaching the youth, you have all sorts
of exercises, and now something like this happens and it is just like
nothing has happened?" Bensenberg about-faced. He was still angry
and now he had direction.

Bensenberg ran into Arye Yitzhaki, gave him the news, and kept
on. He soon found himself standing before a half-built house. Inside, he knew, Benjamin Zeroni was at work. Zeroni was an
electrician, but also Bensenberg's classmate, and more importantly,
his Irgun mate. By the time Bensenberg found Zeroni on the roof he
was breathless; he told of the attack and the little boy's death. Zeroni,
beside himself with anger, heaved a hammer across the roof.
Bensenberg left Zeroni and went searching for Abraham Tehomi, who
was at this time still the organization's Commander. Bensenberg remembered the first time he had met Tehomi: Bensenberg was waiting
with other young Irgunists for an officers course to begin. Tehomi
arrived, introduced himself as commander of both the course and
the Irgun, opened up the leather coat he was wearing and pulled from
his belt a parabellum, a Mauser, a Browning, a Steyr, a Baretta and a
Webley; six guns in all. Had Tehomi pulled rabbits from a hat he
could not have impressed his students more. They looked upon him,
as Bensenberg recalled, as a "god."

Now, Bensenberg tracked Tehomi to where he was presiding over
a meeting of the Command, in the rear of a local health clinic. Zeroni
was already there; Zeroni was wielding a threat and a plan.

"We are burning!" boomed Zeroni. The startled commanders
stared, unsure of what was more unsettling: to be verbally assaulted

by a member of the ranks or the fact that they were discovered in a supposedly secret conference. Zeroni's gimlet eyes bore into Tehomi: "I have come to tell you there is going to a rebellion – "

Tehomi took Zeroni by the elbow, pulling him and Bensenberg aside. Speaking in a calm whisper as they quit the room, Tehomi asked: "Well, what do you suggest?"

Zeroni laid out his plan: a counterattack at the same spot on the morrow, directed against the Arabs on the train. Zeroni proposed mining the tracks, derailing the train and opening fire on the presumably confused and panic-stricken passengers.

Unflappable, brave and authoritarian, Tehomi was slightly taken aback by Zeroni's imperious vehemence. No immediate rush seemed requisite, he said, certain affairs had to be arranged, consultations held...

"Either you act now – or we will act without your permission!"

Tehomi told them to return with a workable plan and he would approve it.

Bensenberg and Zeroni "cased" the train tracks on Herzl Street. They found that the ground floor of adjacent 4 Yehuda Halevy Street was empty; a good hiding place for a unit of commandos. They worked out the details of the operation, stopped for a beer, drank to the operation's success, returned to Tehomi and received his okay.

The "rebels" retreated to Zeroni's residence to assemble the mine. Haim Dviri arrived and asked to speak with Zeroni, alone.

"People are talking," said Dviri. Zeroni did not even know if Dviri was officially a member of the Irgun. "As a friend of yours from Brit Habirionim," Dviri continued, "I am asking you – include me." Zeroni considered for a moment but Dviri was determined:

"Listen, I must do it!"

Dviri was in.

The mine was ready just after midnight. At 12:30 the Irgun's Tel Aviv commander, Abraham "Dan" Krichevsky, arrived. "I knew it was a mistake to stay here with the mine," thought Zeroni as he ushered Dan in.

Dan brought a message from the Command: Forget the mine.

Why, asked Zeroni, convinced the commanders were worried the effect might be too "explosive," literally and politically. Dan mumbled something about what would happen if the mine failed to explode, if the mission were aborted, if, if...in the end, the "rebels" agreed to attack without the mine.

By 5:00 A.M., ten Irgunists were in place at 4 Yehuda Halevy Street. The buildings at the corner of Herzl Street still bore the shrapnel of yesterday's attack.

Esther Raziel, David's sister, approached in an Irgun cab driven by Arye Ben Eliezer. The car stopped, she distributed the guns and the cab pulled away. Looking back she saw behind her ten men standing in silhouette against the rosy glow of the morning sky. As the cab rounded a corner, she might have discerned Zeroni, slightly apart from the others, holding the operation's only submachine gun – it was a Finnish Suomi, but the exuberant Irgunists fondly called it a Thompson – in the crock of his arm; Benjamin Kahane peering into the shadows of the distant tracks; Dviri, a white cap low over his forehead, cradling his pistol.

Dviri was scrutinizing the chunk of metal in his palm, turning it over and over, weighing the precious ore. He noticed the others stroking their treasures as well. They were like misers joyously fingering gold.

For one dubious moment the squalid buildings, deserted tracks, and rooftop-dotted skyline seemed a lie. But the rhythmic chant of the nearing steel wagons dispersed any doubts.

The ten boyish Irgunists moved to the fence which separated Lilienblum Street from the rails and as the train unknowingly drew opposite its firing squad, they let forth a sudden blinding effulgence of gunfire.

In the first major operation of the Irgun Zvai Leumi, one Arab was killed and five injured.

Soon, the windows of the train were boarded up to prevent future attacks from or upon the Arabs, an idea which had occurred to no one so long as Jews were the victims. In truth, there was no need to seal the windows, for the terrified Arabs never again attacked Jewish bystanders along the route of a train on which they themselves were passengers.

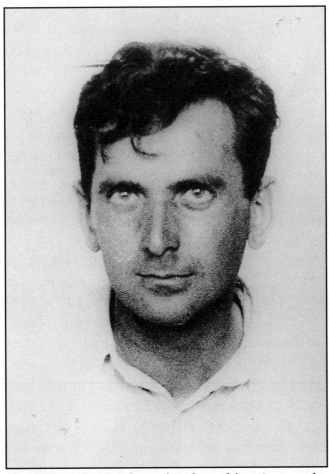

Abraham "Gideon" Tehomi, founder and first Commander of the Irgun (Jabotinsky Institute photo)

Embattled Irgun Commander Abraham Tehomi stepped onto his open-air porch a few moments before the scheduled arrival of the doomed train. The sun was already dissipating the morning mist. Tehomi's inscrutable expression revealed, as usual, little of the conflicts he was attempting to synthesize within. "So, Zeroni thinks he has to force me to take action?" Tehomi thought, an ironic smile undoubtedly twisting a corner of his mouth. "Still," he said softly, to himself and to anyone who might be listening, "I like Zeroni, I really do."

Zeroni and his Lilienblum Street co-conspirators could not have known, but theirs were not the only fireworks scheduled for that morning. Tehomi had invested of his energy heavily. The slight smile on Tehomi's face broadened as he heard, on schedule, shots emanating from north and south, west and east, a veritable symphony of gunfire from all over Tel Aviv. When Tehomi finally heard the staccato of Zeroni's machine gun, he knew that the deadliest operation of that morning was underway.

Sometimes Tehomi was hard put to believe that there were in his ranks those who thought him averse to terror. "I am not opposed to terror," he would try to explain, "but the question is by whom, for what, and where will it lead?" Tehomi opposed the individual, partisan acts of violence which were then, often as not, accomplished in an anonymous hit-and-run style. "We must take responsibility, the acts must be executed by an authoritative body representing a political point of view." And the killing, if necessary, must have an aim: "We cannot and should not compete with the Arabs in an orgy of violence to see who can kill more people. The purpose of our terror must be communicative: to show the Arabs that we can hit them as hard as they hit us, which hopefully will deter them from hitting us in the first place." But where Tehomi most parted way from his fellow officers and even from the one man – Jabotinsky – who with the mere force of his personality wielded more power over the Irgunists than their Commander Tehomi, was in answering, or even addressing, the question of where the terror would lead. "Our escalation of activity," Tehomi believed, "is not merely military but also political. Today we attack Arab gangs, yes, but this will inevitably lead to our clashing with the British. Are we ready to take on the British army? I do not know. Myself, I am ready, provided we are fully aware that this is what we are doing and all of us, including Jabotinsky, choose to do so. Otherwise it is foolish to endanger the existence of our still relatively small army just to kill a few Arabs." An army, an army...this thought gave Tehomi no rest and would eventually have dire consequences for Tehomi himself and the Irgun. Tehomi's intense desire for an army will culminate in the acrimonious cleavage of Irgun ranks that will one day be known as "Gideon's schism," after Tehomi's underground code name.

Tehomi was born in Odessa in 1903. In *Between Darkness and Dawn*, a not very widely distributed memoir of his early years in Russia, Tehomi recalls that on frequent trips to Sevastopol he was most impressed by "tropical trees and flowers, delightful promenades and winding paths, beautiful grottoes...the sublime view of the bay" and, in odd juxtaposition, the nearby "imposing building which contained a panorama of the Siege of Sevastopol...enshrined in niches were statues of the heroes...inside, drowned in profound awesome silence and bathed in dim light, were colossal mural paintings depicting the...siege." Tehomi says he shuddered "with breathless wonder."

When a Russian classmate taunted him, declaring all Jews cowards and offering as proof the "fact" that the Russian military boasted no Jewish officers, young Abraham sought solace from his father, who explained that as Jews were forbidden to enroll in the Military Academy, the absence of Jewish officers was no wonder. "I will go to Eretz Israel and be an officer!" announced the angry schoolboy and future Commander in Chief of the Irgun Zvai Leumi.

In 1919, Tehomi met in Sevastopol a Jew who had actually been a Russian officer, Trumpeldor. More than 70 years later, Tehomi still spoke of Trumpeldor with awe: "He was simply an exceptional person. Exceptional. He influenced me enormously, told me to go back to Odessa; he'd lost contact with his Hehalutz representatives there and wanted me to reestablish contact, to begin organizing. Though I also had my own reasons for wanting to be in Odessa, I went back at his request."

Tehomi stowed away on a ship but was discovered hiding in the hold when it docked in Odessa. His interrogation by the local gendarmes ended in a scene that could have been and was, in fact, written by Dostoevsky: A rifle was loaded, pointed at the teenage Tehomi's head, the order given to cock, aim and...take Tehomi away.

Tehomi helped organize Odessa's Jewish self-defense units during the Red vs. White Russian civil war. He rebelliously began learning Hebrew only when the Soviet government declared it illegal to do so. Eventually he set out for the Land of Israel, a journey that took him through pigsties and haylofts and across midnight rivers in smugglers' boats. (Meeting his contact before crossing the river into Poland, the password was supposed to be "Trumpeldor." "What time is it?" Tehomi asked his apparent contact. "Five to four," the surprised contact answered a bit quizzically. "It is Trumpeldor's time!" responded Tehomi.) One night Tehomi fell from a loft as he scrambled for a ladder and, unable to move, had to be carried across that night's churning river by his brother Anatole.

In Jerusalem, Tehomi rapidly rose to the top of the Hagana's command. He took orders from future Israeli president Itzhak Ben-Zvi and by 1925 was a company commander. "Arabs were attacking Jews then," he remembered in his later years, "especially young women and people on their way to the Old City's Western Wall. I directed the "Kevutsat Mercaz," we struck at Arabs, roughed up troublemakers, I won't say we never took any shots..."

The bombing of the sheik's house? "Oh, yes, we did that. Rather inexperienced then, we prepared a fuse so long, must have been upwards of 60 feet, it jumped like a snake when we lit it but burnt itself out in the middle. We had to return a second night to relight it. The explosion was so forceful, not only did it wreck the house, but two of the newer stones were blown off the top of the Western Wall. I guess the sheik was not at home, I don't know, but no one was hurt..."

By decade's end, Tehomi was Jerusalem district commander for the Hagana, but a burning desire for a more active organization and for a real army led him to leave early in 1931. A Betari friend suggested hooking up with Irma Halperin's Betar School in Tel Aviv. Negotiations between Joseph Katznelson, Moshe Segal, Eliahu Ben Horin, "Dan" Krichevsky and Tehomi led to a merger of Tehomi's former Hagana men with Halperin and Rosenberg's Betarim, many of whom also listed the Hagana on their resumes. Tehomi assumed command of the Irgun Zvai Leumi, also known then as the Nationalist Hagana.

Six years later, the turmoil in Eretz Israel was all too reminiscent of the dark days of 1929. Spitting dissatisfaction with the official Hagana's failure to stem the '29 Arab riots had split the organization and brought the "activists" together in the IZL. Now, again, "activists" were agitating for a more violent campaign against Arab killers. Tehomi was probably aware that Zeroni and his friends had organized the "Grumblers Group."

Zeroni: "Actually, we called ourselves 'the Smartubekim Group.' You see, there's an Arabic curse, *kusmartabuk*, and we were so upset at the paucity of IZL activity that this curse was often on our lips, sort of bursting forth of its own power. Se we chose to call ourselves the 'Smartubekim,' and set up chapters in Jerusalem, Tel Aviv and Haifa, with smaller groups elsewhere, and we constantly lobbied for operations against the Arabs, to be carried out with Irgun approval."

Tehomi was no mild-mannered milquetoast, he just had other dreams for the Irgun, other views on the goals of anti-Arab terror. "My God," thought Tehomi, "we are going to need a real army soon, not just a half-underground, half-aboveground militia. The Arabs are going to try to destroy us and the British occupy our country. We should

109

be working to unite with the Hagana to be that army. What is the point of rushing war with the British when we are unprepared?"

Tehomi, Uri Zvi Greenberg and others met Jabotinsky in Vienna towards the end of 1936. Greenberg attempted to be appointed Jabotinsky's deputy and failed. Tehomi's offer was even more startling. Enough, he said, with the internal machinations and bickering. "I'll resign from the IZL and head a smaller group of, say, fifty fighters dedicated to terror versus Arabs."

Asked years later if this had been a serious offer or merely a political gambit to force Jabotinsky's hand, an attempt to frighten Jabo into restoring Tehomi's tarnished authority, Tehomi seemed taken aback: "The offer was certainly serious. One never joked with Jabotinsky."

Not only was Tehomi prepared to join in crimson combat with the Arabs, he was prepared to lead the crusade. As long, that is, as it did not endanger the unprepared Irgun ("I admit it, I accept responsibility: I spent too many of the years from 1931 to 1936 procuring weapons and not enough time preparing us for battle.") and as long as the authority for the terror originated with Jabotinsky on a political, not solely military, plain. Jabotinsky told Tehomi, "I have not yet decided" about terror and its implications.

Tehomi returned to the battlefield determined to allow only enough terror to alleviate the pressure within the ranks and instill a hopefully edifying fear in the Arabs. But the word "army" reverberated relentlessly in Tehomi's head and he had more or less decided that for the sake of a Jewish future in Eretz Israel, the IZL and the Hagana he had left six years earlier would need to reunite.

In truth, "Gideon" Tehomi and many of his bent in the IZL had all these years been negotiating with the Hagana. A year earlier, Aharon Heichman and Hanoch Kalay (Strelitz), two of the brightest and bravest of the Irgun commanders, had practically abandoned all other activities to work full time on thwarting Gideon's planned honeymoon with the Hagana. The Betar contingent in the Irgun – people like

Rosenberg, Nissim Cohen, Segal, Heichman – felt that ideological chasms lay between the IZL and the Hagana, that the Irgun's ideology of offensive action could never mesh with the Hagana's infatuation with defense. Tehomi began sidestepping his Betar subordinates, secreting arms caches for future use by his unified army; Rosenberg began organizing nighttime meetings of his Betarim to ready them for the coming conflict. In Nissim Cohen's words, the Betarim "became an underground within an underground."

Rosenberg believed unification with the Hagana would mean the end of the Irgun, "the Irgunists will be swallowed up by the Hagana and our ideology will disappear. Tehomi will never get anywhere with the Hagana leaders, they won't let him."

Tehomi: "I must try. We need an army."

Rosenberg: "The Irgun is supposed to be that army. Merging with the Hagana will simply wreck the IZL."

But Tehomi saw the Hagana as the natural foundation for the army: "The men who left the Hagana with me formed the organizational basis of the Irgun. The IZL grew from the Jerusalem branch of the Hagana. We developed the attitude of a conspiracy, we acted like a movement, we initiated so-called terror tactics. Most importantly, in Jerusalem there was a feeling that this was a mission we were shouldering."

Rosenberg could not have disagreed more: "As I see it, the men of the Betar Officers Training School were the kernel from which the Irgun grew. And there would not have been a pool of youth to draw on for membership, and the IZL would not have had an ideology to inspire it, without Betar, and the political backing of Jabotinsky."

This, for Tehomi, was itself another trouble: "Jabotinsky's trying to overwhelm the IZL, turn it into an arm of his Revisionist Party. We need an apolitical army! This is why I must leave..."

Rosenberg had no qualms about Jabotinsky's authority and saw the Hagana as far more political than the Irgun. He recalled that Tehomi had left in '31 because the Histadrut was trying to pull all the strings. "I left three years earlier partly for the same reason. I didn't want to fight under a red flag. I also wanted to shoot before I was shot at, not after." Did Tehomi think things would be any better the second time around?

Tehomi reasoned he would take thousands with him into the Hagana; they would be a force the Hagana would have to reckon with. Rosenberg decided to fight any possible merger with the Hagana, confidant "the thousands" would stay with him. Yet he continued to respect his opponent.

Rosenberg: "I remember my first skirmish with Arabs in Jaffa, back in '21. I organized eight *landsmen* from my city in Russia. I was the only one with a gun, which didn't shoot. We did have sticks though! Fortunately the Arabs were more afraid of us than we of them!"

Tehomi: "We started with so little. That's why I spend so much time on procurements of arms."

Rosenberg later admitted that Tehomi had had no choice, when he took command "we didn't have one hundred guns in all the land. I'd have done the same in his position."

So the internal intrigues and political squabbles continued, waiting impatiently for one straw to break the organization's back. The spring of 1937 brought two.

The first was an arms cache which simply disappeared in Tel Aviv; the sleight of hand was the "magic" work of the Sdan group of Birionim, but few even knew of Sdan's existence, and Tehomi more logically blamed Rosenberg's Betarim. The second straw was a cafe in the Arab village of Yazur.

The ides of March were unmerciful that year. From March 13 to March 16, two Jewish shepherds were murdered, then two residents of Yavniel, and one of Rosh Pina. On the seventeenth, a bomb exploded on Jerusalem's Jaffa Road, creating more consternation at the brazen attack than actual injuries.

On one of those mornings, Benjamin Zeroni was, as usual, up early reading the papers. Zeroni was quite a character, a true friend, a bit odd, perhaps, and impatient, a famous temper, sometimes abrasive. A born rebel, he was in the mid-1930s at a particularly rebellious period in his young life. All conventions were prey for his hotheaded individuality. Like his friend Arye Yitzhaki, Zeroni wore britches and riding boots. He created a tremendous sensation in this portentous outfit, scooting around on his motorcycle. He took his attire seriously. Zeroni felt it the last word in fashionable chic as well as an eloquent statement of individuality. He was more often than not accompanied by a large, more than just a tad vicious, attack dog. Only when the time came to go deep underground did Zeroni abandon the ostentatious behavior. Well, the britches and boots, not the cycle. Different? Yes. Odd? Maybe. By his own account, he was a "smartubek." And one of the most impatient of young Irgunists.

At about 16 he had shared his first – though most assuredly not his last – jail cell with Ahimeir and Segal after the Shiels demonstration. As a group leader he had taught younger charges the proper use of guns and mines. A year before he had held the machine gun in the train attack. Afterwards, to afford this strangely apparelled swashbuckler a release for his obviously pent-up energies, his commanders sent him for a stint of guard duty in Zofit, near Ramat Hakovesh. The first night passed quietly, the second as well. On the third night Zeroni turned to his companions and declared: "Guys, I don't see any Arabs here. What say we go out and look for them?" They looked for four days – for all his bravado, Zeroni and his guards were young and did their share of trembling in the dark orchards – and found not a single trespasser. Zeroni was inconsolable. He returned to Tel Aviv and demanded "a border area. Give me an area, put me in charge, if an Arab does something, I'll act, I don't want to have to come begging for your permission after the fact..."

Zeroni patrolled Tel Aviv's Yemenite Quarter where Arabs were almost always hurling stones and shooting haphazardly at passing Jews. He roamed the streets with a loaded pistol and an itchy finger but uncovered no Arabs causing even the least bit of trouble.

While on an arms-purchasing mission to Warsaw, Zeroni bought a small nickel-plated FN pistol for a girlfriend back in Tel Aviv. They split up before he could make the presentation and he kept the gun, which he used for instructional courses he was leading. Following one lesson, Zeroni wrapped the gun in a newspaper, wedged it under an arm, and sped off on his trademark motorcycle with the inverted handlebars. At the Star of David intersection, a policeman atop a wooden platform was directing traffic. As Zeroni zoomed by, the newspaper remained comfortably tucked in his armpit but the little FN dropped at the cop's feet. The momentum of Zeroni's scooter carried him on as pedestrians gawked and a puzzled cop assessed the situation. Before anyone could move, Zeroni insouciantly reversed direction, sped back, scooped up the pistol and disappeared.

At 5:30 this March morning, his hands shook as he held the paper and tears softened his rough veneer. He sped over to Tehomi's house and woke the Commander.

"Haven't you heard? Slaughtered! Slaughtered with knives! They were just going to get a drink of water, the kibbutzniks were slaughtered with knives – "

"If they're kibbutzniks, the Hagana will handle this one – " reasoned Tehomi.

"They're Jews. Never mind the Hagana – " and Zeroni was gone.

Zeroni met two more Grumblers, Benjamin Kahane and Arye Yitzhaki, later that day. Zeroni and Yitzhaki were Irgun buddies. Their friendship soon turned into a business relationship as well: Yitzhaki was a plumber, Zeroni an electrician, and Tel Aviv's building boom often found them crossing pipes and wires. The trio decided that Zeroni would command the operation. Benjamin Kahane would drive the motorcycle. Zeroni rode in the bucket on a test run to Jerusalem to personally assure himself of Kahane's road skills. "You are one wild driver!" exclaimed a dizzy Zeroni at journey's end. "A real champion cyclist. You'll do fine!"

Who would accompany Kahane in the bucket seat and toss the bomb? Lots were drawn. Zeroni lost. Arye Yitzhaki would go. On March 22, Kahane careened his cycle to a rolling stop a few feet off the Jerusalem-Tel Aviv thoroughfare. Yitzhaki leapt out, hurrying with his deadly cargo towards the bustling entrance of the Yazur cafe. A final step forward, a raised arm, a hurled grenade – and there before Yitzhaki were deformed walls, flying doors, shattering glass, the dead and the injured falling over one another in utter confusion. In the midst of which Yitzhaki went unnoticed as he slid back into the idling cycle. Kahane fired the engine and sped away.

The IZL Command was fury incarnate. Suspicion immediately fell on the impetuous Zeroni and his sidekick Yitzhaki, who at the hour of the attack had been mysteriously AWOL from his officers course. Tehomi flung his words at Zeroni: "Did you do this?!" Zeroni answered that he had not, noting to himself, for honesty's pitiful sake, that Tehomi had not asked whether he had commanded the operation, just whether he had executed it. Tehomi was not actually all that concerned with Zeroni, he was far more interested in discovering whether Rosenberg had been behind this unauthorized action, which of course he had not.

Yitzhaki heedlessly "broke" during his interrogation, and with a shrug of his broad shoulders admitted rather blankly, "So I did it, is it really a big deal?" Tehomi felt personally betrayed by Zeroni's having lied to him. If he had considered pardoning the action, which was in his eyes an inexcusable breach of discipline, he could not countenance the lie. He ordered Zeroni and Yitzhaki expelled from the IZL.

The grenade at Yazur tore down not only the walls of a café but also the already unsteady walls of the Irgun. The partisan action highlighted two diametrically opposed responses to the daily murder of Jews by

Arabs. The activists, the Betarim and the rank and file wanted to fight with any means at their disposal, while the militarily inclined officers with less commitment to Jabotinsky wanted to graft themselves back onto the Hagana to form an army. When the smoke cleared at Yazur, Gideon's Schism rent the IZL. Commander Tehomi gallantly refused to order the troops to join the Hagana. He offered every member of the IZL a free choice as to his personal future.

Rosenberg explained: "We love Tehomi, he is a good Commander and loved...Gideon has despaired, he is not satisfied with Jabotinsky, he didn't get the help he wanted from Jabotinsky, I think this is one of the reasons for his return to the Hagana." Rosenberg urged the troops to remain within the Irgun. Eighteen hundred Irgunists stayed with Rosenberg; about fifteen hundred went with Tehomi to the Hagana.

Historians writing from padded armchairs decades later may generously choose to justify both Rosenberg and Tehomi. Tehomi's forces were absorbed into the Hagana without a trace. The Hagana leadership broke almost all its agreements until, finally, a frustrated Tehomi took the path many of his men had already chosen: no longer able to justify his presence in the Hagana, he left. (During the Second World War Tehomi served with French Intelligence directing operations in Lebanon against the Germans.) But Tehomi had been right – the Jews did need an army to repel Arab armies, and the Hagana filled this role in 1948.

Rosenberg kept the IZL together. Newspapers around the world were reporting that since the Jewish reprisals had begun, Arab attacks on defenseless Jews had slowed. Thus, the IZL had little choice but to step up its onslaught. One day they would be ready to take on the British.

Tehomi's departure inaugurated the short-lived Bitker era. Bitker's Command consisted of Rosenberg, the chief of staff and Tel Aviv commander; Abraham Stern, whom Tehomi had personally brought back from Florence to be his assistant in Jerusalem; David Raziel; Aharon Heichman; and Hanoch Kalay. The foiled bank robbery, a literal and figurative linguistic-gap with his underlings – and an unsolved murder

Commander in Chief of the Irgun, Moshe Rosenberg, inspects the troops in Tel Aviv, 1937. (Left to right) Arye Posek, David Stern (in dark shirt), Rosenberg, Zvi Sofer, Aharon Heichman (Jabotinsky Institute photo)

the police were beginning to unravel, the winding trail from a body found in the Yarkon River leading just a little too near IZL portals – encouraged Col. Bitker to turn the reigns over to Moshe Rosenberg.

Rosenberg was ever the first to admit his drawbacks. He had a civilian business to manage, was as concerned with procuring weapons as Tehomi had been – to the detriment of other activities – and was always more of a military figure than an underground man. But with or without Rosenberg's enthusiastic support, the skies nonetheless darkened for the unfettered Arab gangs of Eretz Israel in the coming months. "We blackened many of their days," as Joseph Kremin puts it.

By now Kremin was one of the IZL's top operatives in Jerusalem. He'd just spent eight months billeted in the house of one Mr. Arochos in the Yemin Moshe neighborhood. He and his Irgun contingent – his deputy Rafael Saban, foot soldier Zvi Meltser, and others – shared their headquarters with the local Hagana branch. They shared the telephone, the single one in Yemin Moshe, too. Meltser was operator: If the caller gave the Hagana password, Meltser passed them the receiver; if the

117

Irgun password was given, Kremin took the call.

The Hagana man explained his orders to Kremin: "We'll disperse troublesome Arabs with the clubs we have." Kremin's incredulity was instinctive: "Clubs? We have guns." The Hagana representative continued: "The Hagana will not shoot at Arabs unless Jews are killed first." Kremin brought the conversation to a quick conclusion: "If they come within 150 feet of here, we're opening fire."

When danger raised its ominous head, the defenders opted for a shield of darkness. Meltser, the local electrician – he and his brother ran an electrical-appliance shop on Jaffa Road, near Mahane Yehuda – climbed to the roof and cut the cable supplying power, blacking out Yemin Moshe. Except, in the distance, one stubborn lamppost lit half the neighborhood; fifteen feet high, its bulb lay at the end of a six-foot protrusion. Meltser pulled himself up the pole and swung onto the extension. With one arm he hung monkey-like; with the other he unscrewed the bulb, to the cheers of the locals.

When the danger seemed imminent, two Arab policemen with rifles arrived to afford "official" protection. Meltser locked the two in a closet and turned the rifles over to more trustworthy men for the night. In the morning, the weapons were returned and the Arabs were sent on their way.

Melster's first real operation was mining a road near an Arab village. The Arabs there had been assaulting Jews, the Irgun decided to return the favor. Saban took Meltser and Miriam Rubovitch to the site. Meltser, again the electrician, laid the mine; after the explosion he rewound the cable and they went home. Soon, Meltser's courage, more than his technical aptitude, was in demand. An Arab gang leader had made contact with the Nazis; he was marked for assassination. Kremin watched from a distance as Meltser, in a raincoat, turned the collar up and his chin down, bidding for anonymity in the midday Jaffa Road crowd. Across the street from a police station, near today's Zion Square, an Irgun operative identified the target. Zvi approached from behind, rested his gun on the Nazi agent's back, and fired three times. Meltser's anonymity died with the victim. An English sergeant gave chase. "I'm young," thought Meltser. "Gymnastics – I know. Soccer – I know. To run – I must also know." He finally lost his equally athletic pursuer by dipping into a half-constructed basement, then ran a few more blocks and enrolled himself in a local medical clinic for an afternoon of treatment. Eventually he exchanged his coat for the doorman's and, again inconspicuous, returned to his electric store. "Did you hear, there were shots on Jaffa Road!" exclaimed his brother. "No," replied Zvi, "I was taking R & R at the clinic..."

When Gideon called an assembly of troops to announce the unification agreement with the Hagana, Joseph Kremin was there. He heard Tehomi declare, "We need a Hebrew army!" and explain what must be done, but felt "satiated with such promises." He harbored no animosity toward Tehomi, on the contrary, he considered him the very epitome of a "gentleman," but Kremin wasted no time. He tracked down David Raziel in Tel Aviv and brought him straightaway to Jerusalem. The life-and-death importance of this move must be gauged by the calendar. It took place on a Saturday. Raziel was a deeply observant Jew who had never before driven anywhere on a Sabbath. That he agreed to was a sure sign of the urgency he felt. They had to get to Jerusalem, they had to organize a new Command, and they had to confiscate as many arms caches as they could for the benefit of the newly weaponless IZL, half of whose caches were now destined for the Hagana. Kremin explained: "We've reached an agreement about splitting the caches but the other side isn't keeping to it. But...they don't know we've appropriated the Hagana's storehouse of arms in Jerusalem!" With these surreptitiously won arms in mind, Raziel, Kremin and a few associates began planning what soon came to be known as "Black Sunday."

Today, Kremin's round, jovial face breaks freely into laughter at almost any opportunity, and it matters little to him whether the occasion is a discussion of his military triumphs against Israel's enemies

119

or, perhaps, a sarcastic jab at his own stone silence regarding those triumphs. Interviewers and historians are easily won over by his friendly laughter but have a harder time penetrating the myths of two genera- tions past. "Some things – it's best stay buried," he winks. "Don't even ask – I'm not going to answer," he warns. The intoxications of fame and historical immortality seem to him like whiskey to a teetotaller. "I have never regretted not speaking," he says, and Kremin was, if this be possible, famous for not speaking. On secret IZL missions to Po- land he never attended Jabotinsky's popular lectures for fear another Eretz-Israeli might also attend, recognize him and send word of his presence in Poland to others who had no need to know. In all his years in Warsaw, he enjoyed the delights of a sidewalk café but once.

One assumes that few of Kremin's neighbors in a coastal town just outside of Tel Aviv are aware that the perpetually chuckling man they meet in the corner grocery was, as IZL representative for illegal *Af al pi* immigration, personally responsible for bringing over thirty- five thousand Jews out of a European hell in the three years preceding World War Two. Hundreds were literally pulled from the waters off sinking ships and brought to safety under his direction. So he has earned a right to smile, and if silence has served him well for half a century, a curious interviewer had best not argue.

But a guest in the Kremin home, while trying to pry secrets from the elderly patriarch, will most likely be served tea and biscuits by a petite woman obviously adept, after years of practice, at being as un- obtrusive as possible. Bat-Zion (Daughter of Zion) Kremin will sit as far away as possible; she may fiddle in the back room or read an old paper in a corner. Most strangers come to delve, unsuccessfully, into Joseph's life, she knows. Few know that before she was Mrs. Kremin, she was Bat-Zion Neeman, a typically vivacious, carefree teenage girl – in the service of IZL intrigue and terror.

All sorts of messages and telegrams arrived at the Neeman's Hashomer Street home in Tel Aviv, and Bat-Zion passed them on, comprehending almost none. The problematic bank robbery was a bit stickier. No Irgunist wanted to be spotted talking to the still-at-large Birionim after that debacle, for British detectives were sure to be close behind. The job fell to 15-year-old Bat-Zion, who with a teen's paradigmatic spunk sauntered into the appointed café to twice meet a fugitive Birion and receive messages for IZL Commander Bitker. She was not fully in the picture, but she understood the news was, to say the least, "not very pleasant."

Should a houseguest find the conversation winding its way to Black Sunday, to explosive days in Jerusalem of yore, that guest would do well to include Bat-Zion in the exchange. "I may have had a hand in it," Joseph is likely to say, "I'm not sure I remember." Bat-Zion will remember.

"I had once been ordered to Nissim Cohen's house," she has told the few who have thought to ask. "I arrived early one morning as ordered, but the mission was canceled and I was dismissed. They must have been impatient, for I was quickly given orders to report Sunday morning. I was given a suitcase filled with arms, a huge suitcase ("Bigger than she!" Joseph will now recall) which we put on the roof of an Egged bus. I had the keys and a bodyguard for the ride to Jerusalem, which, when we got there, was crawling with British. By the Mahane Yehuda marketplace the army was stopping all vehicles. My bodyguard had been sitting to the side, as if traveling separately, but when he saw what was going on he panicked. He whisked by me, slowing just long enough to whisper 'You don't know me,' and got off at the first opportunity. (Joseph: "I was worried about her, I didn't know her then but we knew someone was coming, and I knew her bodyguard was in pretty poor health, tubercular, I think...") Loads of cops mounted the bus; they poked around and told us to continue. Apparently they were more suspicious of outgoing Jews than incoming. We reached the station at Jaffa Road near Ben Yehuda Street and getting off the bus I met Raziel. He was white. I don't know what color I was, but he was white. There he was in the midst of this chaos, the man who had organized it all, hunted by the British, and now I had brought him a suitcase full of illegal arms. He put me in a cab to Shoshana Spitzer's, his future wife. I ran up her steps, knocked, gave her the suitcase, ran back and left Jerusalem without even stopping for a glass of water."

On November 14, 1937, five days after five Jews had been murdered in Kiryat Anavim outside Jerusalem, at 7:00 A.M., Joseph Kremin and Shlomo Trachtman shot two Arabs, one fatally, on Azza Street near the Workers' Dorms. Half an hour later two Arabs were shot, again one fatally, near Bet Israel. An hour or two later, Zvi Meltser delivered a gun to an Irgunist waiting in Romema. An Arab bus was attacked there, three Arabs were killed and eight injured.

Bat-Zion shrugs. "I don't think I should have been sent that day. The papers called it Black Sunday."

Nissim Cohen, too, admitted to an abundance of errors in those early days underground. Prudence and discretion were not the bywords of that era. Sometimes teenage panache, speeding insouciance or even feigned imperturbability were the recipe for hair's-breadth escapes from peril. At one point, Nissim Cohen found himself in Tel Aviv transporting a suitcase of his own. Like Zeroni before him, he was an instructor, and instructors were responsible for bringing and removing all tools of their trade. Cohen moved under cover of darkness and assumed the darker the better – so he drove his cycle without lights, a "foolishness," as he put it, which attracted rather than deflected the attention of an alert member of Tel Aviv's police department. The cop lost no time in letting his attention drift from the lights to the bulky suitcase. "What is in it?" he demanded. Cohen, a bit pathetically, tried: "Dirty laundry?"

"Show me," persevered the officer. To which Cohen could only muster: "No." The cop noted that if he took Cohen to the station, Cohen would surely show him there. In desperation, Cohen tried pluck: "You know what? I see you're Jewish. I'll tell you – I have a suitcase full of arms and ammunition." An incredulous lawman retorted that he did not believe this story either. "Show me!" he challenged, and Cohen suggested they step aside where he would, but now the cop was himself a bit nervous and of lagging spirit. "Really, don't be afraid, come on, I'll show you," Cohen comforted...and he did. "Ah," exclaimed a relieved cop to a far more relieved Cohen, "I thought you were a Communist with manifestos. Go on, get outta here already!"

Sometimes Lady Luck played her decisive hand. Cohen was again ordered to dispatch a suitcase to Jerusalem. His wife dressed to the nines and Cohen watched from a distance, perhaps quivering with the same emotions with which Miriam had watched the baby Moses float off into dangerous waters. A sentry beheld the hapless Mrs. Cohen: Get moving, he urged, take that suitcase and keep moving. But the load was too heavy for this *grande dame*, the Englishman realized, and as the Egyptian princess had lifted Moses, he now lifted this precious cargo himself and strapped it to the auto's roof. The suitcase did not make it to Jerusalem that day, but in the confusion following its confiscation at a roadblock, Mrs. Cohen was luckily allowed, in fact ordered, to ride towards home.

Occasionally neither luck nor chutzpa were sufficient. Twenty-five-year-old Jacob Kotik carried his arms suitcase unaware that he had been double-crossed, set up by an informer. The British hosted Kotik that Sabbath in a solitary-confinement pit of the Jaffa Prison, the first stop on Kotik's harrowing journey to death row.

Another Sabbath guest who enjoyed the gracious hospitality of the British Prison Authority was Rachel Ohevet Ami. Rachel was 20 according to the papers, 18 by her own account. So full of energy new listeners often missed half her rapid-fire speech, her verve and zest won hearts while her courage won respect. Her jet-black hair and matching eyes, her dark Yemenite skin and her fluency in Arabic afforded her an inconspicuous entrance to Arab crowds. Most of the time. Bright teeth revealed by a constant smile, playing off her dark complexion,

Jacob Kotik (right) as constable in Zichron Yaacov, 1936
(Jabotinsky Institute photo)

won her friends even in Bethlehem's Prison for Women, where for half her sentence she was the sole Jewish political prisoner in a society stocked with prostitutes, thieves, murderesses and prison guards.

Rachel had walked slowly up the narrow hill to the Jerusalem Central Prison, the stone wall of the prison compound to her left, the heavily guarded radio station on her right. She was dressed for the occasion, garbed in a tailor-made colorful – and ethnically Arab – dress. Her head was scarved as befitting a devoutly modest young woman. Friday morning was visiting day for the prison's Arab inmates – petty thieves, wife beaters, cold-blooded killers and gang members whose hands were dripping with Jewish blood. Rachel's tiny hands struggled to carry their load. She would be one of dozens of "relatives" with fruit-filled baskets for imprisoned loved ones. Rachel's bulging basket packed more of a punch than the others, however, for under the fruit were metal shards, a timing device set for 11:00 A.M. and seven pounds of explosives. As planned, Rachel paid an Arab boy to carry the heavy gift into the visiting area, which consisted of no more than the prison yard's double barbed-wire fence, across which inmates on one side and family and friends on the other would shout, all vainly trying to be heard over the cacophony. At the fence, Rachel reclaimed the goods. The Irgun's culinary preferences failed them at this point: The pita-bread in Rachel's basket was Jewish, not Arab. The boy received his cent, thanked his benefactress and reported her to the police. The IZL had scheduled 11:00 A.M. for a strike at a British government installation – the prison – and a strike aimed specifically at Arab gang members and their families. Instead, at 11:00 Rachel was interrogated by the infamous Ralph Cairns. Within the week the young girl was sentenced by a military court to life in prison. After the Second World War, having served seven years, her sentence was commuted.

The pita was not the only out-of-place prop in the sanguine drama enacted by Jerusalem's IZL branch that Friday. The *mise en scène* itself was awkward. For no matter what evils were perpetrated "outside," in the open civilian world, a prison's ground was more hallowed to its inhabitants than a church. No Arab Quasimodo needed shout "Sanctuary!" to remind Jewish fighters that no matter how many of their brethren he had maimed "outside" – inside, they were brothers. Any other attitude would fast escalate into food poisoning, backstabbing, nighttime strangling, full-time civil war. No person would be able to eat, wash, sleep or walk. So an unspoken agreement was signed and sealed: The war stops at a prison's gate. Inside, the British are the only enemy. That war continues.

The Jewish prisoners of the Jerusalem Central Prison, ignorant of the IZL action, were now to bear its brunt. The intended Arab victims were furious – had some of them or their relatives been killed the Jews most certainly would have been eliminated with no time for formalities. Yehezkel Altman felt that this was his lucky day when instead of being stabbed to death he was put on "trial" by teeth-bared Arabs. At least a few moments remained for a he-had-no-idea-what-kind-of *deus ex machina* to bring the perilous plot to a happy end. Sgt. Shvilli, a Jewish prison guard, had managed to lift Haim Dviri and Buchko from their respective workplaces and lock them in a cell for their own safety, but he had not gotten to Altman in time. Altman took center stage.

Scene: The courtyard of the Jerusalem Central Prison. Walls of Jerusalem stone, dulled gray with the years. A stone floor, smoothed after decades of exposure to the elements. Occasional apertures lead to the basement workshops. Barbed wire above; beyond, gray skies.

Cast: Dozens of justifiably bloodthirsty Arab convicts; one Jewish ex-policeman, Y. Altman.

(As the curtain rises, Altman is escorted to a nook in the southeast corner of the courtyard, a three-by-five ensconcement situated between the outer walls of the infirmary and the solitary cells. Moslem preachers exhort the worshipping faithful from this corner every Friday morning. This Friday, the Preacher is Judge, the faithful are a chanting lynch mob, and a gaunt, silent Jew is among the Moslems.)

Judge-Executioner: Your sister used a visit to you as an excuse to kill our families!

(An Arab fluent in Hebrew – and Yiddish, too, incidentally – translates for the defendant.)

Altman (thinks quickly): First of all, she is my sister – *(Aside:*

126

She is not, of course. But I'll take whatever cards are dealt)
– so the others are not involved. This is between us and has
nothing to do with Dviri or Buchko!

*(The translator translates, the mob seems willing to settle
for the blood of Rachel's presumptive brother.)*

Altman: Secondly, we are fighting a war, remember? If you
are allowed to bring bombs to centers of Jewish population
why should Jews be forbidden to do the same? After all, we
are learning from you...

Judge: But why here, where we are defenseless and may also
get hurt?

Altman: You talk of defenseless?! Of not using bombs against
the defenseless, who cannot carry arms? Why did you murder
those two nurses-of-mercy in the Jaffa Hospital? It's not
enough they were there to care for you, to tend to your sick!
How could they have defended themselves when the Arabs
of Jaffa butchered them like sheep? You talk of justice, of not
being "allowed" to bring bombs, or not planting them in
particular places, or attacking certain areas? In war there is
no justice. Nurses who saved the lives of many of your Arab
brothers in Jaffa were killed in cold blood and you're looking
for justice...

*(As the translator proceeds the chanting turns to rumbling
and the rumbling gradually to a silence so deep the sweating,
stationary Altman thinks to himself he can hear the flutter
of a fly's wings. Slowly, without being ordered to do so, without being urged, with not a word spoken, sullen Arabs begin
to leave, one by one, then in groups of two or three, and finally
in larger numbers. Altman is left alone with the translator.)*

Translator: It was the mention of the nurses. You undermined
their masculinity and humiliated them.

★ ★ ★

127

Moshe Rosenberg had been with the IZL in its prenatal days, as instructor and deputy commander of the Betar School. He had negotiated the Irgun into existence with Tehomi and chivalrously, for the acknowledged benefit of the IZL, let Tehomi be its guiding Commander in Chief. He had held the organization together during Gideon's Schism and ensured the depleted IZL a future. As IZL violence increased and the circle around him closed, Rosenberg's friends urged a retreat to Cyprus, after which Jabotinsky appointed David Raziel the IZL Commander.

Much time passed before Rosenberg finally returned, deciding to ignore Jabotinsky's warning that "they'll arrest you there." "I prefer sitting in prison in Eretz Israel to sitting in Warsaw," Rosenberg sighed. But by then a different cast of characters was prominent in the Irgun Command.

Aharon "Dov" Heichman was district commander for the Tel Aviv area at the time of the changing of the guard. Actually, he thought Raziel a bit similar to Rosenberg: Both seemed to have been weaned on military milk, soldiers from day one; but neither was an underground fighter. In any case, when Rosenberg passed from the scene several of his ablest officers lost interest in the IZL as well. Lieberman, Rosler, Sofer – they had been the Irgun in Tel Aviv. Heichman was a district commander with hundreds of battle-happy troops and few officers capable of leading them into the fray. He had to bring young blood to the IZL leadership, his eyes had now to spot the best of potential commanders.

"Arye Yitzhaki is one courageous guy," thought Heichman as he slated him for the command of Eighth Company.

So begins the sanguine ballad of Arye Yitzhaki, a ballad not sung in Tel Aviv today, a ballad the words of which were never written, a song the beat of which is street explosions, the rhyme of which is repeating gunfire, the tune of which is unbridled courage, the rhythm of which is Yitzhaki's life. Yitzhaki lived hard and fast, and though his death was slow and painful, it was in tempo. No streets are named

Yitzhaki in south Tel Aviv though this was his lair; no sculptor's hands preserve his image, though his hands were gifts to the dream of Jewish statehood. Myth is an unpredictable creature and her choices are not subject to cross-examination. History will smile at its ironic footnote, that Israel's enemies, Arab and British, knew this son of Israel far better than Israel herself.

Yitzhaki's family moved from Poland to Jaffa in 1924 when he was ten. He joined Betar at 14 and lost no time in making his way to the new IZL. Zeroni first met his future friend and comrade in arms when they both enrolled in an officers course given by Tehomi. Yitzhaki was blond, robust, not very tall, but stolid and firm. He was not one to enter into ideological discussions, to debate philosophical niceties. His prowess was practical, not theoretical. He sought activity, lived for the "next" operation. All who knew him agree that courage was his outstanding attribute. He feared nothing.

Sadly noting that "we have cases of folks shooting 11 bullets at an Arab and hitting his finger," Heichman hand-picked two groups of Irgunists to be trained in the art of "instinctive shooting." These groups, one from Ramat Gan and one from Tel Aviv, became known as the "Very Few," the elect IZL shootists. Off to the side of a deep, dried-up oasis in Tel Benjamin, targets were placed under overhanging sand and stone, and there the groups attained proficiency in drawing quickly, aiming instinctively and shooting to kill. The Tel Aviv group included Avner Ehrlich, who had some years back felled a mounted Englishman at a Brit Habirionim rally; Bensenberg, who had accompanied Zeroni to the verbal assault on Tehomi that led to the revenge attack on the train; Yaacov Meridor, future Commander in Chief of the IZL; Ben Arzi; Max Goldman; Shlomo Pozner; and Yitzhaki.

Yitzhaki's free time was spent in endless conversation with Heichman, who grew to think of him almost as an adopted child. By night, Yitzhaki would often steal through Heichman's second-floor window just to swap yarns. Every time Yitzhaki left, Heichman could only think: "How full he is with faith, what heart-and-soul dedication...and what golden hands, such technical aptitude!" Rarely did Yitzhaki visit without begging for an operation to be part of. Eventually he took his meals by Heichman, practically living there.

Yitzhaki was one of the youngbloods agitating for reprisal attacks on Arabs during the increasingly frequent Arab massacres of Jews in 1936-37. It is doubtful that any of his friends would have been overly astonished to see Yitzhaki, one morning, prone in a lot vacant except for broken bottles and half-eaten tins of preserves, hugging the pebble-strewn ground tighter than a snake's belly, hidden to most eyes in the morning shadows of adjacent homes and offices, a machine gun protruding from his outstretched arms as if it were a natural extension of his swarthy limbs.

Bat-Zion Neeman (Kremin) waited on Engel Street across from the lot, the long folds of her raincoat billowing in the brisk dawn breeze. At her side, red-headed Itzhak Liebowitz sat calmly warming the engine of his motorcycle. An observant, slightly paranoid passerby might have noticed that Bat-Zion's out-of-season coat was long enough to conceal a machine gun should, by any chance, someone lying in that lot across the street wish to pass her one, and that she could easily leap into the cycle's passenger seat, and the cycle could in no time at all speed to the corner of Rothschild and disappear into traffic. Should the need arise, of course.

A bus transporting Arab workers from Jaffa approached the government Bet Hamodidim (Land Surveyors Building) at the corner of Yehuda Halevy and Shenkin. This was no clandestine operation. The hour was 8:00 A.M., the sun-splashed main streets already dotted with workers hurrying along, overhead laundry lines on the side streets rapidly filling with the day's loads. As the bus pulled into view a shot rang loud and clear – loud enough to draw the attention of those on the street, clear enough, in fact, to draw housewives and stay-at-homes to their windows. Bat-Zion and Itzhak waited for the rapid report of the machine gun. It is a machine gun, she thought, its purpose to fire many bullets in rapid succession, hitting the target and frightening away morbidly curious onlookers. Alas, the single leaden bullet that had sputtered forth was sent on its mission alone, and silence reigned on the street. A few seconds, no more, an eternity passing with each, and of a sudden Yitzhaki was running from the yard, springing over bags of garbage, extending the gun as he reached Bat-Zion, pausing just long enough for his plaintive eyes to communicate that the gun had jammed, and he was off. Bat-Zion knew she was being watched, she knew the porches were by now crowded with spectators. No matter, she "hid" the gun under the coat, leaped into the cycle, Liebowitz gave gas and they left their Engel Street audience behind. Perhaps by this time Tel Aviv was no more shocked by gunplay than Dodge City would have been some years ago.

As the terror campaign by Arabs against Jews continued, the IZL carried its own version of eye-for-eye justice deeper into the heart of hostile territory. Nissim Cohen took a couple of young vigilantes to the Arab shuk in Jaffa. Should they be discovered, they knew, their fate would be that of Yaacov Raz, whose Arab robes were torn from him in the Jerusalem shuk when a native shouted "bomba!" and who was beaten and fatally stabbed before he could be evacuated from the seething market. Today's "bomba" is a time "bomba" packed in a mule's saddlebag. The mule is in starting position on a mixed Jewish-Arab street across from the all-Arab shuk. The animal is treated to a hefty whack and is on its way...Cohen, Yitzhaki and the others watch nervously as their mule halts abruptly, its ears pricked, its forelegs now stiffly braced. Would the idiot beast have sense enough to move a few feet further, into the shuk? But no – "This mule is a real jackass!" exclaims Cohen as the animal turns and heads back to the starting point. Yitzhaki wastes no time. He runs to the animal, jumps on its back, rips open the bag and in the midst of shoppers, workers and for all he knows soldiers and police, he tears the wires and disconnects the timing device from the explosives.

Yitzhaki's feckless courage is winning him a name. He is on the Jaffa-Ramle road, shooting; in a group assaulting the gangs of Salame; tossing bombs at storefronts in Jaffa.

Heichman next sends Yitzhaki to a secret IZL training course in the Carpathian Mountains. Perhaps Yitzhaki develops there his explosive talents, for he returns to Eretz Israel with an uncanny facility for assembling mines, delayed-action bombs and other deadly missives intended for dispatch to anyone standing in the way of Hebrew freedom.

As commander of Eighth Company, Yitzhaki is in charge not only of operations but also of intelligence gathering. One of the foot soldiers under his command is another stocky, squat Polish immigrant, Yitzhak Yzernitsky, who will one day go under the name Shamir. In May of 1939, David Raziel is arrested by the British as he attempts to board a plane at Lydda Airfield. Heichman and Hanoch Kalay are now by process of elimination running the show. Abraham Stern's influence on the Command grows; Kalay turns to Brit Habirionim's old publicist Yehoshua Yevin and Yevin now writes almost all IZL proclamations and wall posters, as well as the entire IZL newspaper. By June the time of revenge is passing, the era of war approaching, as the Irgun concentrates less on Arab and more on British targets. Heichman chooses Yitzhaki to help initiate the "Revolt" against England. "It seems to me a commanding officer should personally participate in actions he wants his men to execute," decides Heichman, sending Yitzhaki to demolish the railroad tracks near the Tel Aviv post office. Heichman orders all company commanders to personally blow up one phone booth, but once Yitzhaki gets started there is no stopping the fireball – he just keeps blowing up booth after booth. This action may seem incidental but is actually coordinated throughout the country's major cities, as a means of gaining hands-on experience in explosives while informing the British a war is on. Because of its scope it eventually becomes a major burden on the government's communications network. Yitzhaki is now 24 years old. The balladeer is nearing the end of his song, the tune is the same but the rhythm grows mournful, only one more stanza remains.

Yitzhaki is charged with destroying the Jaffa post office, to be accomplished by means of letter-bombs, a newly patented form of explosive developed by the Irgun in Jerusalem. Yitzhaki assembles the bomb himself in a room at 11 Lilienblum Street. (What went wrong? Perhaps the hand on the watch was set for a minute before instead of a minute after? Perhaps the device simply shorted?) The building at 11 Lilienblum shakes with the explosion.

Uzi Arnon, also in the room, is taken to the Gruzenberg Street hospital with shards of Yitzhaki's bones lodged in him. Heichman takes a taxi to Gruzenberg, wraps Arnon in a sheet and carries the bandaged soldier to his, Heichman's, own apartment on Pinsker Street, where he will be able to recuperate without the hindrance of British interrogations.

Yitzhaki's situation is hopeless and he is most aware of this fact. He is blind now, one hand missing, the other shattered beyond repair. He knows he is dying and his only worry is whether he will reveal any secret information when he is delirious. When the British start peppering the half-dead patient with questions, he responds: "Dogs! Let me die. You won't get anything from me!"

A detective asks him his name.

And Yitzhaki answers:

"My name – is Death."

★ ★ ★

In the torture chamber of the Central Intelligence Division (CID) headquarters near the Jerusalem Central Prison, Sgt. Cairns approached Zeroni. Zeroni's face and body were raw pulp. He could only imagine what devious punishment the Hebrew-speaking sergeant had in store for him this time. But there were no tools in Cairns' sadistic hands, no physical hint of what was to come. Cairns came up close to ensure the weary Zeroni would hear and hear well. He whispered: "You will die just like your best friend Arye Yitzhaki has died, torn to pieces in an explosion. I will tear you to pieces."

Chapter 4

Cairns Takes A Walk

*The blood of the grandchildren of Bar Kochba, having flowed
through the ocean of our people's blood, down from Shlomo
Molcho through Ben Yosef to Yaacov Raz, already runs in
our veins.*
Yehezkel Altman, inscription in an autograph book given to
jailed attorney Max Seligman in the Jerusalem Central Prison

Zeroni had taken his wild proclivity for destruction on the road.
While the commanding officers of other cities offered intended Arab
victims a wide menu of mayhem, Zeroni prepared but a single course
of death in the northern port city of Haifa. A bomb in the Arab market
caused enough damage to warrant a second; the second, a third; and
so forth. By the time the fifth bomb rocked the Haifa shuk the city's
Arabs were not only tamed, they were cowering. So many Arabs turned
tail and fled that the city was relatively easy prey for Jewish forces ten
years later, upon the establishment of a Jewish state.

For the time being, Zeroni was the prey. Not only did the Arab
gangs hate him, not only were the British hounding him, but the Jewish "left" was more bent than the others were on ferreting out the
"cancer" in its midst which dared use Jewish arms to attack, the new
kid on the block who with seeming impunity had killed hundreds of

135

Arabs. Zeroni's photo graced the walls of most every post office and police station, and showing that face on the street grew more risky each passing day. The time had come to hit the road again. Jerusalem, as always, awaited.

For "Zeroni" any hour anywhere was unsafe. So a Mr."Ben Zvi" took the wheel of a car in Haifa one morning and headed south to Jerusalem. In his breast pocket was "Ben Zvi"'s driver's license and other genuine i.d., created by the IZL's genuine-i.d. department. Cruising the Tel Aviv-Jerusalem highway, Ben Zvi noticed British traffic cops lying in ambush for speedsters. Concerned citizens must look out for their fellow drivers; Ben Zvi followed road etiquette and used his lights to signal oncoming drivers, as if to warn: "Not so fast, British ahead." Opposite Ben Zvi appeared a car with a British driver and passenger, and Ben Zvi demonstrated the brotherhood of nations by signalling them the same warning. The driver waved him to a stop, which did not worry the "legally" licensed Ben Zvi. A hatted Englishman, pipe in hand, stepped out and approached Ben Zvi as he, too, exited his own car.

"Excuse me, sir, may I inquire as to what you did just now?"

"I warned you, of course..."

"And why?"

"The police are on the roadside. Just be careful you do not get a ticket."

"Do you know who I am?" the Englishman asked.

"I haven't had the honor..."

"I'm Spicer. Commandant of Police for all Palestine."

"Ben Zvi. A pleasure."

Ben Zvi and Spicer warmly shook hands, the one's photo hanging in half the other's police stations, and parted laughing.

The city into which Ben Zvi steered his car that afternoon was in ferment. Yaakov (Yoshke) Eliav, "the Mad Bomber" of the city's IZL unit, took an artist's delight in designing exploding letters (local historians credit Yoshke with inventing the letter-bomb, though the actual patent belongs to Irgun electrician Haim Corfu), exploding chocolate bonbonierres and even specially tailored exploding overcoats. Arabs were more often than not the target of Yoshke's technical prowess: He and Zvi Meltser eliminated the leaders of the gangs as they sipped Turkish coffee in the old bus station, across from today's City Hall (they stood on the station's roof holding a shoebox containing four grenades, one in each corner, and a plate of explosives in the center, with the box gift-wrapped for the occasion. Meltser lit the fuse and the two of them, together, each with both hands, pushed the device from the roof); he struck in the Old City shuk, on the very spot on which Irgunist Yaacov Raz had been fatally stabbed; he assembled Rachel Ohevet Ami's fruit basket. But the British, too, were increasingly finding themselves victims of Yoshke's enthusiasm and the Irgun's ingenuity. Haim Corfu blew up the post office with a series of letter-bombs, one of which Yoshe claimed was a made-to-order contraption designed to immobilize his personal nemesis, a sapper whose expertise had already defused several of Yoshke's handiworks. Corfu, who designed the missives, offers a more modest view: The three bombs were all destined to explode in the letter depository, with no loss of life; a poorly constructed connection malfunctioned and only detonated when the unlucky sapper shook it into place.

As the summer of '39 lengthened, with Kalay, Stern and Heichman calling the shots, Jerusalem's phone booths, radio station and British citizens found themselves on the receiving end of Irgun terror. One man in particular, Sgt. Cairns, Hebrew-speaking head of the Jewish Section of the British police, seemed determined to crush the Jewish revolt. Cairns saw himself, not without a bit of pleasure, as a "grand inquisitor" whose holy mission was to crush the Jews. This he set out to do, figuratively – and very literally.

In the summer of 1938, Moshe Segal had created an underground movement in his own image. Brit Hashmonaim's membership card listed seven principles: A Hasmonean is faithful to the God of Israel and is ready to give his life to sanctify God's name, Torah, people and land; hopes for the coming of the Messiah and longs to establish the Kingdom of Israel; loves every individual Jew with all his heart; intends all his actions to be for the sake of Heaven and is of exemplary character and behavior; continues in the tradition of the Hasmoneans and Zealots and is prepared to enlist in the war of liberation; scoffs at cowardice and surrender to an enemy and reinstates Israeli heroism and pride; and obeys the orders of his officers.

In a wall poster issued in the mid-1940s, the Brit Hashmonaim called:

> *Hear O Israel!...Israel will not rise unless we come together as one united people, with true brotherly love and in acceptance of the Heavenly yoke. A united people is the need of the hour...Let us turn our backs on secular education and...raise the flag of one God, one people, one Torah, one Land! Let us throw off the disgrace of the public desecration of Israel's heritage in our own land! From Dan to Beersheba, let us cease to profane the Sabbath! Let us remove unclean foods from our tables! Let us preserve the honor and holiness of the Hebrew family! Let us root out all hatred of our brothers from our hearts!...Hear O Israel!...from the blood of our murdered brethren, from hundreds of thousands of graves in the Diaspora, from the ruins of the Exile, one voice sounds, one command issues: Revenge and Redemption!*

If poet Uri Zvi Greenberg unified the different categories of Jewish life by poetically portraying the religious dimension of freedom fighters – a Jewish soldier prays with his rifle, he wrote – Segal went yet a step further. To him firing a rifle or submachine gun in defense of Jewish lives, laying a mine to lay the foundations of a Jewish state, were indeed prayers of the profoundest sort. Many Jewish prayer services begin with the prefacing remark: *L'yihud Kud-eshey Brich Hu u-She-chintey,* stating that the purpose of prayer is to unify God's Holy Name. Segal recited this verse before every mission: The purpose of our prayer is to unify the Name of God.

Official IZL historian David Niv notes that though the five-hundred-member Brit Hashmonaim was "not small in number, its main importance lay in the quality of its cadres." Among its active members were Meir Medan, later a professor and director of Israel's Hebrew Language Institute; Baruch Duvdevani, scion of Rabbi Elimelech of Lizhansk, Hasidic of spirit and an orator from birth; Mordechai Pacho, a Turkish-born IZL operative with long black sidelocks and beard; Haim Kubersky, future longstanding director of Israel's Interior Ministry; Shar Yashuv Cohen, future Chief Rabbi of Haifa; and Menahem Rusnik, commander of Jerusalem's Old City in 1948. Segal himself held a non-controversial position at the Jewish Agency. "Above ground" he ran Brit Hashmonaim and directed its legal educational network. Underground, he served on the IZL's Jerusalem Command. Dividing his time between his professional, his half-legal and his illegal activities was difficult enough; but Segal surely realized his free time was running out.

Two Revisionist pals arrived one fine day with an offer Segal very much wished to refuse. Sgt. Cairns, they claimed, had arrested a young Revisionist on one or another trumped-up charge and would release him only under one condition: that the reputable Moshe Segal personally sign in Cairns' office a 25-pound bond for the suspect. Segal assessed the matter and concluded it reeked of a setup. Cairns was seeking to save himself the messy public arrest of a Jewish Agency official, or the dangerous arrest of an IZL officer. Cairns had devised a means of luring the mouse to the cat without any noisy, messy traps. Once he had quietly and calmly walked into Cairns' office of his own accord, he would continue walking to prison.

Segal's friends were unconvinced and accused him of abandoning

139

a poor young party member to the horrors of prison. Segal was sure enough of his instincts but...how could he take even an infinitesimal chance and leave the lad to suffer? His fears unallayed but guilt building, Segal submitted to his friends' entreaties and let them escort him to Cairns, but not before stopping to leave his money and diary with his pregnant wife, along with a parting plea to care for their three-year-old son and herself.

Cairns placed the bond before Segal and asked him to sign. Segal signed; as he rose he began, for a fraction of a second, to doubt his own instincts. Was he really going to be allowed to leave? He turned and headed for the door; Cairns called after him: "Excuse me, Mr. Segal, I'd like to take this opportunity to ask you something. Please, wait a few moments." Segal's friends were asked to wait in the hall, then chased from the building. Cairns kept Segal waiting a good couple of hours, under guard of British detectives, then returned for a conversation.

"Please, you will certainly agree with me that under the circumstances existing in the country, the welfare of the public dictates that you be incarcerated."

Segal suggested that certainly Cairns would agree that an Agency official offering social assistance to the needy would be more useful "outside."

Cairns looked Segal straight in the eyes, those ever calm blue eyes. "Please, admit that the truth is with me."

Segal, his poise unruffled, his cool intact, decided that since he was headed for the steel bars of the nearest prison he might as well have his say. Now he looked Cairns straight in his slightly darker and more malignant eyes. "Your sitting here in Jerusalem, the Jewish capital, on that side of the table, and my sitting opposite you as a prisoner, this is the greatest injustice I can imagine. Imagine me, in London, in Scotland Yard, arresting you, an Englishman, and saying to you what you've said to me. Why, you'd tell me, 'Sir, go to your country and do your job there, but this is my country and you are a foreigner. How dare you usurp power and arrest an Englishman?!' Well, Sgt. Cairns, here you are the foreigner. You have no legal right to be here, your actions are criminal and you should be punished accordingly!"

The treacherous Cairns, in a rare soft moment, answered Segal quietly: "I understand you, but I have my orders."

"Yes," retorted Segal, "and I have mine!"

Cairns stiffened, suddenly all detective: "Whose orders?!"

"The orders of my conscience!" Segal replied to a disappointed Cairns. Segal was taken across the Russian Compound's parking area, and the gates of the Jerusalem Central Prison opened wide to swallow their newest guest.

Segal was locked in a room with an elderly Jew named Zvulun Moshinsky and a number of Arabs awaiting trial on various criminal charges. At dawn a heavyset guard woke the inmates with shouts of "Wash the floors!" He extended the squeegee to Segal. "Wash the floors!" Segal looked at his older companion: "We will not be washing floors here." The frail gentleman, not as fit to fight as Segal, nevertheless rejoined: "Whatever you decide, I'm with you." Segal grabbed the guard's club and with a mutual barrage of curses he and the guard struggled for control of the wooden stick. The guard finally announced he would take Segal to the duty officer and Segal quickly assented. The guard took his prisoner by the arm but Segal pulled free and instead held the poor jailor's arm, creating the appearance that he was escorting the guard. As they approached the officer, Segal preempted the complainant and took the offensive: "Tell him we are political prisoners and don't work here! We intend to demand all rights due us in this barbaric British prison!" The officer was as impressed with Segal's orders as, Segal recalled, a Russian soldier had once been with his forceful neighbor's. The political detainees Segal and Moshinsky (for the moment – but all too soon a room full of suspected Irgun sympathizers) would not participate in prison labor. (Moshinsky looked at his incarceration with the power of positive thinking; he was happy enough to be there, he said: "A prison is also part of the homeland, and out of the whole country, I prefer being in Jerusalem.")

Outside, Cairns loosed his hounds. Shaul Berkowitz narrowly escaped capture when a neighbor eyed a phalanx of detectives heading towards his home. "Run, Shaul!" came the cry through one window, and Shaul leaped straight out of bed and through another window. The detectives found an empty room, but Cairns wasn't fooled. Resting his hand on the unkempt bed he declared: "It's still warm." Berkowitz, by then hiding in the closet of a nearby relative, was not found.

At 10:00 A.M. on June 11, a bright summer's day in Jerusalem, Menachem Lewin and Oscar Buchwald began the descent from Ussishkin Street to the Nahalat Achim neighborhood below. Lewin had recently turned a room at the bottom into an Irgun laboratory. Cairns and his detectives surrounded the two boys halfway down the Nahalat Achim steps and pushed them into a waiting van. The laboratory key was in Lewin's pocket; the test tubes, bottles, powders and explosives in the lab were laden with fingerprints. Buchwald went straight to jail. Lewin, whom an informer had fingered as the senior technician, was taken for questioning.

Lewin said so little he barely acknowledged his name. No, he told the police, he didn't even remember where he lived. He was trying to give the Irgun time to "clean" his apartment, and to allow his roommate to escape. Lewin kept quiet and suffered for it, unaware that the British had arrested almost everyone he knew that same morning. Ten friends had been sent to the detention camp in Sarafand.

Lewin was thrown into the barest of cells: just four walls and a cement floor. After a few hours the still unresponsive prisoner was taken to Cairns. Cairns excused himself; another sergeant and two others took his place, and the beating began: punches to the stomach, mostly, some kicks and lots of slaps. Lewin maintained his vow of silence.

The next morning, Lewin volunteered the address of a local cafeteria as his own. The detectives took him along for the search. Cairns did not like being played for the fool; when they got back, Lewin was strapped to a wooden board. Cairns again exited and yesterday's sergeant returned. Cigarettes were extinguished on Lewin's feet; sixty years later he will still bear the scars. Water was poured over his head for half an hour. The punches and kicks continued all along. Every few hours Cairns dropped in, saying with equanimity he'd like to chat; Lewin, blood oozing from every limb, couldn't – or wouldn't – speak. "What's the matter?" Cairns asked on each of his visits, avoiding the pools of blood collecting under Lewin. "Aren't you feeling well?"

The third morning, still bleeding, not having tasted food or water since his arrest, Lewin assumed the Irgun had had enough time to tidy up his room and gave his address: 16 Amos Street. The British found literally nothing there and assumed they'd again been duped by Lewin. The Irgun cleaning service had apparently done too good a job, and Lewin had not had much property to begin with. "All we found was an electric light," the detectives recounted angrily. "Really, that's all I own," Lewin replied. Lewin, no longer able to walk, was eventually dragged back to his cement floor to rest. That evening Cairns took Lewin from the Criminal Investigation Department, across the Russian Compound, to the prison. The two men paused as they approached the gate. Cairns looked Lewin over: "You know what," he said, "you won't leave here alive." Lewin returned the stare: "Mr. Cairns, I don't know who will die first, me or you." Inside, the prison was already asleep; Lewin was left to lie on the cement floor of the hallway nearest the infirmary. He was found there in the morning by Moshe Segal.

Lewin told his story. Segal offered encouragement: "Don't let your spirits fall. The Organization will not remain silent. We will know what to do." Lewin was soon locked in a solitary cell, the second on the left. All things considered, he felt well: "I'm hungry, thirsty and cold," he told himself. "But what can they do to me? Wounds heal. If something is broken, so it's broken. I passed the test. Through the generations many have suffered. I'm just another one in a long chain."

The prison's Sgt. Shvilli told Lewin that David Raziel was two cells down, on the right, across the hallway. They shouted to each other until Raziel was transferred. Lewin remained alone for three weeks. By then his wounds had healed enough for him to be seen by other inmates.

On August 3, a badly bruised Mordechai Pacho was tossed into Segal's cell. At night, as all slept except the aching Pacho and empathetic Segal, Segal listened to his fellow Hasmonean's story. Pacho had been arrested on suspicion of being an Irgun leader. The police soon discovered his identity papers were forged. Cairns had begun his interrogation on July 16. Pacho was shown a list of names and asked to identify any, even a single one, of his Irgun associates. When he denied recognizing any of the names, Cairns upped the pressure. For seven days Pacho's feet were whipped with *falakot*, lit cigarettes were pressed to his ears, he was hung upside down, his fingernails and toenails were pulled out, water was forced down his throat, British and Arab guards marched on his chest. Half his beard was torn out piecemeal. Eleven days ago he had been taken to the prison's solitary cells to "recuperate" sufficiently to allow him to join other inmates without revealing the torture he had undergone. Cairn's parting words were: "Tell anyone what I've done and I'll kill you."

Segal recorded the tragic story in minuscule words on paper so thin it was transparent. The testimony was rolled into the sewn fold of a cloth that covered food prepared and sent by Mrs. Segal; she knew where to search upon its return, found the jolting message and passed it to an IZL contact, who forwarded it to Arye Altman, director of the Revisionist Party's national office. He, in turn, sent it to Jabotinsky, still in exile from Eretz Israel, who was then in London. Jabotinsky brought it to the attention of M.P. Josiah Wedgwood, who raised the issue in Parliament, which called for an end to the inhuman crimes being committed by its Mandatory administration. But the smuggling of reports and underground pickups and overseas contact and parliamentary debate took time. Torquemada, meanwhile, plunged into his work with sadistic glee. No one knows exactly how many Jewish men and women, boys and girls, came under Cairn's bloodstained hands. Jerusalem's new commanding officer, Benjamin Zeroni, was one.

Zeroni's days as Jerusalem commander were still in their infancy. Raziel had been arrested at Lydda Airport; Kalay, till then in charge of the Holy City, had assumed control of the Irgun in Raziel's stead. Zeroni had come to Jerusalem to fill Kalay's shoes. Pretending to be a Hebrew University student he rented a room not overly distant from the Jewish Agency building in Rehavia, a neighborhood of Agency clerks and "establishment" tint not exactly notorious for its support of underground fighters. Zeroni figured the best place for this mouse to hide was in the shadow of the cat's back.

One day after he had arrived to stroll Jerusalem's tree-lined streets and bask in the glow of her golden stones – and, of course, to blow to pieces as many of those stones as he could – his deputy Rafael Saban, with demolitions-man Yoshke Eliav, greeted Zeroni with banter and a briefing. The chatter may have been pleasant but the news was not: The Jerusalem branch was short – not of money, no, that would have been too easy: Zeroni had a penchant for financial appropriations ("I always liked robberies," he will one day reminisce. "Not of private individuals, you understand, but of public institutions..."). The deficit in Jerusalem was far more serious. They were out of explosives. Saban, a stolid, taciturn, immutably businesslike fighter who would not have known a bush to beat around if he walked into one, must have presented the cold facts and left them to speak for themselves. But one can only imagine Yoshke, who had so far blown up a bus station, two cafés, three marketplaces, some buses, several telephone booths, a post office, one radio station, an army barracks, a movie theater (the bombs exploded, Yoshke liked to recall, just as MGM's lion opened its jaws to roar) and several private individuals – one can only try to visualize the forlorn look in Yoshke's eyes as he reported that he had run out of explosives.

The two asked permission to break into Nadav's Weapons Shop in the center of town, on Queen Melisenda (today: Helena) Street. Zeroni asked how they intended to get inside the heavily fortified store. They suggested using the less garrisoned neighboring paint shop as a stepping stone, entry to be accomplished from inside the paint shop through a common wall. Zeroni asked how they planned to transport the explosives. "With your car," they cheerfully volunteered. And why not, wondered Zeroni, authorizing the proposed trespass. "Yoshke, you'll be in charge," were Zeroni's final words to his underlings. "Just don't forget to switch the car's plates when you use it."

The hush of an August Sabbath eve lay upon Jerusalem as Yoshke's team penetrated the paint store with no noticeable difficulty. The recitation of Kiddush and Sabbath songs wafted from nearby Jewish homes, where families gathered to celebrate the day of Divine rest, as three Irgunists simultaneously went to work. The thick inside dividing wall proved sturdier than expected and dawn was about ready to break as the drills at last discovered explosives at the end of the tunnel.

Haim Corfu, one of the tired burglars, left the scene of the crime and fetched Yoshke, who brought the keys to Zeroni's car, which Yoshke had left parked outside Nadav's store all night – long enough, perhaps, for a kindly neighbor to fulfill her civic duty and make note of its license plate number, a number which, perhaps, Yoshke had forgotten to remove. The car was loaded with the prize. According to newspaper reports, a quarter ton of gelignite and dynamite and one thousand detonators constituted Nadav's "contribution" to the Friday-night thieves.

The weaponry was destined for a drop in the Valley of the Cross, but by the time the car pulled out, the British had posted the day's roadblocks and the valley was unreachable. Corfu and Yoshke tucked the haul away under a construction site in Rehavia for the day. After dark they moved it to the valley, to be buried by Saban.

Next day Saban, in Zeroni's passenger seat, escorted his C.O. to the stash for an inspection of the site. As Zeroni lollingly drove up

Jaffa Road, passing Zion Square, an Arab traffic cop asked him to stop. "Mind if I get in?" he asked. Zeroni suspected nothing but instinctively ordered Saban to slip away. The cop ordered Zeroni to head for Police Headquarters in the Russian Compound. Zeroni knew something was wrong, but only afterwards did he learn about the plates. "I held out against the police, the Arabs and the entire socialist movement dogging my every step in Haifa," Zeroni laughed with, amazingly, no hard feelings. "And now this!"

Cairns was waiting for Zeroni. The prisoner was taken to a long stone building on a concrete foundation, with barred windows near the slanted roof, wooden partitions dividing the structure into cells. The partitions did not reach the ceiling; only the final partition before the duty guard was topped to the roof with iron fencing. Zeroni had entered Cairns' playground. When the radio was turned to full volume to drown out screams, Zeroni's trouble began.

Cairns asked the questions, Zeroni refused to answer, the torture commenced. Cairns asked again, Zeroni replied "incorrectly," the torture recommenced. Zeroni shot a warning to Cairns: "If my friends find out what you're doing they'll kill you, you'd better be careful, they'll really kill you – " Cairns smiled, massaged his holstered pistol and recited in fluent Hebrew the Psalmist's words, *Gam ki elech bigay zalmavet lo ira ra ki ata imadi*: "Yea, though I walk through the valley of the shadow of death I shall not fear for – " here Cairns again patted his pistol – "*you* are with me."

According to testimony given later by Zeroni, three British guards held his arms and legs while Cairns beat him about the head, back and neck, pounding him under the ears until he was about to lose consciousness.

The following morning Cairns began pulling out Zeroni's hair while shouting: "Are you crazy? You want to die? By us death is not quick! You'll die, but slowly. We'll torture you three times a day: morning, afternoon and night."

Zeroni was stripped naked and strapped to a table, his underwear stuffed in his mouth to muffle the shouts. Cairns donned a rubber glove and crushed Zeroni's testicles one after the other, repeatedly, then raised the prisoner by his testicles and slammed him back down onto the table. When Zeroni's eyes clouded and his consciousness began to fade, Cairns varied the pain by whipping the soles of his victim's feet. Maneuvering his tongue, Zeroni forced the gag from his mouth and shouted for dear life. The treatment ceased just long enough to allow for the sealing of windows. "You dirty Jew, you dog!" foamed Cairns. "I tell you to talk!"

At day's end, wrapped only in a blanket and oozing blood, Zeroni was carried by Arab inmates and laid in his cell.

The new morning found Zeroni still unable to stand, much less walk. He was dragged to Cairns, who fondled a photo, removed from Zeroni's Rehavia room, of Zeroni's girlfriend. "How pretty, what a lovely lady," Cairns licked his lips. "We'll find her, you know, and bring her here, you filthy bastard. You know what we'll do, we'll rape her right in front of you. Ah, it will be fun! I'll have her myself. Then we'll strip her and do to her just what we're doing to you..." Thus Cairns opened the day's beatings which continued till blood spouted from Zeroni's mouth. "We're just beginning," laughed Cairns. Zeroni was taken to a different room, Cairns again beat and crushed his testicles. Then another detective stood on one side, Cairns on the other, each with table drawers. From both sides they shoved against Zeroni's head.

Cairns left for a moment and returned with pitchers of water. A clothespin sealed Zeroni's nostrils; when he opened his mouth gasping for air the pitcher was emptied into his lungs. Zeroni's stomach swelled with each pitcher, his lungs pounded, his heart thundered. An hour and a quarter and nine pitchers later the water seeped uncontrollably from Zeroni's nose and mouth. "You stinking insect! We have pipes to bring us an endless supply of water, bastard!" taunted Cairns.

A brief respite. Then Cairns consulted his associates and brightened with an idea. Cotton was placed on Zeroni's thumbs, rope already hanging from the ceiling fastened around the cotton. When the table was pulled from under him Zeroni was left hanging by his thumbs. The indescribable pain continued until his pulse ceased; Zeroni was let down, but only long enough for the ropes to be wired around his feet. With Zeroni hanging upside down, Cairns whipped his legs with wooden sticks. The soles of Zeroni's feet were soon raw. Cairns resumed crushing Zeroni's genitals. Finally he was dropped to the floor where Cairns and company spit at, kicked and walked over him. At day's end, Zeroni was wrapped in a blanket and left in his cell.

Three days passed without food. When Arab prisoners brought him water he was barely able to sip it through broken, bloody lips. Every morning Zeroni was literally pulled by his arms, his legs extended limply on the ground, to the day's torture. Freezing ice water was poured on his back, cigarettes burned into his palms. Cairns threatened to bring Zeroni's aged aunt and uncle for treatment, to have his sister raped by an Arab inmate. Zeroni's nose and mouth were sealed, Cairns removed the gag when Zeroni turned blue. From the third day to the fifth Zeroni was prevented from sleeping. Cairns ordered Arab guards to hold his eyes open. On the fifth day Zeroni was allowed to taste food. No one offered any explanations but Zeroni was not tortured that day; he had no idea why his conditions had suddenly improved, but he took a chance and asked to be moved from his cell adjacent to the malodorous lavatory to one less inducive of nausea. Miraculously he found himself transferred to the cell closest the guard.

Thus far Zeroni's testimony, recorded after the event.

Zeroni decided that come hell or high water – and both had indeed come as far as he was concerned – he would escape that night.

Broken of body but not of spirit, Zeroni scaled his way up the stone wall and wooden partition to the screen. A rusty razor – left, perhaps, by another unfortunate prisoner with unrealized dreams of liberty? – aided Zeroni in peeling away the tiny squares of the screen until, just before daylight, he finished boring a hole wide enough for his head.

Assuming that the guard's rhythmic snoring would fade along with the dark, Zeroni grabbed a rafter the other side of the aperture and pulled his body through. He shimmied down the wall and found that the Saint of Escaping Prisoners had again smiled on him, having kindly left the key in the door. A slow and noisy turn failed to stir the slumbering guard; Zeroni slipped out, clambered up and over the Russian Compound's wall and he was free. Bruised, starved and sleepless, wobbly and soon wanted – but nonetheless free.

He could not go to his own room, he reasoned. He remembered an old acquaintance from Betar, the only address he could think of, and headed for Joseph Dukler's. At 4:30 A.M., Zeroni pounded on Dukler's door. Dukler was famous for overguardedness bordering on paranoia, and he could barely stutter his questions.

"Wh...wh...who's there?"

"Open up!"

"Who's there?"

"If you don't open it I'll break this door down!"

Dukler opened it a crack, keeping the chain locked. Zeroni's foot was instantly in the doorway.

"Uh...uh...where are you coming from?"

"OPEN THE DOOR!!!"

Once Zeroni was inside, Dukler did not bother with questions. He dressed and took Zeroni to Shoshana Aboulafia's rooftop apartment, near what was to one day be Israel's first Knesset building on King George Street. Zeroni borrowed a dress and with a little makeup was soon a rather attractive Mrs. Zeroni, thank you. Rafael Saban picked up his "wife" and arm in arm they strolled romantically over to an IZL man at the French Consulate, where Zeroni hid until Abraham Stern arranged his transfer to Tel Aviv. There the High Command fed him sour cream and cheese until he won back some of his former sturdiness. He, in turn, related his story. When Moshe Moldovsky, Jerusalem district commander, suggested the elimination of Sgt. Cairns, the High

Command approved and sentenced the torturer to death. Heichman left for Jerusalem to oversee the operation and select the appropriate means of dispatch.

Knowing that Cairns packed a pistol ("Yea, though I walk through the valley of the shadow of death...") and probably wore a bulletproof vest, guns were not to be the favored means. Knowing that Cairns every day followed the same footpath to and from his Rehavia home tipped the scales in favor of a mine. Heichman cased the area from Shoshana Aboulafia's apartment, coincidentally where Zeroni had hidden but also with a panoramic view of the entire area. A mine, he decided, would do fine and would also facilitate the retreat of the fighters, who could set it off at a safe distance by remote control. The time had come for Yoshke to go to work.

At 3:00 P.M. on August 26, 1939, the head of the CID's Jewish Section Ralph Cairns and fellow officer Ronald Barker joked good-humoredly as they passed Shoshana Aboulafia's. They turned up towards Rehavia Gardens, with Irgun eyes tracking their every step. Cairns was an hour and a half late; the Irgun trackers had despaired of his arrival and were taken by surprise when he finally put in an appearance. Shocked into action, they got their signals crossed: By lifting their hats, they informed Haim Corfu that Cairns was walking alone. Corfu, hidden behind a stonemason's shack, looked for a solitary figure and saw two men. Fortunately, he had seen Cairns the day before and recognized him now. Cairns and Barker walked past Bet Hamaalot, onto the same well-trodden path and between the same two trees as always. Corfu peered out from behind the shack, 90 feet away from the trees under which his mine was planted. He applied his finger and the mine tore Cairns to pieces. Barker died, too, and he was buried as befits a British officer; but of Cairns, only his hat, a feather at its side, remained floating slowly to earth through the dust and debris.

Chapter 5
Meanwhile –
A European Interlude

*Ten will remain, ten Jews bleeding, a remnant / testimony
there once was this...sort of...nation on Christianity's tragic
ground... / ten will remain, necks of lambs, eyes as birds in
the mist... / In the midst of time we had a great eclipse of the
sun. / As I walk the roads I see my mothers rocking dear
dead children to sleep in their laps / Patched pieces of my
dead / birds / on the roads of Europe. / East, west, north,
south...what tears in the shadow of the cross!*
Uri Zvi Greenberg, "In the Kingdom of the Cross," 1923

As the Jewish youth of Eretz Israel experienced demonstrations,
arrests, prisons, and, finally, gallows, as the dauntless defenders of
Jerusalem and Tel Aviv were transformed into the embryonic offensive forces of underground armies, as the ideological precursors of
resistance gave way to the foot soldiers of redemption, Europe stag-
gered towards war and once-vibrant Jewish communities
metamorphosed into sepulchers.

All the doomed efforts of the Irgun in Europe were two-pronged:
to purchase weapons and train soldiers for the battle in Eretz Israel;
and to evacuate as many Jews as quickly as possible. Menahem Begin,
future Commander in Chief of the Irgun, was still in Warsaw heading
Polish Betar. Nathan Friedman-Yellin (later known as Yellin-Mor) and

Israel Scheib (who adopted the name Eldad), future leaders of Lehi, were also in Warsaw. Stern was traversing the ocean trying to draft forty thousand troops for a planned invasion of Eretz Israel, which would open the homeland's shores to the millions of trapped European Jews. Uri Zvi Greenberg was in Poland urging Jews to leave. His visions of the murder of Europe's Jews were 15 years old, and only now that the disaster was upon them were the mass of Polish Jews reaching desperation in their desire to escape.

Dr. Israel Eldad's untranslated memoirs, *Maaser Rishon*, offer a revealing glimpse of Poland on the brink*:

Time is not an immovable tunnel, equally wide for its entire length, an apathetic instrument allowing events to flow through. Time lives and spins, widens and narrows, an active participant in all that flows through her. She resembles a knife, a dagger. An individual can permit his fingers to toy with it, knowing that only one edge is sharp and dangerous, but as he approaches the end the blade grows ever thinner and soon only the tip remains, nothing to take hold of, no place to stand, no room to play. He runs or he is impaled. Now, if the individual were the sole owner of this knife he would know how to treat it and control it. But, alas, many are the masters of daggerlike time, and in their hands it is transformed into a living, unpredictable creature. Before you can recoil you are trapped on its edge, its tip, between heaven and earth...

The last six months preceding the beginning of the war were terrifying, awful. Great masses of Jews bursting with

---

* Excerpted from *Maaser Rishon*, by Dr. Israel Eldad, translated and printed by permission of the author.

fear and bursting with desire mobbed the streets. I do not think that the war of partition and the establishment of the Jewish state in 1948 witnessed such a wave of Messianic desire. Maybe because in the interim, six million flames had been extinguished, maybe because the Underground's war in Eretz Israel had released, little by little, the desires and energies that had accumulated. But in the spring and summer of 1939 every Betar chapter and every Irgun cell was a powerhouse and together they erupted, stirred, were stretched to the limits awaiting the great release that would, that must, come.

After years of empty discussions, the Zionist movement and the Mapai (Labor) party and the Jewish Agency and the Histadrut labor union were suddenly as irrelevant as if they had never even existed. No more Jewish National Fund, no more immigration certificates, no more of their endless negotiations in London, no more of their *havlaga*, restraint. All these disappeared, slowly but surely, from the hearts and minds of all. Independent strength, made ready to act by a recognition of historical responsibility, was accumulating. We ceased to be an opposition, within or outside the Zionist Organization. We began to breathe the air of a legitimate liberation movement. The military courses, the independent aliya, the great plans for large-scale action, the first steps towards an independent foreign policy – all these at last put the Nationalist Movement on the right course – one or two years too late.

Courses teaching weaponry and preparation for aliya, courses for arms and for turning illegal aliya into the "national sport" of our youth! God in heaven! If only we had acted earlier!

Now, Jabotinsky says there will be no war! Jabotinsky

explains why war will not break out now! He uses logic! He's never been wrong!

Why was he wrong this time? Because with all his heart he did not want this war at this time, when we were not yet prepared. In this hour of great progress, to be suddenly stopped? No, no, there will be no war. And his logic bowed to his will and to this necessity. War would spell total destruction.

These were the last, tense months of the Freedom Movement in the Diaspora.

Jabotinsky is scheduled to arrive in Poland; from Riga or Kovno he is coming to Vilna. He will be here for urgent consultations.

Uri Zvi Greenberg and Dr. Arye Altman come from Warsaw to meet him. Sunday, 18 Iyar 1939. I arrange a festive reception at the Vilna Betar chapter. Jabotinsky has not yet arrived. I take the two visitors from the train station straight to the Betar chapter. The two visitors? In truth, I hardly know Dr. Altman and he doesn't interest me in the least. Not that I have ever heard anything disparaging about him; no, he just does not interest me. Only two things exist for me: At the club, five hundred Betarim are standing in line, five hundred matchsticks ready to be struck, five hundred ready to be lit, five hundred bodies ready for action, five hundred throats thirsty for a Sovereign Kingdom that is theirs, five hundred stomachs hungry for the War for that Sovereign Kingdom. And Uri Zvi, here he comes, the man I see as the Burning Bush. He will strike the matches. Seven days ago Uri Zvi had set aflame the pages of the *Moment*: "AZZA-ACCO!" he wrote. Acco (Acre) symbolizing Ben Yosef who was hanged there, Azza symbolizing a would-be immigrant who drowned off the shores of Eretz Israel, whose body washed ashore in Azza (Gaza). I decide that our chapter will greet Uri Zvi not with the slogan "Tel Hai" but with "Azza-Acco!"...

The bodies were ablaze. And Uri Zvi was ablaze. He was set ablaze when five hundred uniformed torches wrote in flames across the air: AZZA-ACCO! Uri Zvi was moved and said whatever he said, I do not remember what he said. I do not know whether I noticed then, whether anyone noticed. A fire was raging in the chapter, in our hearts, in our blood. I do not know the name of everyone who stood in line that day. One was Mike Ashbel, that I do know. He managed. He managed to get out. He managed to fight in an Irgun unit and he was captured in the south, in Azza, and he was sentenced to death and he had his sentence commuted and he fell in the attack on Acco Prison. And if the five hundred from Vilna had managed to come, and the five thousand from the Vilna Region, and the fifty thousand who stood ready in Poland, their blood roaring: AZZA-ACCO!, if they had managed to come, then surely -

We would today be sitting not in our truncated state, between Azza and Acco, but between the Nile and the Euphrates as destined, as necessary.

That same night, Uri Zvi sat in my house and read to me and to Eliahu Slotsky (whose soul was beautiful and who often said Hebrew grammar was itself poetry) his ballad about the funeral of Slermeyer, a Jewish student murdered by Polish students in Lvov. The terrifying ballad contained in its darkness all the darkness that was to descend on everyone, on everyone there. The ballad has been lost. The poet left it with his mother; she and it were lost together...

I moved to Warsaw in August 1939.

Uri Zvi took me from the editorial offices of the *Moment*

156

to its rotary room. Uri Zvi, the lover of myth, the "irrationalist," revealed himself as a lover of technology, with a particular fondness for printing machinery. How the verbal spirit assumes body and flesh and becomes print! I have little interest in machinery. I prefer watching the man standing next to the machine. Uri Zvi says that the machine, too, is a miracle of humanity, an arm of man, the fruit of his creative mind.

I stand for the first time facing the most modern rotary machine in the world, imported now for the most widely read Jewish newspaper in Poland, a machine which has become the property of the Nationalist Movement.

Back upstairs in the narrow editorial office, Uri Zvi burns. The lava gushes as from a volcano. As is natural for lava, it consumes and destroys. As is natural, it leaves in its wake ashes fertile with life and riches and power. The newspaper has assumed a new form and a new spirit...

Here comes the guiding hand. Under Uri Zvi's hand the splinters fly off, away towards the horizon, and one, one is the current flowing towards Redemption. The ground is burning underneath everyone's feet in the Diaspora. Jabotinsky explains, justifies, analyzes in the pages of the *Moment*. Uri Zvi marches as a pillar of fire at the head of the paper, across the wide, burning columns. I am invited to edit the literary section, a flashlight alongside the fire.

And Jews are standing on the streets of Warsaw, gathering, their own sparks gathering around this pillar of fire.

The streets of Warsaw...

I saw them, too, for the first time as I watched the rotary press. The streets are also rotating. They suck in, they spew out, suck in, spew out, countless tens of thousands. Each cog rushing to perform its function. Some with beards, some without. Some with canes, some without. Some with covered heads, some bareheaded. With briefcases or packages, in workclothes or religious frock coats. They run, they are alive – though somewhere out there knives are already ready for their white necks. Somewhere out there the bricks are already being laid for the crematoria. And they are rushing, rushing still. One feels like shouting into the ears of the runners: Stop! For God's sake, stop! You are running on the precipice!

No one stops. The present is devouring the future, in every mouth. You cannot worry about life when you must worry about bread. The cog cannot contemplate the fate of the machine, nor of what rolls from the presses, even if he is alive, even if he is a Jew who by virtue of being a Jew must think in universal terms. Stores in small villages yawn without customers, the young yawn without work. The brain experiences a boring, a boring into the brain. In Warsaw, the boring mosquito is not heard. The wheel rotates above the din and the din is not heard. And now the fiery flame leaps from the pages of the *Moment* and sweeps all in its path; it cannot be withstood. Soon everyone will be looking towards the same redeeming horizon, soon. The rotation is being steered, direction has arrived.

I lose my way in the streets of Warsaw, as one dizzy from the spinning. Vienna is larger than Warsaw and I was there for six years but Vienna is a village compared to Warsaw, a mere village. The Jews, too, were quieter there, mellower. In Vienna, apparently, the news is still printed with hand-operated presses. In Vienna, traffic is still brought to a halt to rescue a dove caught in electric wires. In Warsaw, the twentieth century is erupting. Whether I like it or not. Vilna is more quaint, more spiritual, but Warsaw is reality. Rotation is reality. You adjust to it, learn to control it – or you stay somewhere off to the side stammering about ideals and liberalism and conscience and "the world will never allow it." In Warsaw, you feel that the world will indeed allow it. There is nothing that cannot be done by the rotation, quickly and with precision. If you grasp it, it will build you a grand kingdom, measured and drawn and fine and proper. If it grasps you, it will slice your flesh piece by piece with the same exactitude and speed.

This was Warsaw in August 1939. This was the state of our people in August 1939. The entire old world, all of yesterday's politics, all the little blue JNF boxes that amounted to one big yawn, all the empty words of the Zionist organizations – all these were as if they had never been. On one side – Hitler. On the other – the British White Paper outlawing and making impossible escape to Eretz Israel. Between them – one path only, the path of rotation, the once-only Movement for Liberation, the act of conquest. And the revolt has a song, it has commanders, it has tens of thousands of soldiers, and an entire nation floating upon the water.

If only time, time, time will not wrap itself around our necks too tightly. To breathe, breathe, breathe. This is the load on our hearts.

And behold, from the rotary wheel, news:

An act of reprisal by the Irgun Zvai Leumi against Arab rioters. Arabs killed. Arabs stricken with fear.

The hand-operated presses of the men of yesterday's Zionism, the men of the shekel and the charity boxes, tap out their curses on the avengers. But the public is glad, is relieved. The heart is glad. No longer will the blood of Israel be cheap.

And headlining the *Moment* is an article by Zev

Jabotinsky: "Amen!" Not everyone realizes how heavy was Jabotinsky's heart as he wrote this amen. Uri Zvi practically pulled it from him, and he edited it, too (what courage – to edit Jabotinsky!), excising all the softer material, all the gentler passages which would not have passed through steel, which were inappropriate to a rotary machine. The rotation of the twentieth century cannot digest softness. It lacks mercy. "Amen" said every Jewish soul in its depths, deep down, even if the mouth were mumbling disavowals.

In contrast, there are no such internal struggles of the soul in the editorial offices of the Irgun newspaper. The bosses are Samuel Merlin and Nathan Friedman. Seventy percent of the material is supplied by Dr. Y. H. Yevin, who sends his articles from Eretz Israel under seventy-seven different names. In the editorial offices of *Di Tat* (The Deed), the ground is being prepared for the future conquest of Der Yassin; the laws of revenge – as good for our day as for the days of Joshua Bin Nun and King David – are being taught. And the youth, both its legs still in Poland but its thoughts and desires and emotions far from this Poland which it does not want and which certainly does not want it, this youth reads *Di Tat* and already sees itself among the orchards and the mountains of the Galilee and Jerusalem, on the battlefields of freedom.

I find myself lost in the rotating streets of Warsaw and I attempt to adapt my Viennese-Vilnaese soul to the new pace.

The rotation has not yet reached the Betar Commission, only recently established by Menahem Begin, the recipient of all his energy, which will yet be the bridge between the Betar and the conquering Irgun. It has been arranged for members of the Commission to receive high-level military training, enabling them to be both political and military leaders. My position is in the cultural section...

Educationally and militarily we are still in the preparatory stages. But in one area we have already entered the era of rotation: aliya. Thousands upon thousands are making aliya freely, an army of liberation in the making. One more month, one more month, one more month. Each Betari, each member of Brit Hachayal, each member of an Irgun cell who reaches Eretz Israel – is a great additional force worth tens or even hundreds of "pioneers" trained in restraint, who long with all their desire for a higher quota of legal immigration certificates. These so-called pioneers are healthy enough in body to repel the Arabs and the British but they are sick, sick of soul, mumbling about revolution while gazing woefully at...Chaim Weizmann...

Time, time, time is rushing towards the edge with terrifying speed. We must hurry the revolution.

A family update, but one that speaks of the times: My wife is whisked to Lvov. Her brother has disappeared. Seems he acted independently. Alone and with no money he crossed the Rumanian border. Caught in Tschernovitz, he was beaten and returned. Ten days before the war.

Temperatures rise with the signing of the Molotov-Ribbentrop Agreement. Depression spreads in the Commission offices when Menahem returns from the Rumanian border. The last transport was stopped and no one knows whether it will be permitted to cross into Rumania. More than one thousand people on the border. It appears to be the border between Poland and Rumania; it is actually the border between salvation and destruction.

Menahem enters my room and asks how my work is progressing. I answer, "Not well, there is no proportion between what we are doing here and what is about to happen to the world." Menahem smiles, gives me his usual patron's slap on the shoulder and says, "It does not matter, Israel, we must continue."

The hand continues to pen plans, pamphlets, articles, but the heart is not in them.

When the war finally breaks, the situation at first seems clear. This is a war against Hitler; three days later the Jewish masses rejoice opposite the British Embassy, celebrating England's entrance into the war. A heavy stone lays on our hearts. We had lost in the race with time.

Menahem attempts to continue with business as usual. The optimists are saying we will hold out, the British squadrons are already on the way. The pessimists are saying we will hold out for a year. Menahem prepares instructions on how to behave in either case.

Menahem Begin declared this "an historic photograph." Aharon Propes, founder of Betar (left) and Menahem Begin (right) saluting Zev Jabotinsky (center), as they inspect Polish Betarim (Begin: "Such wonderful youth that are no more…")
(Jabotinsky Institute photo)

On the third day, Uri Zvi bursts inside. Israel Epstein and I are in Menahem's room.

"What are you doing here?!" shouts Uri Zvi. "Get out immediately. It's all over!"

We do not understand.

Uri Zvi points to a map of Poland, to the Bug River. "The Russians will move to this point. The Germans will come from the west. In two weeks it will all be over!"

He was only off by a week.

Uri Zvi urged me to leave Warsaw with him. I, of course, will not leave the Commission without an order to do so. Had I left with Uri Zvi, I might have crossed the still open border and reached Eretz Israel two years earlier than I eventually did.

One day a bomb fell on the *Moment* building. The building collapsed on the modern, new rotation.

We left Warsaw on the seventh day.

We were scattered, on every road, by foot, by car, by train. We were scattered and so were the rotating cogs, the paper balloons, the lead geysers. We were scattered and so were the plans, the visions, the lives. We were scattered and so was the one great opportunity for a Majestic Realm of Israel established the easy way, in an act of tremendous liberation. We were scattered.

The result is no secret today. What happened to our people is no secret, nor what happened to the revolution. The revolution did not take place. Not the liberation from others, not the liberation within ourselves. We were too late.

The war came to the rescue of the Mapai-Weizmann regime in Zionism. The rotation was destroyed. The provincial, hand-operated "Zionist" machine remained.

The same regime-machine that withheld immigration

certificates from people like Dov Granek and Dov Gruner because they did not belong to "their" political party.

Look at the few who made it. Look at Dov Granek, tall and blond, the scourge of the British, look at Mike Ashbel, at Dov Gruner, at Abraham Amper. Look at these few and know:

Tens of thousands like them remained there. Dov's for Israel. Lions, panthers for Israel. How can our blood not cry, when it knows what could have been done here in Israel, if another ten thousand, another five thousand, like them – were here! For they were there, they were ready, they longed to give their blood – here! Look at what the few have done, and know what could have been done if the many had made it, the many whose dear bodies were charcoaled into nothingness, into awful, barren nothingness.

Chapter 6

The High Command Goes To Jail

Arise, get out of the ruins / You've sat long enough in the Valley of Tears... Arise, get out of the dirt / Put on your garments of glory, my nation. **Rabbi Solomon Alkabetz, "Lecha Dodi"**

No hourglass holds an unlimited amount of sand. So little time remained. Cairns and Barker took their final constitutional on August 26, 1939. For them, time had already run out.

Now Yoshke's sands were running low and he was running fast. Already gracing wanted posters with a price on his head, he knew that to be caught today meant almost certain death. For months his arc had been the grim circle of terror and counterterror. For that, he might get 15 years. But the British would show little mercy were they to link him to the assassination of the head of the Jewish Section of the CID. Yoshke, wigged and mustachioed for the occasion, fled to Tel Aviv where the IZL was pleased to billet him in the "safest" of its safe houses, a third-story apartment, Aharonovitch Street, number six. Yoshke's time was running out.

T. J. Wilkins wasted no time donning the hat that Cairns had sported. Cairns had not left him much else. A feathered hat, a job and a message. Wilkins took the job as head of the Jewish Section and he heard the message: Don't mess with the IZL. A dedicated British officer, Wilkins intended to do battle with the Underground. He also intended to wear his hat for many more years and, therefore, to keep his hands as clean as possible in this dirty war. Wilkins has, it seems, more time than the other characters about to gather on Aharonovitch Street; alas, his time, too, will one day run out.

Jabotinsky has for years been predicting war in Europe, and simultaneously praying such a war would not erupt. Most Jews have ignored the great orator's heartfelt pleas to evacuate Europe. Their leaders charged that Jabo was himself stoking the fires of anti-semitism which, Jabo correctly saw, were already flaming and needed no help from him. The masses were slow to move and those who began the trek found that Britain had closed the gates of their homeland. Time was running out, that final week of August 1939, for the Jews of Europe.

Jabotinsky in desperation conceived a plan as daring as it was reckless: The Irgun will seize the radio stations and government buildings of Eretz Israel and hold them at whatever cost for at least 24 hours. One more in a long line of illegal immigration ships will just at that time, coincidentally, reach the Tel Aviv beach; among its poor huddled masses will be one Vladimir Zev Jabotinsky returning unexpectedly and forcefully from ten years of exile. The Zionist statesman will immediately declare the first provisional Jewish government in two thousand years. If – or rather, when – the revolt is crushed by the British, the government will already have a life of its own and will continue to function as a government in exile, lobbying abroad for international recognition. Jabotinsky knew that such a government, once declared, would be partner to any negotiations and partner to the armed conflict about to rip through Europe.

Haim Lubinsky had arrived in Europe fresh from a successful meet with the great Jewish American jurist Brandeis. Lubinsky had sought and won Brandeis' support for the Irgun's American outfit, the American League for a Free Jewish Palestine. The elderly Supreme Court justice had agreed with Lubinsky's statement that Britain's Mandate to rule Palestine "meant above all and first of all free immigration by Jews." Brandeis concurred with Lubinsky's conclusion that therefore "there is no such thing as illegal immigration of a Jew to Palestine, and if Britain stops them, it is a breach of international law." The High Command's personal messenger at this point felt confident enough to go for the prize. "Look," he said, "could you do me a favor? Write me a check for...one dollar." The old-but-spry man seemed puzzled until Lubinsky explained that Brandeis' moral support was far more important than his monetary support.

Lubinsky and the dollar landed in London but were soon summoned by Jabotinsky. They rendezvoused in Vals Lebain in the south of France. Early one morning Jabo asked Lubinsky if, hypothetically, he thought the IZL could execute an action along the above lines; Lubinsky told Jabo he would have to consult with the other members of the High Command. The next day Lubinsky was dispatched by Jabo to submit his coded plans to the Irgun Command for approval and coordination. Two letters were elsewise forwarded, communicating details relating to the establishment of an incongruously crucial soap factory. Lubinsky carried the key which enabled the letters to be decoded. The idea was for Jabotinsky to be seabound by October. But Jabotinsky had no more time than his beloved Jews of Europe.

One by one, the members of the Irgun High Command – excepting the already arrested David Raziel – made their way to 6 Aharonovitch. Kalay, the de facto commander; Dov Heichman, Tel Aviv's C.O.; Lubinsky, representing Jabotinsky; and Abraham Stern, called Yair ("The light will shine"), Tehomi's former Jerusalem adjutant, a zealot with plans of his own. Yair had laid a network of Irgun cells across Poland which were just about ready, and the IZL Command expected to have forty thousand "illegal" immigrants overwhelm the shores of Eretz Israel in a coordinated beaching – not of immigrants, but of well-trained soldiers. Forty thousand trained soldiers! The Irgun will not be ready to execute this operation until sometime in 1940. The IZL's dreams have, ironically, only as many days and nights as Jabo's daring plans. The High Command has no more time than the Jews of Europe. With the thirty-first of August, all the dreams and plans of all the Jews of all the world will turn to dust and ashes.

Wilkins presses his hunt; Yoshke assumes the identity of a newly arrived, and therefore relatively innocent, Czech immigrant; Dov, Kalay, and Yair have arrived at the Aharonovitch safe house; Lubinsky carries Jabo's grand designs. Characters are in place, the stage is set. The drama is just beginning when the curtain falls.

Yoshke opened with a report on the successful elimination of Zeroni's torturer, then exited to the entrance room as the members of the Command turned their attention to more secret business. Jabo's idea failed to fan their imaginations, the general feeling was the IZL would not be ready in October. Stern paced, tall and thin, in suit and tie (as always), a slight pallor the only visible sign of sleepless nights spent planning the early morning smuggling of Zeroni, in a car trunk, to Tel Aviv, then the vigil to ensure his health, and now the anxiety over the arrest in Warsaw of a Polish contact. Yair himself expected to be leaving for Poland at a moment's notice. This morning, he had asked his wife Roni to pack a suitcase so he could set out on the morrow. Worry and overwork were unable to dampen the severe courage of Stern's speech, nor dim the apocalyptic vision blazing in his eyes. He argued most vociferously against any October adventure, which would certainly entail the crushing of the Irgun – and hence an end to their own forty thousand plans.

Eliav lolled about his room, the muffled discussion of the Command not quite discernable. He stopped, stood fast, cocked his head, laid an attentive ear to the front door. The dull sounds he heard were no longer words, but steps; no longer from inside, but from the stairwell. He peered through a crack in the door. Ascending the broad stairway were Wilkins, the Tel Aviv and Jaffa police chiefs and several British policemen. Eliav warned the Command just as the detectives rounded the stairs and demanded entry.

Eliav stalled the British, whose shouts of "You've heard our orders...Open the door!" and "Stand back, we'll break in ourselves!" grew in agitation and urgency. White smoke wafted upwards as the Irgun Command frantically torched as many documents as possible. Parched flakes of coded invasion plans fell to the floor as Lubinsky scrambled through a window and into the apartment below, his pockets stuffed with more documents than they could hold. He begged forgiveness of the surprised couple whose sleep he disturbed, entreated them to remain silent and made a beeline for the bathroom where he emptied not his bladder but his pockets, in a mad race to shred and flush as many of the incriminating papers as possible before his inevitable capture. He was, however, trapped there, and when the British threatened to use force against the apartment's residents, Lubinsky surrendered rather than endanger his innocent hosts. After taking Lubinsky into custody, some unfortunate representative of the British empire was assigned the task of "cleaning" the toilet. Heichman followed Lubinsky out the window, but even as he was shimmying down a water pipe, he had already espied the contingent of police below, pistols at the ready.

Yair and Kalay authorized Eliav to open the door and the enemy poured in, eyes gleeful at the fine catch, fingers on triggers in case any of the prey offered them an opportunity to display their marksmanship. Wilkins, hunting for Cairns' killer, never realized he had him in the guise of the albeit illegal Czech immigrant. The British were far too busy basking in the glory of having netted the High Command to pay any attention to a poor greenhorn.

The five arrestees passed Thursday night, August 31, in the Dizengoff police station. Their interrogation Friday morning was interrupted by the frantic entrance of a disheveled clerk whose voice was cracking with either weariness or desperation as he announced to everyone and to no one, not bothering to distinguish between his superior

169

officers and the manacled prisoners, that at five that morning Germany had invaded Poland.

The Second World War had begun.

* * *

The prisoners were transferred first to Jaffa Prison, infamous domicile of the wildest lice colony west of the Jordan and, soon after, to Jerusalem. The Command was quartered for the better part of a week in the CID barracks from which Zeroni had previously escaped; they, however, were bound hand and foot, night and day. They ate with the steel shackles, slept with them, sat in the lavatory with them – and with the door open, under constant, if embarrassing, surveillance. Excepting these awkward moments and the daily interrogations, the chains linked them limb by limb to their beds. A week later the police had failed to assemble enough evidence for a trial, leading the British to opt for "administrative detention," locking them up without trial. Finally sequestered in the Jerusalem Central Prison, the Russian-built edifice across the lot from the CID building, the five were kept in separate cells for another week.

The Russian Orthodox have always had a soft spot in their pious hearts for the Holy Land and in the mid-1800s they trickled in steadily, wonder in their eyes and prayers on their lips. Every decade or so the trickle of pilgrims would surge. A keen-witted social historian reviewing annual tourism figures should be able to gleam with unerring accuracy the sites of the Czar's family's vacations. Two thousand tourists one year and ten thousand the next imply that in between, a grand duke had ignited the passion of the Russian peasantry by making the journey to Jerusalem.

Jerusalem had difficulty enough dealing with its own impoverished peasants, much less with these sudden influxes of the Romanovs and their fans. The Russian Imperial Treasury donated half a million rubles, the Russian people another six hundred thousand, and ten prime acres on a hill overlooking the Damascus and Jaffa Gates of the Old City, just opposite today's Jaffa Road post office, were purchased. The slope had millennia ago been used by the armies of Sannecherib as they besieged the Jewish capital; now the multidomed Trinity Church rose, then a string of hostelries, one star for the common folk, two, three or four star for monks or VIPs. The main hostel was built to hold eight hundred pilgrims; by the 1880s, according to Stephen Graham, an English journalist who had hooked up with the Orthodox, nine thousand were arriving just for Easter.

The British drove the Turks from Jerusalem in 1917 and brought their own logic: If pilgrims were suited to the spartan conditions of the Russian Compound hotels, prisoners would be even more so. Some bars on the windows, iron doors on what became cells, a little barbed wire here and, of course, a gallows there, and: presto, the Jerusalem Central Prison (JCP). No doubt the British had done the utilitarian thing. Soon the walls which had housed abstinent monks hid boozing deputy wardens; the sills upon which the pure of heart had rested their arms, palms raised supplicatingly heavenward, became rests for arms practiced in thievery and stained with blood; though, soon enough, the hands of freedom fighters would painstakingly etch holy Hebrew names into the cold stone sills.

Visitors in the '30s entered the Compound from busy Jaffa Road. By the '40s they would need passes to get past the coils of barbed wire behind which the nervous British hid from the Jewish underground. To the right were the CID headquarters, easily recognizable by a stately columned porch (which in coming years will be blown up by the Irgun, along with the accursed building, twice). Further right was a government hospital (from which Stern Group radio broadcaster and future Knesseteer Geula Cohen will one day escape, garbed in Arab clothing brought her by an Arab supporter from friendly Abu Ghosh). The huge prison lay on the far slope, unseen from Jaffa Road, practically invisible even from Trinity Church. Family members stopped at the front yard's wire fence, as Rachel Ohevet Ami had done. If a "guest" were

171

expected, the gates opened.

Within the solid rectangular citadel, two open-air courtyards were divided by a backbone of cells, showers and toilets. In the east court-yard, to the right as one entered, Altman had stood "trial." In the west, Jabotinsky had once stood alone to hear his sentence pronounced. An injured prisoner, the likes, for instance, of Dr. Israel Eldad, the Sternist ideologue brought through JCP's main entrance in a body cast, might be taken down the long hall on the right, past the solitary cells, to the infirmary. Ahimeir and Jabotinsky had taken the even longer hallway on the left to cell number 18, at the far end of what would one day, years after their own releases, be almost a "Jewish wing," including Rabbi Arye Levin's famous makeshift Sabbath synagogue.

Now, this morning as every morning, Haim Dviri strode to his "office" near the prison entrance. Dviri and Buchko were neither "politicals" nor detainees this time around. In '33 Dviri had used his journalist's i.d. to obtain special privileges; in any case the Brit Habirionim trials were plainly political. He was no journalist now; he was, professionally speaking, a bank robber. Still, Warden Steel remembered him fondly from his earlier sojourn and viewed Dviri as something of his protégé, perhaps because in a prison of several hundred illiterates, at least with Dviri he could have an intelligible conversation. Dviri was given the peachy job of prison librarian.

The library was just to the right of the prison entrance, the same entrance which visitors to the "Hall of Heroism" use today, over which the Prophet Isaiah welcomes his guests, in Russian, to Jerusalem. Just beyond the guards' stand, at which two policemen whiled away the days recording all who entered the hallowed halls, lay the rooms which today's museum signs describe quaintly as the "reception" area. "Reception" does not quite get to the bottom of what actually transpired in the area. An individual convict returning from leave, or a row of tick-infested killers returning from weeks of hard labor – the sweat of summer's hamsin still waiting for a first shower – all stooped over,

172

pants down, as guards searched buttocks for smuggled cigarettes which, if found, had to be extracted...

Against the far rear wall of this heartwarming reception area was the library. Dviri was also in charge of lettering: signmaking for the prison, or gravemarking for deceased British soldiers. But the sweetness lay in the books, for with them Dviri had free reign of the prison. Even inmates in solitary confinement were entitled to a Bible; Dviri was a one man welcoming committee for the new guests.

This morning, as he absent-mindedly dusted off his best seller, *A Thousand and One Nights: Arabian Tales*, about the only literary work ever requested by the Arabs, each cell usually containing one sheikh able to read it to the others, Dviri shot a glance across the reception room and entranceway. The door to "Steel's Table" was open, that table at which Steel had held court once a week, deigning to receive prisoners with special requests. Dviri himself had only been received at "table" once, for the Jewish inmates refused to wear the ungainly sackcloth uniform intended to humble prisoners wishing to address His Holiness the warden. In any event, the recently retired Steel was no longer behind his table, and the door to the storage area to its rear was also open, and pacing solemnly back and forth was what appeared to be a polished gentleman impeccably – and as far as the prison was concerned, improbably – attired in tailored suit and tie. Curiosity piqued, Dviri borrowed a wooden cross not yet assigned a grave of its own and etched in chalk: "Your name?" When the prison's best-dressed resident acknowledged Dviri's inquiry, Dviri tossed him the chalk. The prisoner found a piece of wood and wrote: "Yair – High Command," flashed it to Dviri and immediately erased the message.

Dviri's first stop was the kitchen where he ordered Chef Buchko to prepare special meals. By day's end Dviri had managed to find the five newcomers, even bringing Yoshke Eliav, the only one in the solitary wing, some thick soup, along with a note from Yair concealed in a book.

After a week of internment in separate cells the Command was reunited in the Jewish detainees' room, cell 48; Moshe Segal, Itzhak Gurion, and Dr. Shimshon Yunichman cleared them a place of honor by the wall opposite the steel door. Years later, Heichman recalls the setup: "Arab prisoners today have it far better than any of us, Jew or Arab, had it then. We were twenty-plus in a room, we slept on *bourges* (intertwined rags), on the floor, when you woke you rolled the *bourge* up like a carpet, that was all the property you had. The bathroom was a *kardel* (bucket) near the iron door, which filled up every night. In the morning it was emptied. The stench was great, the food poor." A prisoner's social standing was discernable by the location of his *bourge*. The farther from the *kardel*, the more his cellmates thought of him. "They took good care of us," Heichman says."They honored us, all the time, all the prisoners, even the old-timers."

Jacob Kotik had once, a year earlier, asked a friend of his, an important Revisionist with "protection" on the outside, to influence the warden to have him transferred to a cell with at least one other Jew in it. The Revisionist happened to be quite close with Steel, they were members of the same Masonic lodge, and he made the request himself. "I'll do anything for you," replied Steel with an indulgent smile. "But two Jews in the same room, never. There would be an escape."

Steel virtually lived for the joy of outsmarting escape attempts. Every two weeks the inmates played "musical cells," lining up in the courtyard with their *bourges*. Steel's strategy was designed to thwart the development of conspiratorial bonds and the digging of tunnels. The calling of the prisoners' names and new cell numbers initiated a mad dash, everyone intent on being first to his new room, to set his *bourge* down farthest from the *kardel*. Those inmates who found favor in the eyes of the authorities – say, perhaps, by informing on fellow convicts – were called first. They slept farthest and they slept best. In a crowded room, the inmate called last could not get very much away from the overflowing *kardel*. In the darkness of night, its exact location was always something of a mystery to the bleary-eyed inmates. Sleeping in its vicinity was a precarious proposition. Steel's recent departure had brought many changes to JCP life, not the least of which were "Jewish rooms," one for the convicts (cell 23) and one for the detainees (cell 48).

Altman, Kotik, Dviri and Buchko had already been sentenced and, as full convicts, had a full day's work. The detainees had no work, no place to go, nothing to do. "We argued a lot. Endlessly," says Heichman. Other than reading Dviri's literary contributions to the cell, they had few options.

The two main subjects of discussion were the war and...the war. Yair Stern began at this time to develop his theory regarding the Allies and the Axis. He argued that during the First World War, a Jewish network called NILI had operated in Eretz Israel, supplying the British with crucial information concerning Turkish troop strength and location. The small NILI group was shunned by the entire Jewish community, hunted more often than not more doggedly by their fellow Jews than by the Turks. But NILI believed the Turkish regime was rotten and doomed; NILI's contributions to the British war effort had played a part in bringing about the Balfour Declaration in favor of a Jewish National Homeland. Yair believed in 1939, and through the war's early years when the Germans were advancing through country after country, before the Final Solution had been implemented or even fully formulated, that the Allies were going to lose. "Contacts that we may be able to form with the Axis may, therefore, be able to save the Jewish community in Eretz Israel. If not, if the Axis loses, people will say I was insane. I'll have to chance that." So argued Yair.

A second argument focused on a strange message received from David Raziel. Their de jure Commander had been under arrest since May and had already been transferred from the JCP, where after sitting in solitary he had shared Moshe Segal's cell and kosher food, to Sarafand Detention Camp on the coastal plain. From Sarafand, he

175

ordered the IZL to issue a proclamation announcing the cessation of operations against the British for the duration of the war. Upon the arrest of Kalay and his Command, the command fell, by order of succession, to Zeroni. Zeroni sent Raziel a curt reply: "Israel is not widowed yet." In other words, the organization exists, someone is in control, not to worry. Raziel again ordered Zeroni to issue the declaration; Zeroni knew he had in any case "to cease operations, for at this time we do not have the ability to act," but he refused to declare this publicly. "To stop a war one wins political concessions. We have to negotiate before surrendering."

Raziel again ordered Zeroni to issue the proclamation, this time invoking the authority of Jabotinsky. Zeroni was so far down the line of succession that his own authority did not originate with Jabotinsky. Understanding that Raziel did hold his position by virtue of Jabotinsky's authority, he decided perhaps he would have to issue the blasphemous proclamation. Zeroni took counsel with Yevin, who wept openly when he heard Raziel's order. "You cannot do this," he abjured Zeroni. "I have been given an order," Zeroni protested. Yevin's voice rose: "What! He is in jail, he can't give orders!" Zeroni tried Uri Zvi Greenberg, who replied in the same vein as had Yevin. Again Zeroni tried his luck with Raziel: Why don't you escape, we'll organize it, you can run the organization when you get out. Raziel was losing patience: Just do what I tell you, he ordered. Someone, finally, wrote Raziel's proclamation and it was issued in the name of the IZL.

Yair's position was diametrically opposed to that of his old friend Raziel. The Germans were one type of enemy, the British another. As long as they occupy our homeland, Yair explained, the British must be fought regardless of world events. In any case, a Jewish state with open borders would afford a haven to Germany's persecuted Jews, whereas the British blockade condemns these Jews to remain where they are. The argument was never resolved; Raziel, in accord with his ideology, lost his life on a mission for the British against the German-allied

Iraqis, while Yair split the IZL and formed the Stern Group, known officially as Lohamei Herut Israel (Lehi), or the Fighters for the Freedom of Israel.

Rabbi Arye Levin visited the prisoners and provided the Irgunists with another matter for discussion. Rabbi Arye Levin was a gentle white-bearded minister known affectionately as "the father of the prisoners" because of his years of dedication to imprisoned Jews of all political – and criminal – stripes. Lewin remembers, "At the time we had nothing. No pencil, no paper, not even a toothbrush, not even underwear. But we had one thing: Reb Arye Levin. Just to see him, to shake his hand, was all we wanted." On one of his visits, Rabbi Levin informed Segal that his wife had just given birth to a girl. Segal, no slouch when it came to prison life, seemed at the point of breaking. He longed to be with his wife, to see the infant. The Command convened in special session to choose a name for the newest addition to the fighting family. The suggestions flew fast and furious but Segal's own choice carried the day: Uzit, meaning strength. "That's what the Jewish people needs these days," argued Segal, clinching the vote.

But now Segal was not the only man in the pen thinking inward thoughts. The High Holidays meandered past the guards, the fences, the doors and the steel bars and made their way into the cold cells and into the warm hearts of the Jewish arrestees and detainees. The High Holidays are so atypical of the holidays of other nations that they may be said to be typical of the Jewish calendar: a mesh of stark contrasts, a roller coaster ride of the spirit. The soul-searching stocktaking of the Rosh Hashana New Year holiday, the ten days of repentance, the awe of the stirring shofar blasts, the abstinence of the Day of Atonement – yet these are holidays, somber worship services followed immediately by festive family gatherings, days sanctified by both prayer and wine. The shofar and the awe passed through the prison's steel doors but not the families, and no matter how thick the bonds of brotherhood, each of the fighters was made a bit more introspective than usual by loneliness.

As Yom Kippur approached, Jerusalem's Jews made their way to countless synagogues throughout the Holy City, and countless *minyan* prayer quorums convened to chant the haunting "Kol Nidre." Cell 23 of the JCP became one of these synagogues. Moshe Segal, acting as *gabai*, or beadle, approved lawyer Max Seligman's request to lead the service. (Seligman had been arrested in May; he had bribed a police officer to divert British patrol boats long enough to allow Jewish refugees from Europe to reach the beaches of the homeland.) As Seligman sang, and during the silent portions of the prayer, Yair stood in the left corner of the cell, *mahzor* prayer book in hand, and if he moved at all such movement was imperceptible. At service's end, Yair asked Segal what would be the traditional thing to do, and Segal suggested learning *Mishnayot*, the passages of the ancient Mishna which describe the Priestly Yom Kippur service in the Temple. Dviri had already arranged that prison guard Reuben Effendi would leave the prisoners, who had converged on cell 23 from their respective rooms, behind these bars after the prayers, and so both Segal and Yair were able to read:

> The High Priest...would walk in the Temple Shrine until he stood between the two curtains which divided the Holy from the Holy of Holies, between which was one cubit...He turned to the south and walked to his left, alongside the curtain, until he reached the Ark of the Law. He reached the Ark...piled the incense upon the coals and the entire Temple filled with smoke...Once the Ark had already been removed [in the Second Temple], a stone was there...called the Foundation Stone...and on it he put the incense...
>
> He confessed saying thus: Dear God, Your people Israel have trespassed and wronged and sinned before You; Dear God, forgive the trespassings and wrongs and sins which Your people Israel have trespassed and wronged and sinned, as it is written in the Torah of Moses Your servant, "For this day

you will be forgiven and purified of all your sins, before God will you be purified." And the Priests and the nation standing in the Temple Court, upon hearing the explicit Divine name pronounced by the High Priest, bent and bowed and fell on their faces declaring: "Blessed is the name of His glorious Majesty forever and ever."

Moshe Segal would never forget the emotion which visibly gripped Yair as they read of the Jewish nation gathered on the Temple Mount bowing as one when the High Priest of Israel pronounced the ineffable Divine name as part of the service of the Day of Atonement. Two years later, Yair was to formulate the Principles of Rebirth, a credo for his underground movement. The eighteenth and final principle Yair listed for the rebirth of Israel is: The rebuilding of the Temple as the symbol of redemption.

But this is 1939, and not much is needed to return the imprisoned freedom fighters from the heights of Mount Moriah to the Valley of the Shadow of Death. The conversation must have gone something like this:

Haim Dviri reviewed the ups and downs of his prison career. He'd been a journalist, a "political" with special rights, when he first sat in the early '30s. Now he was a criminal and had fewer rights, though by virtue of his position he had the run of the prison. But he had also been to the valley of death and endured there the scorching sun, the starvation, the beatings and the whippings of the Nur Chams work camp.

Aharon Heichman was singing and Dviri was reminded of the time they plowed 450 dunams of agricultural land in Ramat Tiomkin, near a few scattered shacks and a single road which are today called Netanya. The Jewish National Fund (JNF) owned the land, legally at least, but the Arabs of nearby Abu Kishik tried by plowing, trespassing and occasional acts of more violent nature to take possession of the plot. The

Jewish Agency provided tents and food, and Jewish residents of the area joined with Betar members from Kfar Saba and Hagana veterans to "conquer," or reestablish Jewish ownership of, the disputed territory. Dviri clearly remembered Heichman's organizing presence, but Heichman needed to be reminded of Dviri's volunteered appearance.

"You guys went to all sorts of actions, didn't you?" he responded wryly, recalling for the unfamiliar the tale of what would one day be known as the "conquest" of Ramat Tiomkin:

"We had arms, but the Arabs informed on us, the British came a-searching but didn't discover any. The Arabs attacked, day and night there were fights, but we didn't use the arms we had then, because we had connections and knew when the British were on the way. We fenced off the land, though mostly it was a human fence; we kept the Arabs away while we worked the land. Wherever they plowed we undid their work. Eventually they had enough, and the courts ruled in our favor, too. The spirit was great, but I wouldn't call this activity especially heroic..."

Somebody pointed out that another Kfar Sabaean was present: Jacob Kotik. "Ah, but I arrived there in 1933, I was in Betar and Heichman was commanding officer. I knew him and his wife, but to us they were real old-timers. Which is to say, they were there a year or two before me."

In '33, Altman was also in Betar, in faraway Rumania, though not even the seas and miles could keep the latest developments out of his life. He had been setting up Betar chapters in every hamlet he could find. "One of our members went to Eretz Israel, joined Brit Habirionim, and at some point returned to our village on a visit. From him we learned that the Birionim were engaged in combat with the British, that the British concocted a census to 'prove' that there were not all that many Jews in the country, and Abba Ahimeir organized a boycott of the census." Altman admitted he was stirred by the tales of the downing of the German flags in Jerusalem and Tel Aviv. There in the room with Altman was Dviri, who had felled the flag, and just about everyone in the cell had pulled down his share of census broadsides, even Heichman, who had never been a Birion. In any case, the Rumanian expatriate visiting Altman's village had finally asked Altman why he had not yet gone to Israel and Altman's future was sealed. Chalk another one up to the Birionim.

But now that Altman's holiday-time memories had made the long journey back to Rumania, they wandered on their own and found his mother. He recalled a prison visit by the beloved Rabbi Levin (he was known to everyone in the room as 'Reb Arye,' whose arrival was awaited, according to Kotik, as if it were the arrival of the Messiah himself).

Reb Arye told Altman he had gotten a card from Altman's mother, from Odessa. "My mother wrote that on the day of my sentencing, it was a Friday, at the exact hour, she was resting, and at that moment she felt worried; then she saw her father, who had died in the early '20s, and he assured her that 'Yehezkel will be alright.'" Altman's mother had not even known anything was wrong until that point. But his mother's deceased father had one more stop to make that fateful day. "I, too, that first night on death row, dreamt of my grandfather, with his Herzl-like beard."

Altman was not the only alumni of death row in the room; Jacob Kotik grew pensive. It had been one very long year, precisely.

"My first Yom Kippur in prison I was in a small solitary cell, sentenced to death..." Kotik had been sentenced to death in August 1938. Someone asked for his story, and this is the story he told:

"If you want, I can begin at the beginning. I was born in 1913." Before he was able to decide whether reminiscing that far back was cost-effective, Kotik realized he could not stop, for this was no clichéd opening, this was his story and more. "I have five sisters. Our home is in Poland, in Czekeno, near Bialystock..." Kotik's five sisters will later die in nearby Maidanek. Of this horror Kotik is still unaware. Kotik's father was held as a POW by the Austrians in World War One. "By the time he returned, my father didn't recognize me and I didn't recognize my father...My mother handled the business. My family ran a bakery and my mother also sewed." Kotik's father doubtless expected to find the family anxiously awaiting his return. The poor man "thought he'd find us wanting, but business was booming. Mom, even with six kids, really knew how to manage..."

The Kotik siblings were an eclectic lot. "I learned in a yeshiva in Bialystock; our family was traditional, and Zionist, too. One sister was a member of the Revisionist youth movement of those days, Masada, she learned in a seminar in Grodno, another sister was in the left-wing Poalei Zion, another in the right-wing Poalei Zion, the others in Betar. I joined Betar in Bialystock while I was still in the yeshiva." The 15-year-old Kotik had been won over or, in his words, "turned on to the Betar idea," by Jabotinsky himself, who spoke in the city.

"About twenty of us went to *hachshara* (training and preparation for aliya) in Zelba, and there I waited for an immigration certificate which didn't come; then there was another *hachshara* elsewhere. I waited for a year for that certificate which never came. I was constantly pestering the Betar council for the certificate, but the Jewish Agency had us blacklisted.

"Finally my sister, the one in Grodno, she knew Itzhak Yellin, who was visiting Poland from Eretz Israel...She gave him a letter; he turned red, told her to wait five minutes, went to Propes, the Betar Commander in Poland, and five minutes later Yellin was back. You have a certificate, he said, you can go home, it'll get to you there...My sister? Everyone wanted to make aliya! But they didn't get certificates, a certificate was worth millions, it was a prize." Kotik knew the inestimable value of that document and so did his sister, who used her connections to procure the treasure not for herself, but for her brother. Neither she nor he, of course, knew that Jacob was headed for death row in Eretz Israel, while his sister was headed for Maidanek.

Kotik made his way, "very hungry," via Trieste to the Holy Land.

He found farm work in Kfar Saba. "In fact, they still owe me money..." They will still owe him the money fifty years later.

Employment and sustenance were not the only things on Kotik's mind. His Betar and Irgun activity continued unabated through the 1930s, until his arrest on Tel Aviv's Allenby Street with the suitcase full of arms.

"Well, that day wasn't overly buoyant. On the Sabbath, and what a hot Sabbath it was, they put me in the *zinzana* (solitary-confinement cell). Before that I'd been interrogated at the police station. The officer asked if I had anything to say but before I opened my mouth he added *red gornisht* in Yiddish, and I got the hint, whatever there is to be said should be said in court.

"Ah, Jaffa, Jaffa Prison and its lice. There were no newspapers there, in fact there was nothing there at all. When I was transferred to Jerusalem, what a difference! Of course even here things aren't thrillsville, but compared to Jaffa! And here I found my friends and was greeted with love..." Dviri was first to spot the new arrival. Kotik: "We knew each other from Brit Habirionim. He gave me soap and toothpaste. It was as if he gave me millions. I was pretty pitiful, after all that time in the Jaffa *zinzana*."

Altman, too, was an old comrade in arms. Kotik recalled: "In Zichron, in '36, we served together as policemen, sharing shifts of guard duty. That was the same time the Irgunist Shmuelevitz was killed, I knew him well..."

Irgunists were not yet boycotting court proceedings against them and Kotik participated in his trial, at least up to a point. As the three judges passed sentence, Kotik rose and declared: "Long live the Jewish state on both banks of the Jordan River." Then he sang *Hatikva*.

Dviri: "It was the first political speech at a sentencing!"

Kotik's attorney was less impressed than Dviri. "He kicked me. Said it would hurt my chances for a pardon."

But the scene was emotional and the spectators moved. Afterwards several friends testified as character witnesses. "Yoske Vilner, I'll never forget him, a good friend, he testified with his head held high, though he was on the police force and he risked quite a bit by testifying. Back in Jerusalem I had just enough time to see Dviri, who passed everyone the word I'd been sentenced to death, even as I was on my way to this prison's *zinzana*. Down the stairs, third on the right. Ezra Effendi, as he was escorting me, spoke from his heart: 'They won't succeed in hanging you in Jerusalem.'" Ezra had tried comforting the doomed man. Altman had done the same: "I tried cheering Kotik up, telling him they wouldn't hang him, but this wasn't easy, after Ben Yosef and Schwartz had already been hanged."

The new boy on the cellblock chose an interesting neighborhood. Abdul Magid and Issa el-Abras (Darwish), the two Arabs whose confession in the Arlosorov murder case had been ignored by the Revisionist-hunting British police and Jewish establishment, had taken up temporary residence in solitary as punishment for one or another infraction of prison etiquette. Other cells held other Arabs awaiting the hangman.

"All the time I was in that cell I sang, killing time...One of the Arabs wept all that same time." Abdul Magid took a critical view of his brother: "Why are you constantly sobbing? Look at the Jew who sings while you cry!" Undeterred, the condemned man wept all the way to the gallows.

Kotik's questionable fluency in Arabic dictated that intercell converse be conducted in Hebrew. He and Abdul Magid became friends. "Darwish was a cold-blooded killer. Magid was also a killer, but not of the Darwish sort, who did the shooting. Magid shined a flashlight on Arlosorov. Darwish shot. Magid described the whole affair, admitted everything."

Easy and sweet – perhaps bittersweet – conversation brought to Kotik's mind hours when social intercourse was not so easily facilitated. "Dviri and I would meet in the bathrooms, because notes could be passed underneath the dividers as we crouched. I wrote a farewell note and passed it just as we heard shouts of 'Kotik! To the office!' I was taken, along with an Arab prisoner, to the warden who spoke first to the Arab: 'Till now you were under sentence of death, now your sentence is commuted to life in prison.' In an instant, the Arab was on the floor kissing the warden's hands and feet. The warden faced me: 'Previously, the Military Commander decided you were sentenced to die. Now your sentence is commuted to life in prison.' 'Thank you,' I replied."

Kotik's commutation brought its own fair share of kisses, though: As soon as he had exchanged the red clothes of the doomed for a standard prison uniform, his comrades filled the quota of requisite kisses and hugs.

"Yes, but I was put in an Arab room, not even with Altman. Steel respected but suspected me. My first run-in with him was on his regular Friday inspection of the cells." Tradition dictated that the servile prisoners extend their hands. Kotik played contrary, explaining to the surprised Steel that "'By us, it is the Law. Only for God do we extend our hands, not for man.' Steel said OK, but ever afterwards he had it in for me." Only when Steel retired was Kotik able, on his own, to move to the Jewish cell with Dviri, Buchko, Altman and the others.

The wicked Haman of ancient Persia, whose thwarted scheme to murder the empire's Jews is celebrated in the Purim holiday, is said to have honed his hatred for the Jewish Mordechai when the latter refused to bow before him. By refusing to extend his hands, Kotik had perhaps stretched the letter of Jewish law allowing Jews to bow only before God Himself, never man, but he was firmly grounded in prison tradition. Segal had refused to mop, Dviri had incurred the wrath of an unbroken-in escort to the Nur Chams stone quarry by refusing to bow to him. The point was never to appear servile and in this the prisoners remained well within the spirit of Jewish tradition.

"Altman and I were the only ones not sitting during the daily countings. Dviri was lucky, he was upstairs, Buchko was in the kitchen.

185

Altman and I were on our own in the yard. At least the authorities had enough smarts not to fight us on this one. They understood it was a matter of principle with us," noted Kotik.

But Dviri's good fortune held only so far as the walls of the JCP. True, Ezra Effendi had put off the overanxious warder from Nur Chams by telling him it was with His Holiness Steel's approval that Dviri did not fall to his knees, but when Dviri refused to bend while awaiting transport to Nur Chams, the insulted warder got both angry and even. Once in the hard-labor camp, he whipped Dviri senseless. Dviri refused to beg for relief, cry in pain or whimper to any extent. By an incredible act of will, his body refused to fall even though he was hardly conscious. When the guard finally threw in the towel, too exhausted to continue, Dviri was the victor. He'd not gone down for any count and not displayed any weakness or inclination to cringe. In Nur Chams, this gave him a TKO over the frustrated representative of brutal authority. Dviri was carried away by his fellow inmates, all of whom, Arabs as well as Jews, paid him hero's tribute. From then on the Arabs freed him from bathroom duty and reserved a space for him at the head of every line.

Just what was Dviri, so at home in this prison, doing in the stone quarries of Nur Chams?

Mordechai Schwartz, a policeman and Hagana member sentenced to death for the murder of an Arab policeman with whom he shared a tent, was then in the JCP. Schwartz was not a happy camper, not so much because of the noose which longed for his neck but more so because the Hagana had forbidden him to tell in court the true story of his "crime." Schwartz wished to tell of the boasts made by his tentmate of how many Jews he would kill when the Arab gangs overran Tel Aviv, of exactly how he intended to rape Jewish women, of the bloody future awaiting Schwartz's people. Day in and day out, the creative cop with the killer's eyes took delight in adding meticulous details to the crimes he and his friends in the then active gangs intended to commit. Whether the tactless Arab raised his gun first is still a matter of conjecture over some sixty years later. What is certain is that Schwartz fired first and that the Hagana ordered all nationalistic implications suppressed at the trial. The obedient Schwartz never gave his prepared speech about busting the *havlaga*, about defending Jewish honor, about the danger he was in that night. No, the Hagana feared that Schwartz might become a model for other Jewish youth, that he might, in fact, become for the Hagana what Shlomo Ben Yosef had become for the Irgun. So Schwartz, ever loyal to those who betrayed him for political expediency, allowed rumors of homosexual advances to worm their way into his case, thereby thrusting the whole case, in most people's minds, into the category of tawdry gossip, and thus allowing himself to be removed from the pantheon of Jewish martyrs.

Dviri befriended the red-robed Schwartz and accompanied him on his daily walks, for those few moments he was allowed out of his death cell. A self-seeking fellow con fabricated a tale of a smuggled saw which Dviri was supposedly delivering to the desperate Schwartz. Dviri was sent to the chain gang; Schwartz was in due time hanged as planned.

Itzhak Gurion noted that considering the welcome they prepare, "the two Haims [Dviri and Buchko] are actually two angels." Gurion himself was brought to the JCP just before Rosh Hashana. He was brought to cell 48 while its residents were taking their morning ramble in the courtyard. The cell was not completely empty, however; though his friends were enjoying the fresh air, Moshe Segal was standing in tallit and tefillin completing his morning prayers. Segal quickly put away his spiritual finery and helped Gurion to settle in.

The next morning, Gurion woke to the sound of Hebrew chants: "The soul is Yours and the body Your doing, have mercy on Your handiwork." Segal and several others were sitting on their *bourges* reciting the penitential *selichot* prayers of the season. Gurion donned his cap and joined in.

As this was Yom Kippur, if any one of the assembled incarcerated

187

were to let his mind sally forth into the corridors of time, surely Moshe Segal, whose name and whose shofar will forever be linked in history books with the Day of Atonement, was he. Segal's mind did not, however, wind its way straight to that day ten years ago for which he won fame; or, if it did, it did not loiter long at that juncture. Segal was wending his way further and traversing not only time but also oceans. He was on his way to Poltava, but the road was hard and he was hungry, hungry, yes, so very hungry. It was the year of the great famine. Segal and his Hehalutz friends were working the land in various settlements, trying to absorb agricultural training in preparation for their immigration to Eretz Israel, while keeping one step ahead of the famine. Finally the hunger reached Novopoltava and Segal's horseback-riding days were numbered. As the famine encroached, the settlers began letting go of their help. One torrid summer day, Segal's "employer" Kremer turned sadly to his charge and spoke wistfully: "I can pay you double. But there is not enough bread here even for me." Segal and a friend, the last of the trainees to have remained under the nearly hopeless conditions, embarked on the road to Poltava. Without travel documents a ticket was unobtainable, so they decided to start by foot and try their luck with the Nikolayev train, some four or five miles away.

"We walked the ten kilometers. The sun blazed above us, and we had no food. We finally struck grass in one field, on which we dined; it was rather bitter..."

They eventually stumbled into the train depot, but getting into the iron horse itself was another matter. No train had been repaired since the Revolution of 1917. "If a train broke down, it was junked." Every time one went out of service, there was one fewer on the tracks and proportionally less room on the remaining cars. "People stood sardine-like on the roof and in between cars; three steps led up to the carriage and on each, passengers were balanced with one leg on and one off." Segal and Haim Hasin reviewed one car after another and found no apertures. They noticed, however, that 99 percent of the fares were soldiers...and they themselves were fortunately wearing khaki. "With aching hearts we split up, hoping one of us might survive. I had my eye on one spot, in full knowledge that it could not contain a person." Segal approached a nurse for assistance, asking her to let him pass...on the heads of her fellow passengers. She convinced the others; Segal climbed up, clambered over and rolled into the hole. "I fell asleep on top of some packages, just under the ceiling, concealing my bootless legs, hoping I appeared military in my khaki."

An officer passed once, twice, finally whopping Segal in the leg and asking for identification. Segal snored, feigning sleep, but the stubborn officer pulled him down and, finding Segal documentless, ordered him to the rear carriage with the other prisoners. The Zeirei Zion and Hehalutz certificates on Segal's person ("kept for sentimental reasons...youth does things like that") would, he realized, be death certificates. When the prisoners were ordered off the train and into a straight line Segal assumed the worst and gambled. *Tovarisch!* he called to the officer in charge. "I won't go!" Segal was told he would be shot on the spot. Desperate, he opened his shirt and ordered: "Shoot!" This the armed officer could not fathom: "Are you crazy?" he wondered. Segal rejoined that without his bag, life was not worth living. The officer inquired sarcastically as to whether Segal wished him to send a special guard to accompany him as he collected his baggage. Segal naively assured him he would return. The *tovarisch*, pointing to his pistol, reminded Segal of what would happen if he did not.

Back on the train a cluster of old women asked Segal what he was doing and he answered them honestly. They prevailed upon him to try his luck with them. He crouched, at their behest, under their baskets and under their long, flowing skirts. He remained awake for the remainder of the voyage for fear one of them might at some point stand up. At Poltava Station, which Segal knew well as a childhood playground, the women informed him that his still persistent hunter was for the moment up ahead and Segal broke for the station's coal entrance, sped to the gate and jumped into the first horse-drawn carriage he spied. His mother exclaimed when she saw her 18-year-old son, who had not eaten for three days, "You look like you've come from the netherworld." "I did come from the netherworld," said Moshe.

Segal's itinerant memories had completed the long, roundabout journey to Poltava.

"Many of my friends had joined Komsomol, the Communist youth league. I knew if I joined I'd get an apartment for myself and my family and a job. Being in Hehalutz meant losing all rights, that if one were starving, death would be the sole option." Obviously, Segal chose Hehalutz and Zionism.

Another year, another Yom Kippur. Kol Nidre night. Segal was standing by his father's side in the local synagogue when he noticed he was just about the only representative of the younger generation there that evening. Poltava's Jewish youth had chosen, almost without exception – Segal's predilection for being the exception evincing itself even then – to attend the gala Komsomol celebration in the Workers Palace. Segal short-changed his prayers that night and headed for the shindig, where his friends were overjoyed to see that "Segal, too, has finally come to join Komsomol, and on the Day of Atonement!"

The youthful audience was engrossed in a Yiddish lecture being delivered by a Communist Jewish apparatchik, the gist of which was that the Gaon (genius) Rabbi Elijah of Vilna who lived 150 years earlier had himself written the Bible, the Talmud, the Midrash and the various books of Jewish law, promoting them as if they were ancient holy books. The orator warned his listeners not to get caught up in the web of "rabbinical clericalism" with its lies and forgeries. Segal's boisterous laughter was especially glaring in light of the otherwise general applause. Segal complimented the speaker on his ignorance, noting for the benefit of the more impressionable crowd that "not even an academy of geniuses could have composed in one generation the inordinately large amount of literature, with its variant styles and languages, such as is contained in the Bible and the post-Biblical Mishna, Talmud, commentaries, legal decisions, Kabbala, etc., etc., etc. – much less could one individual have done so." Segal demanded of the speaker to know what had become of his Marxist materialist realism. "Silly superstitious belief like yours has no place in this new progressive period!" taunted Segal.

Moshe's friends hustled him out as the intensity of the furor grew, but he spent the rest of the night in the palace gardens propounding Jewish ideals and debating Marxist theory with the alienated Jewish youth.

For some, Yom Kippur in the JCP was the sort of experience one remembers for a lifetime. Segal lived every Yom Kippur that way and he would never forget the Mishna he studied with Yair. For others, the wellspring of memories and conversations, the prayer service and song was not much different from other days behind bars, excepting that this day brought with it permission for a holiday family visit. As the twilight deepened, the food brought by these visitors was laid out for the postfast feast. The inmates decided to hold that food in abeyance. They would refrain from breaking their fasts until that year's shofar blower at the Western Wall had been brought in. They knew someone was bound to continue Segal's tradition; it had happened every year since, sometimes by plan, sometimes by chance. They knew someone, somewhere, would pick up the shofar Segal had cast and sound it, and that lad would undoubtedly spend the next few months with them behind bars. The least they could do was to hold dinner for him.

And sure enough, the extra place did not go empty. Quite some time passed, however, even after the official fast had concluded, before the shofar blower was willing to admit his "crime" or even give his name. Who could blame him? Could he really be expected to believe that he was sitting in a cell with the Irgun High Command itself, and with Moshe Segal, the man whose path he had followed?

Abraham Stern thought the boy's taciturnity a sign of character

191

and suggested they leave him be till morning. Segal, the "mukhtar," or chief, of the cell, broke tradition and placed the newcomer far from the *kardel*; Segal quieted the complaints of the cell's criminal elements by displaying the wounds the shofar blower received from the British during his arrest, classifying him as ill and therefore deserving of a comfortable corner of the cell till he recuperated. Reb Arye Levin, who had worshipped with the prisoners and stayed for dinner, managed to steal from the newcomer his name: Yeshayahu Gottesman. As soon as the rabbi had won the name he was gone, undoubtedly to inform people outside of Gottesman's arrest. Heichman began singing Betar songs to win the lad's trust, and by the time the whole cell was singing, so was Gottesman, who opened up and revealed his name to the curious Command.

Gottesman was eventually acquitted of the shofar blowing for lack of evidence, but convicted of being an illegal immigrant and sentenced to six months.

★ ★ ★

Lacking sufficient evidence to convict the High Command, the British soon transferred them to Sarafand Detention Camp where they joined their long-detained de jure Commander in Chief, David Raziel.

Inexplicably, Yair Stern's transfer was delayed by a few days. On Sabbath eve, he therefore rejoined the Jewish political prisoners for services and Ezra Effendi granted their request to leave open the door of cell 23, locking instead the hallway door.

They sat on *bourges* under a bare light bulb, just outside cell 23: a semicircle of "students" with their "rebbe," Yair, at the head, as Dviri describes, with an air of romanticism, the haunting gathering.

Altman, Segal, Dviri, Kotik, Tamari, Lewin, Buchwald and Buchko, politicos isolated from the rush of what was then an awful reality, were unsure how to interpret the confounding events which were permanently reshaping the world. They saw the war as an "opportunity," on the assumption that imprisoned and oppressed peoples, theirs included,

192

would attain freedom in the course of battles which would redraw borders. In prison, hopes clutch even at straws, and the politicos were hopeful. Now Yair Stern, far and away the most dynamic of the Irgun commanders and respected for his firsthand knowledge of the Eastern European cauldron, was sitting with them. They would finally learn what was really occurring outside. They peppered Stern with anticipative questions.

"We assume," said Dviri, or perhaps one of the others, since they were of one mind, "that this war will bring much political upheaval, governments and regimes will falter and pass, the Russian system of government will change and its doors will open to allow free aliya – "

Another prisoner interrupted. "The Jews of Russia, Poland and Europe will flock to Eretz Israel like the Exodus from Egypt – "

"...hungry for sacrifice and glory, with the fires of mastery and freedom burning in their hearts," added a third voice, completing the thought.

Yair surveyed the prisoners, each of whom had pinned his eyes on him, this foggy night on the floor of a prison run by a foreign regime in their land. The prisoners, too, if ever they let their eyes wander from Yair – who they knew would enter history as the great Hebrew revolutionary of the modern age – to themselves, knew that they were a compact squad of freedom fighters, of single heart and single mind. They listened intently to Yair's calm, devastating words, which gave them a glimpse and more of what had been happening in the world during their "absence." Dviri felt the gray prison turn cadaverous.

"My brothers in war and faith. I've listened well to your thoughts and your hopes, which are my hopes as well. With great suffering, pain and disappointment – I must disagree with you. I do not see the war as optimistically as you do, though I'd gladly see things your way, if only reality were in line with your assumption that the war will solve our problem, the problem of the entire Jewish people.

"The war erupted at a bad time for us. The nation of Israel in the Diaspora is not ready for it and neither is the Jewish community of Eretz Israel.

"I've just returned from Poland, with its millions, with its great potential of youth ready at a moment's notice to immigrate and raze the locked gates of Eretz Israel. We began preparing them for aliya. This war nipped these efforts in the bud.

"As for Jews in general, they can be divided into three ideological groupings, the first of which is Zionist and feels deeply the imminent destruction of our people, the disaster speeding towards them. These Jews are willing to make aliya at any price, but the path is blocked, for the Mandatory [British] government has decided to eliminate the rise of Israel and prevent aliya.

"No one will save these Jews. Certainly not the established leadership which is not willing to conduct a meaningful struggle against the prohibition of aliya, feeling as it does a solidarity with the foreign regime...

"The second group is the anti-Zionist Bund which promises its adherents that the 'national' solution for the Jewish people is international socialism, which will solve the problem of Jews everywhere; Jews should therefore avoid the temptations of vacuous Zionism.

"The third and dominant group is one of religious extremists, which in the name of Heaven asks its adherents not to make aliya. This, without considering the anti-semitism and Nazism which crouch outside the door of every Jew in Europe.

"If only these three groups would merge with the sole intention of saving lives and making aliya, the hated British government would be unable to prevent the human stream...

"Not only for the Jews of Europe has the war come at an inopportune time, but also for the Jews of Eretz Israel.

"The community here, like the Jews abroad, is without a leadership worthy of the name, they are without leaders, they are unarmed

194

and unable to fight for their brothers and sisters and parents still in the Diaspora.

"The question of whether we'll even do all that is possible during this war depends solely on us, whether we'll be able to consolidate our forces and bring here that youth we'd begun organizing to make aliya and fight."

Yair finished speaking in almost a whisper. Dviri saw the light at the end of the tunnel dim. He understood that the war would eliminate much potential Jewish power, without kindling any new flames in uncomprehending hearts. The fighters would have to begin anew with depleted forces, fewer weapons and still without the assistance of the visionless Jewish community around them.

Chapter 7
The Underground Rises

A new stage begins today.   Che, *Diaries*

"I hope the both of us – soldiers in the Army of Redemption which fights the Israeli nation's war of liberation – will meet on the front in Eretz Israel," wrote Abraham Stern to his brother, in 1933.

Abraham Stern was, in his own words, "crazy for the Kingdom." Long the most charismatic of the Irgun commanders, Stern knew that his task was to usher in the new stage of the Hebrew Revolution and he was just as certain he would die trying, "falling in battle, the sky a blue flag to our bodies."

Eretz Israel's frontier days were winding up. The focal point of the Jewish forces was slowly metamorphosing from the kaffiyed Arab marauder to the uniformed British imperialist. The new times called for a new type of revolutionary and Yair was it.

Tall, thin, elegant. Intellectual, educated, polite. A deep voice, never raised in argument. Perhaps Hollywood has ignored him only because Tyrone Power is deceased and only Tyrone Power could do him justice. Impeccably dressed even under the most adverse circumstances, his demeanor was usually serious and often reserved, but he was at heart romantic and could, with a performer's charm and the love of a prank, quickly become the life of a party. Yair was often idolized and women found him especially intriguing.

Abraham Stern (Jabotinsky Institute photo)

Yair was an urban revolutionary for the new decade. He redrew the target for Hebrew arms. He had done his share of guard duty, from the rooftops of Jerusalem's Old City to the fields of the Galilee, protecting produce and lives from Arab rioters in '29 and that year's aftershocks. Yet he had developed in the '30s and had done so on the training grounds of Poland, on the unsteady "illegal" immigration routes of Europe, on the covert arms-purchasing missions at which he was so adept. Kremin and Yair sailed together for Italy once, and they were still together as they disembarked in Brindisi. But caution overcame amicability and by the time they boarded their train their destination was identical but their wagons were not.

The giant leaps forward in Jewish life up to Yair had been effected by the likes of Jabotinsky, Tehomi, Segal and Ahimeir. They had taught the Jews of Eretz Israel to fight, to endure prison and gallows, to think in regal terms, to organize armed forces. Yair created the Underground and called it by name: "We live underground! 'Twixt damp basement walls, under a pale bulb, on a floor open to the falling rain." Yair sang of blood and looked death in the eye, daring to glorify his inevitable violent demise, yet his dreams were ever before him: "We in the dark underground have been blinded by the dream: The floor's puddle is – the Lake Kinneret; the bulb's light – the rays of the sun."

The man who could write: "As my father carried a prayer shawl to Sabbath synagogue, I carry sacred pistols...Blessed be he who believes and cursed be he who denies the religion of Redemption and the war of liberation," could also write to his wife: "I should perhaps have been more cruel in our relationship: Had we separated seven years ago, you might today be happy"; or, in another letter, tell her: "My child, do you think I do not know the meaning of 'pain'? I tell no one but I know and know well the meaning of 'pain.' A man would need a heart of stone and nerves of steel to withstand the bitterness and degradation of poverty and wanderings and continual anxiety for everyone and everything, the responsibility for the lives of those who, with me, abandoned all to throw themselves into this insane but magnificent life, this life of battle for a better future, for the happiness of even those who are today willing to turn us over to the hangman. How fortunate that I have faith. Prayer from the heart purifies the soul, strengthens the heart and brightens the world."

"I used to get telegrams and messages and pass them on to the Command," recalls Bat-Zion Kremin. "I don't really know why these messages came to me, I guess they had my address. Yair came once on a Friday night, my religiously observant family had already lit the Sabbath candles. I gave Yair several messages, he didn't write anything, none of the numbers or dates, nothing, it was already Sabbath."

Fellow IZL officer Haim Lubinsky believes Stern adopted a more religious character only after the arrest of the Command, during their near year of detention in Sarafand. But Stern's widow Roni remembers him "telling me before our marriage: Our house will be a Jewish home, you must know this now. You will observe the Sabbath, we will observe the fast days, you will light Sabbath candles, I will go to synagogue." At the time, Roni did not even know which benediction to recite over the candle lighting. Roni says Abraham prayed every morning and "never went to sleep without first reading from the Bible."

Most of Stern's travels from 1934 on turned on the axis of procuring arms for the Irgun and training, in Poland, for the Irgunists. Once or twice, he accompanied IZL Commanders Bitker and Rosenberg to Jabotinsky in unproductive attempts to win authorization for a more offensive strategy against Arab terror. This was before Jabo's Greenberg-edited "Amen," before Ben Yosef's ultimate sacrifice, before the telegram signed "Mendelson." By the late '30s Yair was preoccupied with his forty thousand plans, which became the juxtaposition of his previous goals with his latest: illegal immigration.

Joseph Kremin, IZL contact man for illegal immigration activities, was at one point bogged down in Lebanon. "I knew a boat was expected. Yair sent a note: Do not worry, all will be well. He didn't want me to leave my mission there. Then a problem arose with the boat *Katina*, they had no choice but to send me to Greece." Yair filled in for Joseph at the boat's unloading. The British discovered the boat and shot up the shore. Yair stood on a hill overlooking the area and did not budge, despite the bullets which plowed into his hilltop post. He seemed to regard death as a friend, an acquaintance he expected to find waiting for him wherever he went. Yair left that night only after all the new immigrants and Irgunists were safely away.

In his free moments, Yair relaxed by translating into Hebrew the songs of Goethe and Schubert. He had been the Hebrew University's most promising student of classical Greek and Latin, even being awarded a stipend to continue his studies in Florence, before Tehomi found him in Italy and brought him back as his aide-de-camp. "Yes, I am a soldier and a poet," opens one of his poems; another, "Soldiers without names or uniforms are we / surrounded by terror and death," became the Underground anthem.

Upon the death of Arye Yitzhaki, Yair wrote: "Hold your tears, Hebrew mother / young yet great was the son you suckled / Stalwart Jew, seeking vengeance and freedom / A generation sees itself and its desire – in him."

"Raziel is our military commander," said Nissim Cohen. "But this talented *literatus*, this poet, is our spiritual commander."

Stern, the ideologue, emphasized the educational aspects of revolutionary activity. He initiated the Irgun's radio broadcasts, edited the Lehi newspaper, met personally with as many recruits as possible to imbue them with an understanding of their task.

"I have two boys from France," Yair told Nissim Cohen in 1939. "One Jewish, one not. They know all about radios. You'll be their contact." Cohen found them a safe house. The Frenchmen compiled a shopping list of ingredients necessary for cooking up a radio station and Cohen was the educated consumer. The transmitter fit into a suitcase and the radio station hit the road, always on the move to avoid

David Raziel (Jabotinsky Institute photo)

detection by the British. Most of the material was written by Yehoshua Yevin and by Stern himself.

When the Command was arrested in August 1939, Stern was probably the most prominent of the commanders, certainly the most independent, ideological and intense. But he was one among equals. Only after their chief Raziel decided to halt operations against the British and, on the contrary, enlist in the British effort against the Germans, did this situation change.

Long arguments in Sarafand were followed by long arguments on the "outside" after their release. Segal brought Raziel and Stern together in a Carmel Market apartment in Tel Aviv. "But the courageous,

201

practical soldier Raziel and the uncompromising ideologue Stern just couldn't find common language," concluded Segal. Others brought them together for negotiations in Haifa. A Mr. Maseri put his 89 Dizengoff Street home at the Irgun's disposal. In the summer of 1940, the Command met there. "I'll set them a good table," Maseri schemed, "maybe the food will put them in a good mood." They ate well indeed. But the split was inevitable.

At one point Raziel resigned and Yair was elected the new Commander in Chief, but Jabotinsky soon wired an order reinstating Raziel. Sadly, the two friends parted ways. Raziel felt the British had to be helped to defeat the Nazis; Yair differentiated between the Germans, who fit the Hebrew description of *tsorer* (hateful foes of the Jews in the tradition of Haman, the would-be destroyer of Persia's Jews), and the British, who were the *oyev* (enemy) which, as long as it forcibly occupied the Jewish country, needed to be fought. Any wartime truce with the British, reasoned Yair, could only be based on a solid commitment to further the aims of Jewish statehood afterwards. No such promise was forthcoming from the occupiers. They had only recently issued the infamous White Paper banning Jews from purchasing land in Eretz Israel and barring the immigration of German Jewish refugees fleeing the war and European persecution.

On the eve of Rosh Hashana 1940, exactly one year after the Command's arrest, Stern effectively announced by broadside the establishment of the Fighters for the Freedom of Israel (Lehi) when he published proclamation number one of the Irgun Zvai Leumi B'Israel (the Irgun in Israel) – as opposed to Raziel's Irgun Zvai Leumi in Eretz Israel: "The passing year was one of disaster and destruction: For the Jews of the world – exile. Europe is being totally destroyed. Its Jews have lost all and are imprisoned in ghettos. For the Jewish community of Eretz Israel – a year of lost direction...For the Irgun – a year of restraint...and negotiations...We take upon ourselves three tasks: (a) to unite all those loyal, proud and fighting...in the ranks of the Hebrew liberation movement; (b) to appear before the world as the single representative of the Jewish fighters and institute a policy of eliminating the Diaspora...; (c) to become as quickly as possible a body capable of taking control of the country by force of arms... To ready ourselves for these tasks the fighting force is changing its structure to that of a revolutionary underground..."

Abraham Stern had experienced loneliness before, but it is doubtful that anything other than wild determination could have prepared him for that which would soon be his wretched lot. True, when a child, Abraham's family had returned to Poland leaving him to complete his elementary-school studies in a temporary Ural Mountain refuge. And poverty, and an unfortunate twist of circumstances, soon turned the 13 year old's Ural classes into cleaning home, stoking stove and transporting river water in Siberia. An uncle afforded the young teen a cultured St. Petersburg respite, replete with dramas by Schiller and musical interludes by Chaliapin himself. At 14, though, Abraham was on the road again. This time he was to journey long and journey lonely from Petersburg back to his Polish home, without money, victuals or travel papers. Four years later the still teenaged, but by now weathered, Abraham set out on his own again, this time for Eretz Israel.

Yet if Yair ever thought he had known how lonely life could be, he went further now. Ahead heretofore had always lain family and home, the warmth of community. As he forged the Underground, Yair had to decisively and coldly cut his ties to his family, even to his newly arrived mother. He had few friends with him and fewer who would remain, he could anticipate inevitable defections and certain arrests, he had to wander about with no direction save death.

The underground road emerged from the mist of the strife-torn Irgun. Raziel was confirmed as Commander in Chief by Jabotinsky only shortly before the great statesman, father of Jewish self-defense, founder of Jewish armies and supreme commander of Jewish resistance passed away in August 1940. Jabo's final march, with Irma Halperin at his side as he had been in Jerusalem twenty years earlier, was a review of the ranks of young Betarim training at a summer camp in New York. Yair and Raziel, or "Razi" as Yair affectionately referred to him even after their differences, both tried to garner the support of the Irgun commanders. Segal stuck with Raziel – Heichman says Segal "was among the most extreme in his views, I think he supported Yair all the way, but he was more loyal in a personal sense to Raziel." By his own account, Segal passionately detested recrimination and lack of unity among Jews. Failing, as did so many others, to bring about a meeting of minds between Yair and Raziel, he must have found it difficult to sign up with the man who was, technically, leaving the organization. Nonetheless, several years later, after both David Raziel and Abraham Stern had fallen in battle, Segal would formally enlist in what was not very fondly called the "Stern Gang" and he would bring with him the several hundred members of his religious Brit Hashmonaim. Segal, Kremin, Nissim Cohen, Yaacov Meridor – stayed with Raziel. Heichman and Lubinsky went with Yair but soon renegotiated a brief return to the IZL before ultimately retiring from that organization, too. Zeroni, Kalay, Svorai and Eliav went with Yair.

Rafael Saban met with Zvi Meltser: "Zvi, I've come from the IZL Command in Jerusalem. You've been appointed Jerusalem district commander." An hour later, Yoshke arrived: "I've come from the Lehi Command, you've been appointed district commander for Lehi." Zvi thanked them and asked if they'd lost their minds. He declared Jerusalem neutral territory till all the organization's officers could meet and hopefully avoid a split. When the split was a done deal, Meltser called Jerusalem's officers together and announced, "I want to hand Jerusalem to the command of David Raziel. Whoever agrees, good. Whoever doesn't, I'm sorry." Shlomo Trachtman, Yoshke, Dviri and Yaacov Orenstein left for Lehi, most of the others stayed with Raziel. Meltser himself soon asked Raziel to relieve him of duties so he could care for his parents, newly arrived from Europe, and get married. Instead, Raziel offered him command of Haifa; Meltser chose to remain in Jerusalem. He remained IZL district commander for six months until a suitable replacement was found.

Zeroni and Kalay left Yair the next year after a three-day marathon meeting of Stern's Command in Tel Aviv. Zeroni: "I told Yair he'd make a grand political, but not technical, officer. You can compare it to a government and an army general staff. Yair would make a fine prime minister but not chief of staff...Either Hanoch or I should determine the operations." Zeroni spent three nights combing the Tel Aviv beaches with Segal in an attempt to reunite Stern's IZL with the original IZL. Segal took their memorandum of agreement to be approved by Operations Officer Meridor, who quashed it, leaving Zeroni and Kalay with no place to go but the police, to whom they surrendered. The Birionim U. Z. Greenberg and Yevin put their literary influence at Yair's disposal, and Stern remained in contact with Ahimeir as well.

By the autumn of 1940 Stern had his own organization but it was running on empty. The time had arrived for the Underground to withdraw some hard currency from its account at the friendly neighborhood bank, but, of course, it had no such account, and so the method of relieving the Anglo-Palestine Bank of its reserves became a bit more complex. Zeroni, it will be remembered, entertained a fetish for expropriations from public institutions and in this case the repository was British to boot. "I know the manager of the Ben Yehuda branch," he reasoned, "he's not the type to make trouble, at least not when looking down a gun barrel. He'll do as he's told." Zeroni cased the bank and crafted for the occasion unique masks: weighted pieces of cloth, rolled under caps, which automatically unravelled when the cap was raised. Yoshke Eliav came from Jerusalem to join in and touched up the plan by restationing the getaway car in a side alley. Also participating were Abraham Amper and Zelig Jack, two relatively new arrivals who would soon become Yair's personal bodyguards.

One sunny September day, shortly after noon and immediately

before closing time, Amper and Jack tossed some smoke bombs from a nearby roof. Pedestrians and motorists, fearing an air raid was in progress, scurried into the nearest bomb shelters. One woman fainted. With the street to themselves the foursome nonchalantly entered the northern Tel Aviv bank, raising their hats in deferential greeting and their pistols in tandem. Yoshke leapt the countertop, confiscated the moolah, swirled while simultaneously disarming a bank official's gun and fled with his fellow clients. Zeroni had conceived a parting memento, a newspaper-wrapped package to be left dangling from the doorknob. The clerks and officials were sternly warned not to follow in feckless pursuit, for the bomb would explode if moved. The prudent victims sat patiently for half an hour, till the police opened the package and defused a...shoebrush.

But warning shots fired outside by one of the trigger-happy novices nonetheless set off the chase, and the quartet sped away with upright citizens in hot pursuit. Several roundabout blocks away, the money was transferred to a waiting motorcycle and delivered to the Underground's coffers. But, alas: "They didn't change the plates!" lamented Zeroni. "That's how [one of them] was caught!...I wasn't dealing with such details. I had to give an order to change the numbers?! I had to give an order like that?"

The getaway car's driver in police custody was young and ingenuous and inexperienced in the ways of interrogation. At first he swore to the police he would not incriminate his comrades or speak a word that might cast suspicion on a member of the bank-robbing cabal. The British surprised him by giving him a name – Stern's. According to the CID interrogator's report, the man went pale. The police had their confirmation. The path was slippery and the driver had soon confirmed the involvement of several more Underground members. Eventually, good soul that he was, he offered to let the police know if ever they arrested anyone *not* involved, so as to facilitate the release of the innocent from captivity. But, he insisted, he would not positively identify anyone who was involved. All evidence points to the prisoner's being honestly self-deluded, convinced till the end that he was protecting his friends. Despite their list of names, all of which they had gathered on their own even before questioning the driver, the British managed to arrest, try and convict only one member of the gang: the driver of the motorcycle, Joshua Zetler, who was apprehended five months later.

Notwithstanding a 15-year sentence for this poor-man's Dillinger, the overall score was heartening: the heist netted almost forty-five hundred pounds.

Shortly thereafter, the wherewithal was put to use. The third issue of the Underground paper *Bamachteret* included this item in its monthly news summary: "The immigrants of the ship *Atlantic* were deported from Eretz Israel. The British police were armed with clubs and sticks and they did not spare women, children or the elderly. The immigrants were pushed naked and bleeding onto boats, amidst shouting by the many former inmates of Buchenwald and Dachau among the deportees...On the nineteenth of Kislev at 11:00 P.M. three explosions rocked the Immigration Department in Tel Aviv on Allenby Street...many documents, passports, etc. were burned in the offices. British officials are of the opinion that much damage was done, both in material terms and to the lost documentation. This action occurred about a week after the deportation of the *Atlantic* immigrants."

Stern's boys may not have been as adept at knocking off banks as Dillinger, but then how many British installations did John Dillinger blow up?

The British tightened the screws on Raziel. The police tried threatening, cajoling and even seducing Raziel into informing on Stern and the Irgunists who had broken away with him, or at least publicly censuring them. Roderick Musgrave used political, practical and moral arguments to force Raziel's hand. He spoke of a commonality of interests and also of a moral obligation on the part of the Irgun, and he intimated the consequences of Raziel's not turning over his former comrades. In a typed report marked "Secret" submitted by Musgrave to CID chief Giles on October 19, 1940, Musgrave recounts an interview with Raziel of the day before, held in the Arab restaurant, The National:

"I spoke of the recent activities of the Irgun, and pointed out that some of these activities were undoubtedly attributable to the Stern group, which was also said to have attempted to establish contact with the Italians. How true this latter point was I could not tell, but suffice it to say that [the British] Government held that the continued existence of this group was not in its interests, and we were anxious to trace Stern and certain of his followers. The Revisionist Party had proclaimed its intention of cooperating with Government during the war and had been treated on this understanding to the benefit of everyone concerned. In wartime there were no half-measures and if the Party and the Irgun were on our side then they were morally obliged to regard our adversaries as theirs (as indeed in this case they were), whatever their race or religion. Although we considered the Stern group as working against our interests, the Party had not openly denounced them as traitors to the Revisionist movement. The Party leaders should realize that Government must regard them as responsible for the activities of the Revisionists of Palestine, and that the successful cooperation which had hitherto obtained between the Government and the Party must necessarily suffer if activities such as those attributed to the Stern group were permitted to continue. Apart from the wartime moral obligation, therefore, it was in the best interests of the Party and the Irgun to assist us."

Musgrave's appeals and warnings were to no avail, at least at first. Raziel may have been hurt, angry and organizationally threatened by Stern but he was a man of honor. He told Musgrave he agreed the Sternists were "working against both Party and Government interests," and he well knew he and the Revisionists had promised to help the British during the war, but he "regretted he could not help us to find

Stern...he would not be able to assist the authorities in tracing the members." Raziel told Musgrave he "could not denounce a member or ex-member of the Irgun."

Musgrave gave it one more stab and said that given the circumstances, "a Britisher would not hesitate to denounce a fellow countryman." Raziel replied that were the government Revisionist, he would do so as well. "But," said Raziel, "this is not our government, it is yours."

Raziel may have been fighting for the British, and Stern, against; but they were both fighting for the same goal.

And yet, before parting, Raziel told Musgrave he agreed the party and the Irgun should label the Sternists traitors. Apparently, Raziel said he would try to talk to party leaders about issuing such a statement. Raziel may have been worn down by his interlocutor's arguments, or he may have been genuinely convinced of their correctness; perhaps he was trying to give Musgrave something to work with, to justify their relationship, or perhaps he was toying with him, leading him on, deceiving him. The British sought the Revisionist condemnation because it would, as Musgrave told Giles, "help us to obtain greater assistance from the Jewish police and public in tracing these men."

Raziel also confided in Musgrave that he had heard a rumor that the Hagana's Eliahu Golomb was planning to kidnap Stern and sequester him in some remote place until things cooled off. With the British, the Hagana and the Irgun now arrayed against him, either actively or passively, Stern's solitude was increasing. So was his influence.

"Under Yair's orders we rose to initiate the greatest revolution in our nation's life since we were exiled from our land – to 'forever wrest the homeland from foreign hands,' and to 'renew the Hebrew mastery over the redeemed land,'" wrote Eldad in a clandestine pamphlet published by the Underground in 1944. "After two thousand years of Exile, Yair again ignited the flaming desire for freedom."

Yair Stern – the ideologue, the educator, the poet, who attached so much importance to personally meeting his troops, to explaining to each the meaning of their goals, to stirring the apathetic masses – was not the author of the catchphrases into which he breathed life. The Brit Habirionim had disseminated stencils heralding the "Kingdom of Israel," Segal's Hashmonaim were imbued with a sense of mastery and fever for the Kingdom of Israel and of God. Stern transformed barely legible stencils into rousing anthems, molded raw individuals into armed cells, strung cells together into marching armies, set the agenda for the revolution. Yair put huge blocks of his time underground in the course of several months into the Principles of Rebirth. Some of these principles, as they were published in the second issue of *Bamachteret*:

> **The Nation** – The Nation of Israel is the chosen nation; creator of monotheism; legislator of the prophetic morality; bearer of age-old civilization; great in tradition and in sacrifice, in the will to live and the ability to suffer, in the light of its spirit and in certitude of redemption.
>
> **The Homeland** – The Homeland is Eretz Israel in its Biblical boundaries ('To your seed have I given this land from the River of Egypt to the great river, the River Euphrates,' Genesis 15:18), it is the land of life in which the entire Hebrew nation will live securely.
>
> **The Nation and the Homeland** – Israel conquered Eretz Israel by the sword. In it, Israel became a nation and only in it will she be reborn. Therefore Israel and only Israel has right of ownership to Eretz Isracl. This right is absolute: It has not been and cannot be abrogated.
>
> **Foreigners** – Solving the problem of foreigners through population exchanges.
>
> **Ingathering of the Exiles** – Complete ingathering of the exiles in the Kingdom of Israel.

210

And finally:

The Temple – Building the Temple as a symbol of the course of complete redemption.

Eldad attempted to analyze Yair's influence: "A huge difference in approach separated Yair from even the best of those who opposed him: They admitted fighting was necessary in order to be free, he said fighting was necessary because we are free." The masses, Eldad felt, were not yet speaking Yair's language, were not yet prepared for his message.

Within Yair's personal radius he met with various reactions. Stern was honest enough to print respondents' reservations in *Bamachteret*, as well as his attempt to address their critiques.

Yitzhak Shamir, who later headed the Sternist movement, said Yair's 18 Principles of Rebirth "were not the Torah Divinely revealed at Mount Sinai," he identified with them in general, but not directly with every word. Others did view them as something akin to Biblical texts; Israel Eldad, for instance, who was to share power in the Underground with Shamir and Nathan Yellin-Mor, arrived in Eretz Israel early in 1941. Abraham Amper met him at the port as he met many of the Betarim and Irgunists safely arriving from the European turmoil. Amper was Yair's "missionary" fishing for men's souls, winning converts to the Underground. Eldad's soul needed no saving, he was at Stern's service. Amper scheduled the meeting.

They met in a dimly lit corner of Rothschild Boulevard in Tel Aviv. They talked politics, reviewed articles destined for publication, strolled streets which grew meaner with every Underground operation; they wore their caps ever lower as the populace wallowed in ever growing animosity towards this gang of bombers, bank robbers and self-proclaimed revolutionaries. Yair read his Principles aloud to Eldad and asked the latter to prepare a commentary. Eldad filled 46 pages of a black-covered notebook with his inimitable script. He wrote as he spoke, without stopping for breath. Pages and pages without a word crossed out. Only once on page 24, and again at the close, did Eldad ink out more than two or three words in a row. His version of the Hebrew letter "heh" commences not in the upper sphere but at the line itself, as if an "h" were lying on its side because the penman did not have time to raise his pen after completion of the previous letter. Eldad spoke like this till his seventies, as if he were the first car in a roller coaster pulling his listeners along at breakneck speed the entire course of an hour-and-a-half lecture. At speech's end he did not need to rest but his audience was often gasping for air. "For better or worse," he once confided to an avid reader of his biweekly newspaper columns in the 1990s, "I never edit my writing, what appears in the paper is just what gushed forth."

"The Chosen People – " the commentary begins, "Know that you are son to the ancient Hebrew race and be proud. Let your look penetrate the depths of the generations, seek and penetrate till you reach the root of your race. And you shall stand amazed and in holy awe of that great and wonderful person...our father Abraham...for you he formed a blood alliance with his God and on your shoulders, the shoulders of Isaac his son, he loaded the bundle of wood for the fire which will burn for generations on Mt. Moriah. And you shall raise proudly to your shoulders the burden of your destiny...

"Legislator of prophetic morality – The prophets did not create an abstract philosophic system, or the laws of racing atoms in a material universe. They recognized the laws of life ruling over these two...Flesh and blood – with the spirit of God dwelling therein: This is the prophetic law of life. The rule of will over momentary desires, the rule of the spirit over atoms, the rule of God over idols, the responsibility of the nation for its individuals, the destiny of Israel at the center of the world: This is the law of prophetic morality, the Hebrew nation establishing the law of the living God in the world, Mt. Zion as the center of the fire of life..."

Yair took the notebook, studied it and politely told Eldad that he would have "written it differently." Less effusively, less fire, less pathos; more logic, analysis, practicality. The original notebook remained in Eldad's possession. His commentary to the Principles of Rebirth has never been published.

While a harried but driven Stern furtively laid the casements for the Underground, his former commander and time-tested friend Raziel took his own beliefs to their limits. Accompanied by three Irgunists,

Dr. Israel Eldad (Beit Yair photo)

including 1937's Western Wall shofar blower Sicka Aharoni, and determined not to combat the British occupiers of Eretz Israel à la Stern, but rather to aid them in the world's struggle with Germany, Raziel left to personally participate in the sabotage of oil reserves in Nazi-allied Baghdad. Aharoni says the morning they left Tel Aviv, Raziel hinted at another reason for the trip: "He told me, 'We are going on a mission to the border to strike at one of Israel's greatest enemies.' It was obvious he meant the Mufti," Hitler's ally, organizer of pogroms in Eretz Israel. Aharoni was surprised to see Raziel recite the Wayfarer's Prayer as they boarded their plane, but soon discovered Raziel had also taken his tallit, tefillin and a copy of the Mishna to study. On May 20, 1941, the German Luftwaffe strafed an airport in Iraq, unknowingly killing the en route Raziel.

Conflicting accounts record Stern's reaction to the death of the Commander in Chief of the rival Irgun, whose views and path he castigated in print and on the airwaves. More than one person claims to have delivered the bitter news. But whether Stern wept or went pale, all agree he was visibly shaken. Nathan Yellin-Mor claims that when he told Stern, Yair opened a small prayer book, turned to face Jerusalem and recited the memorial Kaddish for his one-time soul mate.

But there was more than prayer and propaganda to running an underground. Once again, mammon was as necessary for the renegades as oxygen, and the hour was ripe for engineering another bank job. The target this time was the National Arab Bank of Jerusalem, the time: the witching hour. The band of desperados donned British army garb and Arab police uniforms, and for good measure, two "plainclothesmen" trailed along. They rapped on the door of the slumbering bank manager's home, waved imposing-though-forged search warrants under his nose, and drove the drowsy fellow to open his own bank for the thieves. The foraging inside was superficial and it was not long before the "detectives" got to their real business. The still weary banker, however, meekly protested that he could not open the safe as was being demanded of him. He had, it was true, the key...but two keys were required. The Sternists split up, two of them setting off to desperately seek the bank's accountant, holder of the second key. Unfortunately, the real police reached the scene before they returned. The trapped Sternists chose to fight their way out. Bullets flew as they tore out of the bank and fled to freedom, all except for one, for whom the role became the actor and who played it to the hilt, prolonging the masquerade in his British officer's jacket, engaging in natural conversation with the real McCoys. This Sternist received no Oscar for his performance; he did, however, receive five years in the calaboose.

Robbing banks, of course, was merely a sideline, not the linchpin of the affairs of the Fighters for the Freedom of Israel (FFI). Their trade was forcing the British out of their country by any available means, and the *modus operandi* was more often than not violent. The gang much preferred professional hits, and most of those present probably felt relieved, at one summertime Command meeting, when the agenda included the elimination of British Minister of State Lyttelton, then based in Cairo. Yoshke, perpetually trigger-happy in an amiable, innocent, childlike sort of way, if that can be imagined, suggested adding to the hit list some local Jews whose activity was deemed unhealthy for the organization. Out of the question, ruled Yair, there are more than enough people to rub out in the British Criminal Investigation Department. Another candidate was nominated for execution whom Yair also vetoed: He was Australian while the priority was British.

Also at the top of the agenda was the Mizra Detention Camp. Some forty of Stern's charges were under lock and key north of Acco in tin-roofed wooden barracks mutually separated by barbed wire. Every day fewer and fewer were free for activity. The dearth of soldiers was perhaps the only crisis surpassing the lack of funds. Stern hung great hopes on his imprisoned fellows: Mizra, Mizra, Mizra, he would repeat. Moshe Svorai had already escaped from the camp, against orders but impatient to return to action. Now Yair and his officers began readying escape routes and safe houses to absorb a dozen runaways.

Assassination, breakouts and break-ins were the order of the day. Yet never did Yair let go of his main vocation: teaching the Jews of Eretz Israel to be free. He had not only to physically free the land, he had to free people's minds.

Eliezer Sirkis' specialty was radio broadcasting. No towering antenna

215

for him though, and no station for reporting to work in the morning. Sirkis' office was in his battered suitcase. The Sternists suggested that a particular FFI member might like to make himself scarce at such and such an hour, then appropriated the absentee's apartment. Sirkis sometimes preferred neighboring apartments, asking for right of way "to hook up your neighbor's radio antenna." "We put it up shortly before the broadcast. We knew we connected when the vicinity's light bulbs, charged with our current, lit up. We knew we had the right frequency when we heard tens of radios in the neighborhood emitting our transmission." The speakers fled immediately following the show, and Sirkis returned a few days later for the antenna. The emcees tried never to do more than two shows from one site, to limit the chances of detection.

Imagine, in those days before television, men and women, young and old, families and individuals, workers and unemployed, all sitting attentively by their radio receivers on a Saturday night, placidly enjoying musical entertainment or anxiously awaiting wartime news. Static, noise, fine-tuning, the dial is adjusted. The cackling radio hisses a bit, barely audible voices come and go, then at once the reception is clear, the radio in your living room echoes the radios in every apartment on your block, the bass voice drifts into the street through the open windows of Tel Aviv's hot season:

> *The Voice of Fighting Zion, the Voice of Free Zion! The Radio of the Irgun Zvai Leumi B'Israel!*
>
> *As for the "holy enthusiasm" to do every thing possible to aid England...this cannot be until the British government ceases its war against Zionism and allies itself with the Hebrew nation to fight together till victory, the meaning of which is: Farewell to the British Empire; Hebrew rule in Eretz Israel...*
>
> *The Voice of Fighting Zion! The Voice of Free Zion! The Radio of the Irgun Zvai Leumi B'Israel!*

*It is three years since the day Shlomo Ben Yosef ascended
the gallows, may God avenge his blood. Not in the heat of
battle is death approached. With others in battle, he was alone
on the gallows. One of many, one of the anonymous soldiers,
sacrificing for the Messianic ideal not only their youth but
also their mothers, families, all they own: For they know there
is no way other than force.*

And there is no sacrifice other than blood sacrifice.

And the price of freedom is life.

And the victory of the nation is the loss of the individual.

May his memory be blessed!

The Underground's utilities included, in addition to this communications network, a first-class postal service. All letters, naturally,
were hand delivered by mailmen who could be seen on the street even
less than the usually inconspicuous employees of a standard government Post Department. Service was, however, astonishingly speedy
and dependable. Neither rain nor sleet nor overconscientious censors
could stop a contact from delivering the coded messages; only, perhaps, sudden arrest or death at the hand of a suspicious lawman. Yair
maintained an unbroken line of communication even with Mizra
Camp. The correspondence, mostly ink and paper, also included an
occasional pistol to be used in future escape attempts.

The boys inside learned of the arrests and defections outside, of
those who tired of the struggle and dropped out, of those who feared
for their lives and turned themselves in, of those who disagreed with
this or that policy or scheme of Yair's and left him for other paths.
Yair sent the Mizra residents copies of the broadcasts, accounts of the
operations and honest reports of the not altogether cheery situation
underground, especially after Zeroni and Kalay broke with the FFI. In
Mizra they knew that Yair was under tremendous pressure, that he

217

had no pillow to call his own, that the British were hunting him and the Jews condemning him. Perhaps they did not know just how bad things were: Yair, too, wandered the streets suitcase in hand, though his baggage was no transmitter, but rather a makeshift cot. One night he slept in a public bomb shelter, one night in a stairwell. As the police dragnet spread and even Jewish antagonism grew, as his face began appearing on wall posters and in newspapers, Yair had fewer sanctuaries, fewer hours during which he could wander Rothschild Boulevard and Yehuda Halevy Street in soft conversation, and no one who was willing to shelter him for the night. To encourage their beleaguered commander, the men in Mizra dispatched a special Hanuka holiday gift late in 1941: an olive-wood *Hanukia* lamp, with the traditional eight candle holes, one for each night of the holiday commemorating the Jewish victory over ancient Greece.

The home- or prison-made *Hanukia* was, in Svorai's words, the "boys' reply to events outside." They told Yair they would stand by his ideas and would do and give anything to get back to their outside posts. And they attached a one-line note to the lamp: "To our days' Hasmonean, from his soldiers in captivity." As Svorai tells it, Yair's face literally glowed as he held the lamp and the note. He responded personally by letter, telling his students and soldiers what Hanuka meant and means, paraphrasing the holiday prayers in noting how few they were and how many the enemies, yet conscience and necessity dictate: War, war to the end! Their note had struck a raw nerve and Yair, moved, went so far as to hint at the plans being drawn for their mass escape.

A broadside had recently been plastered onto the billboards of Tel Aviv, proclaiming that "In these days when restraint has become tradition, surrender – regularity...With faith, without doubt, with continued readiness for sacrifice, the IZL B'Israel will open an unrestrained war to free Israel and free Jerusalem." Now, to mark Hanuka, the newest wall poster announced that "the torches of Hebrew victory will yet be carried in the hills of Judah and Jerusalem, on Mt. Tabor, the Carmel and Mt. Hermon. Then shall we surely merit the establishment (*Hanukat*) of the Hebrew Kingdom in the land of the Hasmoneans and the establishment (*Hanukat Habayit*) of the Temple on the Temple Mount."

As a man, the trappings of underworld activity aside, Yair exuded warmth, gave fellow conversationalists the feeling he considered them of consummate importance. He regularly launched dialogues destined to soon enough tackle matters of international intrigue with questions the like of "How is – ? Does he really have enough money? What can we do for his little child?" One such Underground family Yair often fretted over was Svorai's, for former Birion and Irgunist Moshe and his wife Tova, a former Betaria, had a little girl, Herut (Freedom).

Tova Svorai recalls the night she discerned that sound for which she pined every night, that furtive scratching at the door of her rooftop apartment (really little more than a converted laundry room, plopped down in the center of a roof in the Florentine section of south Tel Aviv), which signaled the safe return of FFI operative Moshe. The hush was broken at midnight, and Tova ran – or she would have had the small flat allowed for sprinting, but more accurately she skipped somewhat lightheartedly – towards the door, certain that at least for the next few hours she would have Moshe for herself. Tonight Moshe appeared out of the shadows but not alone. Moshe left his guest in the hall and gently pulled Tova aside.

"Tova, I've brought Yair. We were propagandizing for the Underground and he's got no place to sleep, he roams the streets at night with a collapsible cot in a suitcase." Tova responded instinctively: "Our house is his house and the house of any Underground member who needs one." Moshe improvised a pillow-on-wooden-box bed for Yair, royal luxury in comparison with his latest lairs. At first Moshe disassembled Yair's bunk in the mornings, the box sliding under the couch, the pillows on top of it, but Yair's acute predicament rapidly became

Tova Svorai, 1940s

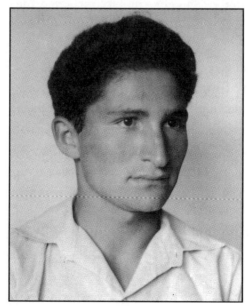

Moshe Svorai, Brit Habironim period

obvious – there was no other place to go. The British were omnipresent, and, worse, the Jewish community – still enthralled with the British – felt no love for Stern's zealots and was searching everywhere for the band of hated revolutionaries on the run. After breakfast Tova would excuse herself to a back room, leaving Moshe and Yair to work at the hallway table on their newspaper, broadcasts and darker plans. My family life, my privacy, she thought to herself, all pale in insignificance compared to the plans and operations: "Faced with Yair's burning vision, all my little dreams are meaningless." Still, to vary the often melancholic routine, Tova surprised Moshe one night by wearing her wedding dress. She had decided to celebrate their third anniversary with the most lavish and wasteful party the Underground could afford. That night Yair, Moshe and Tova did indeed enjoy hot dogs, french fries and beer, and as a sad sign of the hard times, they honestly felt they had eaten lasciviously.

Saturday night: The radios whine, sputter and one by one tune in to the crisp words:

The Voice of Fighting Zion! The Voice of Free Zion!

Hebrew youth! Do you desire the nation's redemption? Do you desire the homeland's conquest? Are you prepared to give your life for the establishment of the Hebrew Kingdom? Join the war, enlist in the Underground army of Fighting Zion, whose flag will one day fly above the walls of a Free Jerusalem.

The radio of the Irgun Zvai Leumi B'Israel broadcasts every Saturday night after the holy Sabbath, at 40-50 on the shortwave dial.

* * *

But now the maelstrom of events was taking its own course, and crisis after crisis would engulf the already reeling organization. The final few months of 1941 and the first few months of 1942 seemed to pass in slow motion. History was not keeping pace with the frantic activity of Yair's mind. It was as if the voice track were running in fast forward towards freedom while the film plodded on towards doom. Yair was describing events and initiating actions that would occur only years later, but he knew only too well that the hour promised little more than disappointment, death and suffering.

One clear January morning two Sternists held up a bank clerk on Ahad Haam Street in Tel Aviv. An incensed crowd, most likely unaware that this was an "official" appropriation, gave chase. Joshua Becker fired high to ward off his pursuers, found temporary refuge in a cellar, shot his way out when a British sergeant discovered him and, as he ran, returned the gunfire which aimed to fill his back full of holes. Becker and his teammate were both apprehended, which in itself was a powerful blow to the short-staffed Lehi. Worse, however, was that two innocent Jews had been killed by wild bullets during the chase.

That night Yair, accompanied by Jack and Amper, his two loyal and heavily armed bodyguards, engaged lawyer Max Seligman to represent the two men who might well be charged with murder.

True, no one knew for sure whose shots had killed the bystanders, Becker's or those of the police. Even if one supposed that circumstances had collided to make Lehi responsible for the two deaths – and Yair time and again harangued his men to take all precautions, to always avoid assaulting anybody but the British forces – still, one could hope that at some future point the Jews would, if not abet underground activity, at least remain neutral and get out of its way. Yet no explanation in this case could have brought Yair peace of mind. Yair was shaken by the killings, no matter who was directly responsible. He overcame his remorse only because he had to continue. But the Tel Aviv citizenry increased the rabidity of its hatred. They hounded the fighters and lay in wait to uncover fugitives and inform on them. The eyes of Tel Aviv were hungry for revenge. The pack was ready at any time to mercilessly fall upon one of the "Stern Gang." Every corner had to be approached with caution and every tree with care, lest some flashlight be shone in one's face by an enraged civilian doing the work of the British police. Lehi old-timers refer to this period as the "lantern nights."

Saturday night. The mission is larger than they are. They must continue, rise and ride again. People must understand, they must be told the truth, they must hear the message so they may one day adopt it as their own.

The Voice of Fighting Zion! The Voice of Free Zion! The Radio of the Irgun Zvai Leumi B'Israel!

The Irgun Zvai Leumi B'Israel is a covenant of freedom fighters whose purpose is fulfillment of the national destiny: (a) Redemption of the land, (b) Establishment of the Kingdom, (c) Rebirth of the nation.

...The body of the nation will free itself from the Diaspora through a complete ingathering of the exiles in Eretz Israel. We deny the Emancipation. We forego the war for equal rights in the Diaspora and leave it to the various types of assimilationists...

The Fighters for the Freedom of Israel fight not for the civil rights of Jews in the Diaspora but for the political rights of the Hebrew nation in Eretz Israel...

Can a Jew in Eretz Israel be a cabinet minister? No! Can a Jew in Eretz Israel be a member of the government? No! Can he be a mayor in a city with a mixed population? No! Can a Jew be a high-ranking officer of the police? No! Can a Jew be, in peacetime, a soldier in the army? No, no! No and no!

The Voice of Fighting Zion! The Voice of Free Zion! The Radio of the Irgun Zvai Leumi B'Israel!

On Wednesday, January 21, 1942, the dailies splashed the news across their front pages: "A Terrifying Crime in Tel Aviv," and within a frame of black mourning, subheadings: "Major Shlomo Schiff is killed in bomb explosion. 2 Jewish officers wounded, and 1 British and 2 Jewish policemen. A mass funeral for the victim; strong condemnation of the gang of thieves lacking any national conscience." Actually, the paper had gone to press early. Killed along with Schiff were Officer Nahum Goldman, a Jew, and Turton, the British hangman of Shlomo Ben Yosef.

The next Lehi bulletin recalled the elimination of Cairns and listed the crimes for which Goldman and Schiff were shot, "and we again warn informers and mercenaries of the foreign regime that if they do not desist nothing will save them from our wrath."

But truth truly is subjective. The two explosions on the roof of 8 Yael Street were quite meticulously prepared by Yoshke Eliav. The first and minor detonation was designed to draw to the scene the Underground's arch-enemies Morton and Wilkins, the second bomb was designed to remove them from the scene. Joshua Cohen, in his teens already one of Lehi's most fearless combatants, lay on a nearby roof, one steady hand on an electric detonator, his motionless eye on the street below. Should the infamous duo avoid their rooftop demise, Joshua was the insurance man who would ensure that a third booby-trap would give them a big send-off downstairs. Tragically, with the luck which was the Underground's lot that fatal winter, Schiff and Goldman checked into 8 Yael first. Schiff was blown away at the portal, Goldman done in by shrapnel. Morton and Wilkins lost no time, but by the time they arrived they were lost in the crowd. Joshua remembered Yair's admonitions not to injure innocent Jews, lifted his hand, picked up his feet and hightailed it out of there. Yoshke, who had invested so much nocturnal ingenuity in the ambush, never, if truth be told, forgave him.

Yitzhak Shamir learned of the events on Yael Street inside Jaffa

Prison. "I was shocked...before my arrest we had discussed the 8 Yael plan and decided against it, for Morton and Wilkins' appearance was no certainty...The less experienced members, who took the place of those who were arrested with me, decided we had been too cautious." Shamir must have experienced déjà vu. A few weeks earlier, already in detention in Jaffa, he had seen Becker being brought in. That operation, too, had been nixed by Shamir, who deemed it too prone to failure.

Yair's cup of misery ran over. He had achieved the sinister reputation of a master criminal and a fifth columnist. The British saw him as a menace to society, the Jewish Agency called him a dangerous beast, Tel Aviv looked upon him as being outside the pale of understanding and mercy. Any minute he and his fighters expected bullets in the back. They knew by now that joy was not to be theirs on this side of the grave. Paranoia seeped into every crack, they began to suspect even former friends of treachery.

Once, the scratching at the door surprised Tova; the night was young, ten o'clock was early, her nervous anxiety was usually more protracted. When she opened the door, Moshe practically fell in, breathless. "Has Yair arrived?" he managed to cough. He and Yair had kept a scheduled meeting in some dark alley. An auto stopped, an Englishman demanded their identification papers, they beat their separate paths out of there. Lead pellets buzzed about them as they fled. No sooner had Moshe regained his composure than the scratching was heard again. Tova opened the door for Yair who immediately quizzed her: "Has Moshe arrived?" The next morning Abraham Amper scratched, coming at Roni's behest. She had heard the shots a few blocks from her intended rendezvous with her husband and needed some assurance that Yair was still alive.

The wanted posters were not sufficient. The police ran ads in all the newspapers. The price on Yair's head was one thousand pounds, a small fortune in those days.

Shamir was soon transferred to Mizra. Menachem Lewin was also interned there and the two of them became the camp's garbage collectors. At the end of each day they wheeled out their cart full of garbage and dumped it on the nearby beach, being rewarded for their labor with half an hour's swim. Shamir received a letter from Yair: The ex-

Palestine Post, January 27, 1942

perienced fighters, known to the police, are being arrested or killed. The new commanders are, naturally, less wizened. The cordon is tightening. You cannot sit "securely" in prison. You must do everything to break out, rejoin us. As soon as possible.

Palestine Post, February 3, 1942

The Voice of Fighting Zion! The Voice of Free Zion! The Radio of the Irgun Zvai Leumi B'Israel!

Neither the kindness of other people nor the world's conscience will grant us the homeland. Hebrew weapons will conquer her from the hands of foreigners, to be for us an eternal inheritance...

The path of conquest is the path of strength, the path of the national revolution, the path of the Hebrew revolt! The Fighters for the Freedom of Israel! They, who have lived days and years underground. They, who risk their lives for the sanctification of God's name and for the homeland. They, sitting in prisons and concentration camps in the homeland...

Hebrew nation! Remember these sons of yours! Hebrew youth! Look for the path to enlist in the ranks of the underground Irgun Zvai Leumi B'Israel.

Go to war for your great and persecuted people, be one of the anonymous soldiers.

Long live the Hebrew rifle! Long live Hebrew freedom! Long live the Irgun Zvai Leumi B'Israel.

The Voice of Fighting Zion! The Voice of Free Zion! The Radio of the Irgun Zvai Leumi B'Israel!

The Saturday-night broadcasts were nearing the season's end, radio receivers would soon be mute, the voice of Fighting Zion was about to be stilled.

The tabloids reported that on January 27, four members of the Abraham Stern Gang were uncovered during a search at 30 Dizengoff Street. Two were wounded in the ensuing gunplay.

Tuesday, January 27, 4:00 P.M. Thirty Dizengoff Street, third floor, a rear apartment rented by Zelig Jack. The Command had only recently met here, Yair putting the finishing touches on the plan to rub out Lyttelton. Now the apartment was but a classroom, but what a classroom: Svorai, Yoshke, Jack and Amper were giving or receiving PDQ instruction in explosives and demolitions in a quixotic attempt to inculcate the fresher commanders with the basic education necessary to any worth-his-salt revolutionary.

The four: A week earlier Jack had had no time to lose. He, Shamir and other prisoners were on their way by rail to Mizra. It was a chance in a million, but betting all on one split second in the course of a train change at Lydda, Jack darted swiftly into the orchards. He slipped shadow-like through the ring of police scanning the fields and flitted past British and Jewish hunters to make his way to Tel Aviv; Amper, a refugee from German-occupied Poland, had precariously dodged the Germans, Poles, and Soviet police to sign up with the Fighters for Israel; the day's lesson over, Svorai was prone in bed relaxing, immersed in *The Memoirs of a Social Revolutionary*. Jack, in the next bed, laid his book down when Amper, sitting aside Svorai's bed, began to regale the rapt listeners with tales of his escape from the many plagues of Europe; Yoshke, a few moments before 4:00, excused himself to the adjacent lavatory. Svorai and Jack heard the door open and paid no attention, assuming that Yoshke was returning. Some incomprehensible question about a "Mr. Schiff" was asked, no one knew exactly who had spoken, nor what the question was, but those inside again assumed it was Yoshke. Morton flung open the door, gun drawn, yelping "Hands up!" to the off-guard fighters, with two detectives not yet inside flailing guns to Morton's rear and Wilkins on their heels. The surprised boys quickly stood and raised their arms high. Morton waved off his team with his left hand and with his right pumped three shots into Amper's stomach. As Abraham was falling, Morton took aim at Svorai, putting slugs into his left shoulder and right thigh. Jack was then shot twice in the stomach. Jack and Amper fell limply to Svorai's bed; Svorai had been knocked to the floor. Morton walked calmly over to Svorai, only his eyes revealing the churning hatred stirring within, and sent another bullet towards his forehead. A slight jerk of Moshe's head preceded the shot, which therefore slammed into his jaw.

Morton's cohorts now entered to claim their share of the entertainment. They spit into the bloodstained faces of their victims, flipped them over, kicked one, dragged another around the room, cursed to their hearts' content. Unbridled laughter resonated from the windows of 30 Dizengoff. Wilkins took two grenades and a pistol from one of his accomplices and snuck them into one of the hanging coats, where they could be conveniently found during a search for incriminating evidence. Morton meanwhile loaded a second cartridge and shot five holes in the bathroom door. Nimble Yoshke, however, had as soon as he had heard the first gunplay jumped through the third-floor bathroom window and, grasping the vines which hugged the water pipe, begun his descent. Innumerable guns blazed from below and the lead shower which followed left Yoshke's derrière in pretty poor condition. No sooner had he fallen to the earth than he was dragged out back and out of sight. The beating ceased only when he finally managed to ask: "English gentlemen, are you not ashamed to beat a wounded man?"

Two and a half hours later Magen David Adom was at last allowed to administer first aid. The four were soon after tossed like so much damaged merchandise into a police van and taken to Jaffa Hospital. Amper and Jack held on for four excruciating days, drifting in and out of consciousness as Svorai and Eliav watched their friends dying. "You'll be joining us, too," one of those about to die said good-naturedly, "and you'll be most welcome provided you bring us the encouraging news that it continues here, the fighting for freedom..."

"Maybe a day will come," gasped the other, "when the Jewish population will know we were its soldiers, not just Yair's soldiers, not just the organization's but the anonymous, ever loyal soldiers of the nation." On February 1, the fifteenth day of the Hebrew month of Shevat, in the early afternoon hours, Jack died. An hour later Amper followed.

Moshe Svorai and Yaacov Eliav recovered and in April were sentenced by a British military court in Jerusalem to life imprisonment.

Hisia Shapiro was Yair's contact, making early morning visits to the Svorai apartment in south Tel Aviv. At first she had delivered not only Underground messages to Yair but also groceries to Tova. As the hatred, pressure and searches outside mounted she arrived earlier, skipped the minimarket chores, slipped in, waited for Yair to answer his "mail" and slipped out.

From the moment she had first met Yair (she had been assigned to be a "contact" but had not been told for whom) she had been mesmerized by his high, wise forehead, his serious, placid eyes. Being in a room with him meant being riveted to him. His appearance and demeanor, she thought, could only be indications of supreme inner strength, tinged with an inner calm. Once, in response to some superficial point in a conversation, Yair seemed to signal no with an almost imperceptible movement of his head. The speaker repeated his statement, claiming that Yair's nod was no more than a meaningless movement. "I don't make meaningless movements," interjected Yair.

Hisia allowed herself, once, to express to Stern her anxiety over his perilous safety. Who could ever take his place, she tried, desperately pleading for him to reduce the hazards which regularly put his life in jeopardy. "Do not talk like that," he testily answered in what Hisia says was possibly the single instance in which he actually appeared angry. "If I die others from the ranks will take my place and continue the war. If I die, Mizra will continue."

The dawn of February 12, 1942, was exceptionally still. A slight morning mist still hung over Tel Aviv as Hisia stole through the empty streets. Tova and Yair simultaneously heard the scratched signal. Who could it be? Jack and Amper were dead. Moshe lay wounded in Jaffa.

Hisia had stopped coming. Yair nodded his approval and Tova opened the door. Hisia entered, explaining that she brought mail which could not wait. Hisia joined Tova in bed in a lame attempt to warm up in the freezing rooftop apartment. Yair had had a sleepless night, he had been writing till 4 A.M. When Yair seemed to be absorbed in the mail, Hisia whispered the latest depressing news to Tova: who had been arrested, what rumors were circulating outside...The word "arrested" was powerful medicine and though spoken in a hush immediately stirred Yair. He insisted on being given the news. The ranks, again, were thinning, the air was poisoned. One rumor had it that Yair had already fled and was comfortably abroad.

Yair sat at the hall table to handle his correspondence. Hisia's urgent message was a Jewish offer of a safe haven if he would agree to an early retirement. Yair thanked his correspondent but refused the offer: "I am not one of those who of their own accord turn themselves in to the police," he wrote. If the incident on Dizengoff Street has opened their eyes and revealed to them the regime's true face, Yair continued, he was prepared to entertain their suggestions for operations against the government.

At 7:30, Yair bade Hisia farewell. "Send all our friends my heartfelt greetings, from abroad!" he smiled as she left.

Tova laid out breakfast as Yair ambled around the apartment. When he thought he spotted two willowy figures on the roof outside, he pressed against a wall. Tova's eyes silently asked for an explanation; Yair indicated the presence of people on the roof who could see through the open slats of the shutters. Tova thought to herself that it was early for the landlord to be hanging laundry outside, but as inconspicuously as possible she extended an arm, opened the inside window, lowered the slats of the shutters, and resealed the window.

She and Yair shared their breakfast of bread and margarine, bread and soft cheese and bread and jam.

Not a scratch, but a light tap at the door. Yair hid in a closet on the assumption the landlord was dropping by and would soon leave. Tova opened the door. Wilkins and company entered. "Why don't you visit your injured husband," he baited her. "I've come to get some fresh clothes for him."

Tova left the intruders in the hallway and brought Wilkins some of Moshe's clothes. Wilkins mocked Tova with seemingly innocuous small talk, harassed her with comments about how Moshe's foolish war had left her and their little girl to the Fates, yelled at her that "You are killers, thieves, all of you, all of Stern's people! You will all face a bitter end, just like Amper and Jack. We will cart you all off to the Nahalat Itzhak cemetery!"

Tova had up to this point retained her composure and silence. She could no longer do so. "Wilkins," she said, "pay attention and listen. I will yet see you all fleeing our country."

The detectives brought in two neighbors to witness and attest to the propriety of the search. Yair's hat was in plain sight; perhaps the police thought it belonged to Moshe. Wilkins scanned the papers on the table at which Yair had been writing; perhaps he did not recognize the handwriting. A tall, heavy-set detective opened the closet door, his hand poked inside, searched pockets, squeezed garments and unavoidably encountered Stern. Yair was pulled out; the detective reached for his gun; Tova jumped in front of Yair: "You'll have to shoot me first!" she warned. Wilkins ordered Stern seated on the couch; Yair sat in the corner nearest the door. The detective who had discovered him sat opposite the couch; with one of his large hands he held Yair's two hands, with the other he held a gun under Yair's nose. Another detective, standing at the door right next to the couch, held a second pistol pointed at Yair's head, at a distance of about six inches. Yair asked Tova for his shoes, which she brought him despite Wilkins' snort that she would now take orders only from the police. About a quarter of an hour passed and two more plainclothesmen arrived, bringing handcuffs for the prisoner. The two neighbors were shown the wanted pictures of Stern from the newspapers but they had difficulty matching the man on the couch with the hoodlum in the photo, for the British had added stubble to the pictured chin to improve upon the criminal image they wished to create. The two women were shown the door. The room filled with detectives. Finally Morton arrived.

Tova was taken downstairs, pushed into a waiting car. Wilkins, too, conveniently left the scene. Yair was lifted to his feet. Morton later claimed that Yair was shot attempting to escape through the window. But with two guns pointed at his head, and both the window and the shutters closed tight by Tova, this was patently absurd.

Three shots were fired. On the street below, Wilkins looked up. Passersby on the street, morning shoppers, local residents, young Bela Kleinspies walking her son to kindergarten, heard Tova cry: "They're murdering Stern! They're murdering Stern!"

Three shots. Three times Morton's gun recoiled smoking. Three times. And with these three frenzied flashes of insanity, Yair died.

His bleeding corpse was wrapped in a blanket and rolled down the stairs.

★ ★ ★

"Darkness is not evil," writes Israel Eldad, not if plans are made within its folds, not if the seeds of life are sown within its cover, not if ammunition for a just war is forged in its hours.

The nights of February 1942 were simply dark. The days, too. Following Yair's murder more officers were arrested or willingly surrendered. The core of the Underground was being whittled down to nothing, and a deep depression was settling over those left.

The day Yair was killed, the air was so full of fear, the police and establishment pressure so heavy, and the ranks of Yair's followers so thinned, that no one printed broadsides to inform the public of what had really happened. The only ones left who believed in Yair's path, who were both alive and free, and who had the courage to risk being

FRIDAY, FEBRUARY 13, 1942   THE

From Dan to Beersheba

TODAY'S POST BAG

TWO NEW FACTORIES will come into being in Jerusalem as result of yesterday's reconsideration by District Town Planning Commission, with Mr. E. Keith Roach in chair, of previous rejection (January 15) of applications to erect diamond-polishing - and wax-matches plants in Givath Shaul and Beit Vegan west of Jerusalem. Permission was granted as factories will be valuable to war ffort, but time-limit was se "for" the duration only".

* * *

FRIENDLY RIVALRY between Australia and India evoked warm cheers in military hospital "somewhere in Palestine" this week: nine Indian officers in tug of war pulled nine Aussie officers over line. Occasion: revenge by Indians for previous week's defeat "BEST WAY TO DEMONSTRATE for recruiting to join the Army yourselves," said Magistrate in Tel Aviv, Dr. Chessin, admonishing four youths before him yesterday for holding unauthorized demonstration, obstructing policeman in course of duty. They were fined LP 2 each or fortnight's jail, bound over in LP 25 each for the duration. All four chose jail to payment.

* * *

TRYING TO EXTORT MONEY from a hotel-keeper in Tel Aviv by posing as a detective, and offering to settle an alleged "offence" for bribe of LP 10, two 17-year old lads, Simon Berkman and Isaac Levitan, fell into police trap. Hotel-keeper sent letter to Poste Restante inv ng writer to come to her o r settlement: detective arrested lad who collected letter. Both were committed for trial yesterday by Magistrate, Dr. Chessin. Late Inspector Goldman organized trap... FOUR GRAMMES OF HASHISH cost Rajeh Hussein Natur (35), of Haifa, six months' imprisonment when he came before Chief Magistrate, Mr. S.W. Weldon, yesterday.

* * *

SPONTANEOUS COMBUSTION OF STORED COTTON WASTE caused fire in Zevah Oriental Paint Industry Ltd. at Kfar Ata (in Haifa Bay area), destroying paint, raw materials, tin worth several hundred of pounds on Wednesday night. Factory itself was undamaged. Hadar Hacarmel Volunteer fire brigade did yeoman work, fighting blaze for three hours until 1 o'clock yesterday morning. Production schedule uninterrupted, factory will resume work on Sunday.... CHILDREN'S CLUBS supported by Working Mothers Organization of Tel Aviv, cat-ering for 750 children every

LEADER OF STERN GANG SHOT DEAD

CLIMAX OF ANTI-GANGSTER DRIVE

TEL AVIV, Thursday. — The notorious gang leader, Abraham Stern, was captured during a raid in Florentin Quarter near the Tel-Aviv-Jaffa border and was shot dead shortly afterwards when he made a bid for freedom.

The wife of Moshe Svorai, another alleged gangster wounded and captured recently, was found in the room with Stern. A reward of LP 1,000 had been offered by the police on January 29 for information leading to Stern's apprehension.

Following clues collected in the investigation of the murder of D.S.P. Schiff and Inspectors Goldman and Turton as well as the subsequent raid on an alleged Stern gang arsenal in Rehov Dizengoff, police threw a cordon around a building at 8 Rehov Mizrahi B, and entered a room on the roof.

Only Mrs. Svorai was found in the room at first but a search revealed Stern hiding in a wardrobe, and he surrendered without a struggle. Continuing their search, police allegedly found documents showing that the Stern gang had planned further illegal acts.

Stern suddenly made a break and attempted to get away through the window, but was shot. He died in a Health Department ambulance on his way to hospital.

Police later found fragments of an identity card made out to one Abraham Hermoni. The address was given as 19 Rehov Sirkin, where Stern's mother and brother live, and his occupation was stated as "teacher." The card bore the signature of a District Officer and the seal of the Tel Aviv District Offices. It was undated and did not bear the signature of the holder.

University Graduate

Stern was born in 1907 at Svulaki (Poland) and spoke Hebrew, Russian and Polish. A graduate of the Herzlia College of Tel Aviv, and of the Hebrew University in Jerusalem he had also attended a university in Italy. He was described as a brilliant student. He leaves a widow, who is a music teacher at Ramat Hashavim village.

Stern had no previous convictions but had been detained for some time in connection with the murder of Police Inspectors Cairns and Barker in a land-mine outrage at Jerusalem.

The room in Rehov Mizrahi B had been rented on December 29 by a bearded man who had given his name as Moshe Bloch, a lorry driver and said

WORLD MUST BE ALL-FREE OR ALL-SLAVE

DR. MAGNES AT LINCOLN MEETING

"God Save the King" and "The Star-Spangled Banner," national anthems of the two great Democracies now linked in the great struggle for human liberty, opened a special observance of Abraham Lincoln's birthday held at the Y.M.C.A. 'n Jerusalem yesterday evening. A large audience included many Americans, Government officials including the Chief Secretary, Mr. J.S. Macpherson, church dignitaries and other notables.

Mr. Lowell C. Pinkerton, U.S. Consul-General in Jerusalem, w in the chair. Dr. J.L. Magnes, President of the Hebrew University, was introduced by the High Commissioner, and delivered the principal address. "The very nature of our cause has made our paths converge," declared Mr. Pinkerton, in speaking briefly of America's and England's common war. The High Commissioner then introduced Dr. Magnes, saying inter alia:

Dr. Magnes has been in Palestine some 17 years, has been President of a world-famous University, of which he was previously the Chancellor, for six years and more, and is not only a great Jew, rightly proud of his race and its achievements, but is a very distinguished scholar and man of affairs...

He would agree with all of us that, if mankind is to be saved, the forces of evil embodied in Hitlerism must first be defeated and extirpated by the forces of the spirit wielded by the free races of mankind. The High Commissioner then described his esteem for Dr. Magnes, concluding:

I also value above rubies the friendship of those I respect, and is as a friend that I like me to think of Dr. Magnes, though on this occasion I have the honour formally to 'introduce' him to you in a far more distinguished role.

Frontiersman to President

Tracing Lincoln's early life as the son of a frontiersman in America, Dr. Magnes mentioned Lincoln's own quotation of a line in Gray's "Elegy" with which he describe his youth. "The short and ple annals of the poor." The speaker used many quotations from Lincoln's speeches to illustrate his character and principles, citing passages from his letters, too, to portray him. Quoting the passage:

I believe this Government cannot endure permanently half-slave and half-free, I do not expect the Union to be dissolved, nor do I expect the Government to fall, but I do expect it to cease to be divided, Dr. Magnes continued, "Can a world exist half-slave and half-free? Must it not become all

DE DR

HO

HA "Stick da Tur ber 6 himself muzzle Dr. 48 year professi turn to can do doubted of mind This d Street jumped manded 16 Pevs Palestin story: "I wa from J Hacarm Bar Glo 'on the Hacarm Avenue, had left up to ob switched and star "After heard a hear the waited proache the sma steering in Europ woollen with on posed m he cried tural Hi self look a gun.

"I wo do and would be repeated leaned t to knock but hit causing h and stun the stree "I sla bent ove and step shots ra ness. To inch fro passed th The seco of the s hole. All took a f straight mel Poli ported th and I re of the cr cartridges live roun ably fale the man "It so cash had in and would ha in any ca

TAXI DE

caught with "Sternist" literature, were a small group of Segal's Hashmonaim. Segal and Medan wrote a poster headlined "Murder!" Haim Kubersky, Shimon Barmatz, Barmatz's future wife Aliza and three other teenage Hasmoneans hung copies all over the country. Their fear was so great they did without the usual bucket boy who carried paste for the walls. Rather than chance being seen with a bucket, they pre-glued the posters and quickly pressed them to the walls of the cities.

Two weeks later the *Struma* sank, hundreds of would-be immigrants drowned because the British would not let them into their own country. Murmurs of understanding were heard in Tel Aviv. Stern's name was mentioned with a measure of sympathy for the first time. But the Underground itself was by then a shell of an organization.

Eldad, heir to Yair's propaganda machine, makes the acquaintance of a small group of pseudo-hermits hiding in the orchards outside of the main cities. Joshua Cohen, not yet twenty, tall and with a bushy black beard, is, according to Eldad, the first he meets who radiates strength. "He claims no authority. His character is his authority." A born partisan, Eldad calls him. His picture is on the walls, he needs direction, but "his eyes are Bren guns."

The thin, brown-eyed, thick-haired Cohen had met Yair but once. In the course of a group meeting each had asked the other one question. Joshua, decrying the scarcity of operations, had stated more than asked: "You mean to tell me you expect us to go back and tell our people that for such and such a reason, we are going to remain silent?" Yair responded in his calm authoritative manner: "That is exactly what you will say." Cohen's fury was transposed into admiration for this man who knew what he wanted and demanded it without even attempting to pander to the whims of others. From then on for Cohen, Stern embodied authority. And Yair's question? Yair asked every person there that night if he or she had a place to sleep. Joshua replied in the affirmative. After the meeting he found a park bench on Rothschild

Joshua Cohen (Beit Yair photo)

Boulevard and fell asleep, not having wanted to deplete Yair's coffers or take any more of Yair's time to deal with the comparatively paltry matters of his own lack of bed and board.

The legend spreads. A lone wolf, the sole remnant of the Stern Gang. One man who does not know what it means to despair. One audacious teen living off fruits and berries, waiting for some mystical magnet to draw the limping cubs of the Fighters for the Freedom of Israel to his lair. And they come. Slowly, one by one. A thousand pounds are offered for Cohen's head, but he roams the fields and when necessary descends upon the city. Joshua Cohen initiates an Underground tradition: He is at all times armed. A pistol is tucked between his shirt and pants. Every member of the Stern Group will from then on be armed. No one will be arrested without first shooting to kill.

Eldad finds Cohen in the orchards. So does one of the first men

237

who, hypnotized by Yair's explicit wish, compels himself to personally execute the command to escape from Mizra. He hides in a bedding and blanket storeroom, rips a whole in a fence, and trots to an idling getaway car. Joshua Cohen's contact, girlfriend and future wife Neha hands the fugitive a new set of clothes and takes him to a forest outside Ranana. There, Joshua Cohen, who had kept the organization alive in its days of total darkness, hands command of Stern's Underground to Yitzhak Shamir.

NEW YORK TIMES, MONDAY, MAY 4, 1942.

PALESTINE DISSIDENTS WAGE WAR ON POLICE

Abortive Land-Mine Outrages Laid to 'Stern Gang' Survivors

Wireless to THE NEW YORK TIMES.

JERUSALEM, May 3—Three recent abortive land-mine outrages have drawn attention again to the activities of the irreconcilable political terrorist group known here as the "Stern Gang," after their leader, Abraham Stern, who was shot two months ago in a police raid on his hideout on the fringe of the city of Tel Aviv.

These attempts were directed against the Inspector General of the Palestine Police, Alan Saunders, and the assistant inspector general, Michael McConnell, neither of whom was hurt, though Inspector McConnell's Arab servant was killed when he picked up a bomb hidden in a garage. That happened in Jerusalem a fortnight ago.

This week-end a land mine exploded just as the car driven by Assistant Police Superintendent Geoffrey Morton passed a spot near his house outside Tel Aviv. The mine, hidden in a roadside ditch and detonated by a man hidding in a grove, damaged the car badly though it did not injure the occupants, Mr. Morton, his wife and two British constables.

Mr. Morton, as head of the detective force of the Tel Aviv area, was responsible for breaking up the Stern Gang.

The Stern group, of whom there are a number of survivors despite the recent arrests of leading members, is actually a terrorist, if appears to have sworn vengeance against the Palestine police force. The Palestine government is conducting a vigorous man hunt for the capture of the remaining members of this dangerous group.

New York Times, May 4, 1942

Chapter 8
The Hebrew Revolution

We fight, therefore we are.   **Menahem Begin**

Five years after that morbid February of 1942, in the heyday of its violent war against the British, the Lehi noted in a tract written for young adults: "Abraham Stern, may God avenge him, was murdered, but Yair lives on in our blood and in our war. And he is more and more alive, strong, pure and true."

Shamir was first out but far from last. Dviri had long before been legally released and had, in fact, been preparing a Jerusalem hideaway for Yair even as the British were gunning him down in Tel Aviv. Dviri and "Grandpa" Judah Leb Schneerson, a survivor of the crimson Hebron massacres of 1929, might have appeared to be poring over the worn pages of thick Talmudic volumes in the Tifereth Israel Synagogue, but rather than debating the wisdom of the sages, they were debating the wisdom of this or that safe house. The disputation resolved itself on Dviri's rented flat in Nahalat Zion. Yair was due to move in on February 13. One day too late.

Dviri's next mission was more sanguinary. After Yair's death, pistol in hand, he tracked the British High Commissioner. He was under Joshua Cohen's orders to do away with the Englishman then ruling Eretz Israel. Dviri and the revolver were there, but as he put it, the Commissioner "failed to keep the appointment we set for him."

Which Way Out—
SURRENDER AND DEATH or RESISTANCE AND FREEDOM?

Do you honor the DEAD fighters who fell in the Warsaw and Vilna Ghettos of yesterday?
Let us also honor the LIVING fighters in the Ghetto of Palestine today.
What happened then in the Warsaw and Vilna Ghettos is happening in our homeland today.

What happened in the Warsaw and Vilna Ghettos?

On the one hand, there were the "official" elders, despairing, so paralyzed by fear they dared not raise a finger against the enemy. Betraying ancient Israel's sacred law of "Vouch ye one for another," they fed korbonnes, sacrifices, to the Nazi monster, five today, ten to-morrow, a hundred, a thousand the day after to-morrow, as the Nazi high priests ordained — and all in the interests of Israel, as they thought, to save Israel!

AND THERE WERE ALSO THE YOUNG, THE BRAVE AND FEARLESS, FIGHTING ISRAEL, WHO WOULD NOT LIE DOWN AND WAIT THEIR TURN FOR SACRIFICIAL EXTERMINATION, AS ONE MAN THEY ROSE AND STRUCK BACK. THEY FOUGHT, IF NOT TO SAVE A PRESENT THAT WAS LOST, THEN A FUTURE THAT COULD STILL BE SAVED.

They were condemned by the "official" elders as traitors and murderers of their own people; ordered to be ferreted out and exposed. "The blood of innocent victims is on their hands," the 'Judenrats' of Warsaw and Vilna proclaimed. "By their wanton acts of violence they have placed in mortal jeopardy the whole life of the Ghetto."

Where did these and similar "official" counsels of our "wise" and "reasonable" elders get the Jews in Europe? What was the result of Jewish non-resistance in Europe? Do we have to be told? Gas chambers and incinerators for all — except those who fled to the woods and fought.

What happened in the Warsaw and Vilna Ghettos is happening in Jerusalem today.

There are our "respected," "responsible," "official" leaders who counsel patience, forbearance, moderation, non-resistance. Like their fellow elders of the Warsaw and Vilna Ghettos, they would plead, reason, deal with the enemy. They would lighten the Jewish burden, which alas! is already heavy enough, they say.

AND THERE ARE ALSO THE STALWART, FAR-SEEING, SELF-LESS YOUNG MEN FOR WHOM THERE IS NO DEALING WITH AN ENEMY BENT ON ISRAEL'S DESTRUCTION, WHOSE ANSWER IS ACTION, ACTION, AND MORE ACTION.

What has been the result of "official" Jewish policy in Palestine? Destruction of all civil liberties, slow economic strangulation, impending dismemberment of our Homeland limb by limb.

WHILE YOU HONOR THE FALLEN HEROES OF THE WARSAW AND VILNA GHETTOS, REMEMBER THE DEAD AND LIVING HEROES OF THE PALESTINE RESISTANCE WHO FOUGHT AND FIGHT TO THROW OPEN THE GATES OF ERETZ ISRAEL TO OUR HOMELESS BRETHREN, WHO FOUGHT AND FIGHT TO ERASE THE GHETTO FROM THE FACE OF THE EARTH.

Help them carry on the fight!
Learn the lesson of history before it is too late. There are only two ways out:

SURRENDER AND DEATH or RESISTANCE AND FREEDOM
Fighters for Freedom of Israel (Stern Group)

Distributed by
AMERICAN FRIENDS OF FIGHTERS FOR FREEDOM OF ISRAEL, Inc.
227 West 46th Street, New York 19, N. Y. — Circle 8-4680, Ex. 18
Duly authorized to collect funds for the Palestine Resistance Movement.

Document published by U.S. supporters of the Stern Group

Shamir called for Dviri and sent him to scout for potential civilian sympathizers. Dviri returned to Shamir with the news that he had finagled a contribution which according to the donor's instructions could only be used to cover the cost of a true-to-life printing press. One newspaper reader had obviously strained his eyes on the substandard stencils long enough, and the Underground now had the first press worthy of that name.

Segal resumed his Brit Hashmonaim and underground labors. Arrested again and detained without trial in Latrun, he led regular Talmud lessons there. The Talmud is a stream-of-consciousness compendium of discussions of every aspect of every Jewish law, its subjects ranging from two oxen which collide to two people claiming ownership of the same prayer shawl, from what time to recite prayers in the morning to what is the meaning of life. Meltser, also under detention, remembers, "No matter what the subject, Segal always managed to bring it to the conclusion: 'You have to fight for Eretz Israel.'" Meltser organized the cleaning of the camp's kitchen before Passover and convinced the commandant to supply plenty of kosher-for-Passover meat and wine for a seder. Segal, with a little help from Meltser and Grandpa Schneerson, led that year's Passover seder just before Segal was again released. Meltser heard that the first thing Segal did "outside" was go to the British authorities and demand Meltser's release, taking upon himself responsibility for the latter's good behavior, a dubious and dangerous proposition at best; but Meltser was indeed freed.

Segal then answered Shamir's call and reported to an old wreck of a building in Pardess Katz. It provided well-disguised cover for the seat of the Lehi Central Committee. "I read the Hashmonaim paper," recalls Shamir, "and was familiar with their ideology. I knew it was important to meet, and described our movement as Segal listened." Shamir wanted Segal on his team but made no bones about wanting more. He asked Segal to bring over the entire Hasmonean movement en masse. "Moshe Segal replied: 'You are right. Your path is right. I am with you.' The result was we opened a branch of Lehi in Jerusalem."

241

Segal was appointed the FFI's representative there. Shamir eventually assigned him a deputy. "That turned out to be Joshua Cohen," Segal was able to laugh when he recalled the story. "The first time we met, Cohen began talking freely, nonchalantly." Segal interrupted: "That's how you talk!? Stand at attention!" The baffled Cohen did, but for the rest of his life never forgot the incident. Cohen never before and never again stood at attention for any man.

Segal and Shamir continued to meet. Once in a while Shamir, his beard dyed red for the occasion, would drop by Segal's home; at other times they would meet in a Rehavia synagogue with Gemara-laden *shtendas*.

Nathan Yellin-Mor was the third rampart, along with Eldad and Shamir, of the Sternist triarchy. He dug himself out of Latrun and resumed his responsibilities. On Christmas Eve 1943, Yoshke Eliav ingeniously talked his way out of the Jerusalem Central Prison. First he convinced the warden to exploit his electrical prowess in the service of what was to be the best-lit Christmas tree in the city. The warden's shack was just beyond the prison fence, but the warden was game. Eliav and Moshe Bar-Giora went assiduously to work under the suspicious eyes of a rifle-wielding Arab guard. The eyes grew less hostile as time passed and nothing untoward occurred, until both Eliav and Bar-Giora assumed a stymied, woebegone air. The empathizing guard adopted their worries as his own; if the tree was not completed he, too, might be blamed – or so he reasoned with a little intellectual help from Eliav. Yoshke told him all was ready, except that he and Bar-Giora had to complete the circuits outside. Who would hold the electric wire in position on the ceiling? Yoshke beamed with a possible solution: The watchman could use his rifle to attach the wire to the ceiling. Yoshke's parting words were not to move, for the slightest movement would bring with it electrocution. Eliav and Bar-Giora, plug in hand, walked out of the wooden cabin and just kept walking till they were out of the Russian Compound. They split up then, with Eliav finding temporary refuge in Segal's house as the Underground worked to schedule transportation to safer quarters outside Jerusalem.

Eliav's partner Svorai was also destined to escape, but his chance would materialize only years later. He joined 11 others from both the Irgun and the Lehi who tunneled their way out of JCP cell 23 into a nearby sewer. Svorai's first hiding place was in the home of Shlomo Goronchick, who would one day shorten his family name to Goren and add the title Chief Rabbi of Israel.

Ironically Segal, even after his release, continued to spend time in the Jerusalem prison he so wished to leave. "He came on the Sabbath to pray with us," Kotik recalls admiringly. "And every three months, like clockwork, he would visit me, for I was eligible for one visit every three months." Kotik was at one point notified by the authorities that he, too, was to be freed, though the exact date was not supplied. Back in cell 18 Zetler, Becker, Svorai, Levstein (Eliav) and Altman threw Kotik a party, but the next day he was still there. So that night they partied again. "The happiness was so immense they kept making me parties; it got so I had to ask them to stop, the release obviously wasn't finalized yet."

Kotik, 50 years after the joy and the pain, the impatience and the celebrations, reaches for a pile of envelopes atop a shaky cabinet in a one-room apartment facing the sea. Out from one envelope comes an autograph book. This book is filled with the sometimes warm, sometimes humorous inscriptions not of classmates but of cellmates:

"You've seen and had your fill of many evils within the walls of this accursed building," wrote Svorai on February 5, 1943. "The refinement you've undergone in this torturous furnace will give you the strength to endure and overcome the trials and suffering for which our people does not lack."

Nitchko, Hisia Shapiro's husband, wrote: "I would like to bestow upon you a title of honor, comrade in the movement and training and aliya and times of hunger for bread, whose head is hoary with suffering, and all this before the age of 25. And at 25 the 'law' put Death

before you, a crown of payment for your deeds...You are worthy of the highest description any of us can merit: Idealist."

One Saturday a disbelieving Kotik heard his name called with the delightful addition of the word "free": "Jacob Kotik *fraj.*" Kotik instinctively refused to go, determined not to sign the release forms on the holy Sabbath. "If you don't leave now, who knows what will be tomorrow," he was told. Kotik had no civilian clothing, he could telephone no one on the Sabbath, and outside a light rain was falling steadily. With nowhere else to go, Kotik headed for Segal. On the way he met Pacho, the same Pacho who had snapped his own *fraj* at Dviri's suggestion when another prisoner of the same name had been ordered released. "Pacho accompanied me to the Segals, I got my clothes, washed up, and towards evening Segal and I made our first visit to Reb Arye Levin. We kissed, he had tears in his eyes from joy...he shared some wine with us. This was just before the afternoon Mincha prayers; Reb Arye stopped whomever we met on the way and begged them ecstatically to 'Share my happiness!'"

Soon enough Kotik and Shamir found each other, and Shamir at one point actually became Kotik's roommate at 14 Yarden Street. "Don't you think this is a bit dangerous?" Kotik once inquired of the FFI Commander. Shamir casuistically responded, "They'll never imagine that I'd live with a man once sentenced to death!"

While Kotik, Altman, Segal, Svorai, Dviri – these men whose suffering had been the bricks of the Hebrew Revolution, whose sweat had been its mortar, whose blood had given it life, these first individuals who went underground with no friend but their courage to accompany them – while they crawled to freedom under cover of the black of night or walked upright through swinging prison gates (gates which in many of their cases bore a closer resemblance to revolving doors, considering the number of times they were arrested in the years before and those to come), Shamir's induction efforts, Yellin-Mor's diplomatic and public-relations work and Eldad's inimitable ideological proselytizing were

Back from the gallows: Jacob Kotik (left) and Yehezkel Altman after their release from prison (Jabotinsky Institute photo)

meanwhile winning hundreds of adherents for the Underground. By 1943 Menahem Begin had made his way from Poland to Eretz Israel and by 1944 he was commanding the IZL in the combative spirit of his Underground predecessors. The Hebrew Revolution was in full swing with massive battles being waged by fighters who had not yet been born when Tehomi collected arms with Rosenberg or when Segal sounded his shofar at the Western Wall. By the mid-1940s several thousand sons and daughters of David were taking shots at the more than ninety thousand British Goliaths occupying their country. And their aim was just as deadly as the young shepherd whose slingshot slew the Biblical giant.

The IZL lads stood at the Jaffa Road entrance to the Russian Compound. Straight ahead lay the onion-domed church, but they were not penitents. Behind the church lay the prison, but they were not visitors. To the right lay the hospital, but they were not ill. Their eyes hungrily took in the multi-columned stone building on the left: Criminal Investigation Department (CID) headquarters. In one of the most heavily guarded compounds in the country, their sights were drawn on the torture chamber itself.

Uninvited guests often prefer side-door entrances and so did the attack force. Fifty years later, just behind a sidewalk hawker pushing cassettes, a steel door lies tucked into the corner of a Russian Compound building across the street from the former CID. The door is firmly and forever shut, but the British occupiers lacked the prescience to seal it way back in the spring of '44. One morning a curiously forlorn ladder appeared outside the door where it rested comfortably for several days. The ladder seemed forgotten but was not. Every day IZL scouts paid homage to their wooden colleague to ensure that it had acclimated to its new home. As the Passover holiday approached, the IZL delivery boys entered the building through its other portal on Jaffa Road and left one hundred kilograms of explosives under the stairway behind the steel door, all neatly packed into matzoh boxes. This is the sort of matzoh which will upset a lot of British stomachs, thought one of the messenger boys.

With everything in place, IZL teams set forth that night from behind Shoshana Aboulafia's apartment building off King George Street. They entered the Compound through the Jaffa Road door. Several men were detailed to dispose of the British guards stationed on the inside of the single possible entranceway to an area otherwise surrounded by barbed wire. Pleasantly surprised to discover no guards at that station, these men joined in the more important work. One team assumed positions outside the church to cover their comrades and harass any police leaving the CID building. As the ladder and explosives were being carried across the street to the CID, a British officer passed by, hand in hand with a young woman. Fortunately, she seemed to absorb more of his attention that the dozen or so fighters carting boxed bread of affliction to the nerve center of the secret police. "We watched his eyes watching his female companion and let him walk on obliviously," says one of the Irgunists. Several men scrambled up the ladder onto the porch and delivered the matzoh. The plans allowed for a 20-minute warning – enough time for the attack force to safely evacuate – but a shot from one alert guard somewhere became the signal for an all-out gun battle. Asher Binzamin shouted in flight that he was wounded and met with the general laughter of his buddies, one of whom retorted skeptically that perhaps Asher did not notice that he was successfully running a pretty fair distance at a jolly speed for someone supposedly shot up. But Asher was running on will power only; his leg and abdomen were shot through with British lead. He died later. Joseph Avni and others carried the cadaver to Mahane Yehuda and phoned the police. The immediate members of Asher's family were the only people present at the nighttime funeral of "Sergeant Avshalom," as he was known, the first casualty of the Irgun to follow Menahem Begin's formal proclamation of the Revolt against England in 1944.

In Jerusalem, the CID wing of the large building fell apart. One British officer was killed, several were wounded. One Irgunist was captured and sentenced to 12 years. That same night, the police headquarters in Jaffa and in Haifa joined their Jerusalem counterpart on the road to smithereens.

The British were down but not out, at least not yet, and they naturally rebuilt their investigatory headquarters, stately columns and all. Bad habits are hard to break, though, and that steel door in the corner building, with its inconspicuous Jaffa Road entrance to the otherwise heavily guarded compound...that door seemed so inviting the Underground could not resist. A year and a half after the Passover rumble, the IZL and Lehi put their heads together and devised a Christmas gift for their playmates in the CID. Joseph Avni returned to the scene of his earlier escapades and deposited a small amount of explosives near the CID door. The uninvited holiday guests poured in, each carrying as much of the holiday dinner's fare as possible, all of which was decoratively laid out inside. A punctual 20 seconds after the last charge was placed on the portico, the deed was accomplished, the building and porch only rubble. The famous pillars which, perhaps, had been waiting patiently and faithfully for the inevitable return of those whom they had served so well in springtime, once again obligingly disintegrated.

An Underground unit stationed on a porch of the Generali Building at the intersection of Jaffa and today's Shlomzion Roads had already poured oil on the road below and now set the street afire. This both kept innocent passersby away from the scene and hampered potential British pursuers. The team retreated from Levitsky's law offices – they had been granted safe passage, but to deflect suspicion from the friendly secretary who'd mapped out their route, they broke a door down to give the impression of a break-in – and sped off. The demolition group, supposedly under cover of the Underground guns above and the billowing fire below, nonetheless encountered determined British gunfire as they escaped. They realized they were relatively unspottable and therefore safe in the inferno; the enemy's shots, it turned out, were emanating from one or two enraged Englishmen who were unable to take aim or even see the Jewish fighters and were simply spraying the street with as many bullets as they could unload.

The evening's toll: Zvi Aharoni of the Lehi was killed, deputy commander of the operation Dov "Hablondini" Granek (known as "the blond Dov") was wounded and one Irgunist was arrested. Seven British officers were killed, fourteen wounded. At the same hour, the four-story Jaffa police building deigned to again collapse in a similar blast.

Curfew was imposed on Jerusalem, Tel Aviv and Ramat Gan. The British arrested twenty-four hundred Jews in Jerusalem alone, in a mostly vain attempt to track down the underground fighters.

The elaborately planned multi-teamed underground maneuvers

which so quickly and thoroughly broke the spirit of the British in Eretz Israel did not, however, eliminate instances of individual heroism. "Eliezer" found himself called upon to discover the hidden courage within, and in doing so, he gave new honor to the word courage.

Destruction of British Criminal Investigation Department (CID) headquarters in Jerusalem, a joint operation of the Irgun and Lehi, December 27, 1945 (Jabotinsky Institute photo)

At 8:00 A.M. on a Thursday morning the British surrounded the Galilean settlement of Yavniel and went straight to the home of young Menahem Luntz, known in Lehi circles as Eliezer. He saw them drawing near and knew the game was up. He had been tending an injured fighter who was still bedridden in the house. Eliezer walked inside at a leisurely pace and briefed his recuperating friend on the likely developments. They closeted themselves in a closed room off to the side. "Zion," born Shabtai Druker, quite weary and still bandaged, slid out of bed. He loaded his gun and readied a cluster of grenades.

The police pushed open the door and came under immediate fire.

249

Though Zion's grenades did not detonate the British backed out of range of the bullets. Eliezer now had a window of opportunity, a few brief seconds to leap, dash, or jump out of the window, perhaps, or another entrance. And leap Eliezer did – to Zion's side. The savant who said that every man dies alone did not know Eliezer.

British guns exchanged fire with the two desperate trapped Sternists. But when the smoke cleared and the British entered the ominously silent room they found that their bullets had not succeeded in felling the boys. After they had emptied their guns, Eliezer and Zion had saved their last bullets for themselves. At the time of his death Menahem Luntz was 20 years old.

"I wish to call attention to a headline in your paper," wrote a member of Menahem's family in a Letter to the Editor, "that was about 'two thugs.'" She asked the editor's permission to describe one of the two.

"A pure and naive young man, noble, merciful and gentle, modest and generous...Talented, well read and studious. Forged in the hardships of life on a Galilean settlement. Born and educated in Yavniel, he worked in its homes and fields, did guard duty and pioneer's work. His father – righteous, a religious member of Poalei Zion, invested 30 years' life and labor in the land of the Galilee. As did his mother. The boy, after completing his studies at the Teachers Seminary and despite his desire to enlist, felt obligated to choose the lonely path and take upon his shoulders the collapsing farm, and he was just 19. An idealist through and through...making do with the bare minimum...Open hearted, dedicated to his family, with golden hands, his spirit poured forth in flute playing, he was 100 percent Galilean innocence and courage."

With the IZL and FFI and occasionally the Hagana on an unmitigated rampage throughout most of the 1940s, the British government had its hands full trying to explain to the mothers of England why ninety thousand troops had to risk their lives in distant Eretz Israel. This was not the British homeland, it had never been a seat of British culture, no famous Englishman had ever been born here, no English work of art or literary masterpiece ever composed here. Whether the terrain was mountainous or level had no military, social or historical impact on, say, the people or city of London, which lay thousands of miles north. Sooner or later, the Underground reasoned, the British would be forced to admit defeat and retreat.

Meanwhile the British had already exiled 251 Jews to Africa. Several dozen more were flown out the next year. One IZL man, Eliahu Ezra, strolled too near a fence in Eritrea and was shot. Shaul Hagalili of the Lehi ran to apply some first aid and was himself gunned down. Both died.

A rough-and-tumble rally in Tel Aviv got the goat of some soldiers who shot up the nearest living-room windows, killing seven Jews and wounding more than fifty. Around the same time, a curfew was imposed on the northern regions of the country. The residents of several towns didn't take to the presence of the British armed forces in their homes and tried, nonviolently, to hamper their passage. The British, in turn, did not cotton to this noncooperation and killed nine, wounded over sixty and arrested more than three hundred.

The Underground pressed on.

The Irgunists waited impatiently in the safe house known as the "Edison Room." 9:00 A.M...10:00...11:00...11:30...The operation had been scheduled for 10:00. At noon, with the commanding officer still absent, Eliahu Levy took charge and ordered his troops out.

No one in the Edison Room knew then that the operation's official commander was a traitor. He had passed details of the action to the British before skipping town and country.

Two cabs left for Jerusalem's railroad station. One parked opposite the nearby gas station with first-aid accoutrements, just in case events took a turn for the worse. The second vehicle inched up to the station's doorway, made a U-turn and came to a stop facing the city center. As a well-dressed couple emerged from the cab, two of the many Arab porters loitering about the station's steps approached. These two

"Arab" porters were, however, every bit as Irgunist as the spiffy couple. Joseph "Cushi" Levy took their bags inside and rested them ever so gently by a pillar supporting the station's roof. These suitcases were of the sort not usually selected by intrepid travelers. These were that rare brand which, when lifted, convulse in a roar of smoke and shrapnel. Left on their own the suitcases had a half-life of 30 minutes, after which they would in any case do away with the surrounding building.

Sima thoughtfully put a "DANGER – LAND MINE" sign on the luggage to protect the innocent. It was not this warning, however, which tripped up the Irgunists, but rather a jealous Arab porter angry that Cushi had stolen his "clients." This noxious doorman physically assaulted poor Sima who hit him, literally, below the belt. When the unbridled Arab commenced ripping at Sima's dress, Cushi could not really have done much else other than pull his gun and shoot the overenthusiastic shlepper in the forehead. Another shot or perhaps two were fired, and by then the British soldiers lying in ambush, alerted in advance by their man in the Irgun, understood that their moment had come: they opened obstreperous fire in all directions. The stalls emptied in a flash, peddlers and customers and would-be passengers fleeing in all directions. Sima dove into the open cab door, Cushi was right behind her. Azulai was hit in the leg but they were off. Soldiers posted along the tracks, on the hill opposite and on the station roof kept up heavy volleys of fire and an armored car turned in from Hebron Way and added its fire power. The Irgunists shattered their rear window and returned the bullets. Meir Feinstein, driving, yelled, "I'm hit!" and was ordered by a back-seat driver to "Drive! Just drive!" and he yelled, "I'm driving!" and he did. As they sped around the next corner the shooting ceased. Feinstein drove up a dirt alley towards Yemin Moshe. From there Cushi, still dressed as an Arab porter, walked calmly through Jaffa Gate. Marching Legionnaires, headed for the fray at the station, asked him if he knew what had happened, amicably suggested getting off the streets, and then moved on. Cushi thanked them and took the No. 3 bus to town. As he was changing his clothes he heard the railroad station erupt.

The only British casualty was the sapper working on the suitcase. The police followed a trail of blood from the abandoned cab and arrested Meir Feinstein whose left arm, broken by 19 bullets, had to be amputated. Azulai was caught and sentenced with Feinstein to death by hanging. Azulai's sentence was commuted to life. Meir was put on death row in the Jerusalem Central Prison.

On another occasion, another curfew was imposed up north. This time the entire settlement of Biria was carted off under arrest. Even that is relatively tame if one considers the day the army took over the Jewish Agency building in Jerusalem, killed five Jews elsewhere and relocated over sixty-two hundred Jews to detention camps.

In addition to imprisoning the Jews already living as citizens in the country, the British continued trying to keep other Jews out. The destruction of European Jewry impressed the British as little after it had occurred as it did while in progress. The British did all they could to catch Jewish refugees on the high seas or on the beaches, in order to send them anywhere but Eretz Israel. By 1946 the preferred destination was the concentration camps the British had established in Cyprus, which they promptly filled with the downtrodden Jews they caught.

One night, as several hundred refugees were attempting to land on the shores of Tel Aviv, the British attacked a Hagana position on the other side of town. An armored car full of soldiers chased 19-year-old Bracha Fuld. The car's spotlight put her in view: she was clearly an unarmed teenager. She was shot, tried to run from the bullets and was shot again and again. When the soldiers got out of their vehicle and picked her up, instead of taking her to a hospital they interrogated her till she died; she was either unwilling or unable to give them any information.

The *Hasmonean*, the bulletin of Brit Hashmonaim, put the matter in context:

"The arms that attached locks and bars to the gates of our country, in order to block the path of those returning to Zion – these arms

253

are stretched farther than ever...There is no limit to the evil, it spreads its net across the world, and now twelve hundred Jews who have been through the seventy-seven rungs of hell and the death camps and destruction have been caught, and there is no place on earth for them to rest their weary bones. The Empire's radio called this, with great fanfare, a tremendous victory...But there is another outstreched arm, the Divine arm, which has written on the wall of this Empire: *Mineh, mineh, tikel ufarsin* [Daniel 5:25: God has numbered your days and is bringing them to an end, you have been weighed and found wanting, your kingdom will be given to another]"

The daily newspaper *Ha'aretz* reported:

"A girl, just out of school, with life and service and work ahead of her, has sacrificed her life..." *Ha'aretz* recalled the Midrashic story of Isaac telling his father, Abraham, that if it were ordained for him to be sacrificed he was ready, "but I feel sorry for my mother..."

The Irgun broadcast the story of Bracha, whose father had committed suicide before the Germans had time to send him to a concentration camp: "Bracha Fuld has fallen in the line of duty. She fulfilled all her obligations. The enemy's bullets killed her body but made her spirit eternal, and our nation will cherish her memory among those of its pure and holy daughters who gave their lives in the war for redemption..."

The Lehi newspaper wrote:

"Blessed among daughters is Bracha. May her memory be blessed. Let her name be remembered for generations. Let her name and memory stir love and hate. Love for this land, our homeland, which absorbed her spirited blood, which received her fresh body. Love for our people, brotherly love. For these she put her life at risk, left a quiet and warm mother's home, went out to the field – to be, in the dark of night, a brick in the a wall of young bodies. Love of freedom, without which there is no meaning to life, and for which death or martyrdom can be holy. These were the loves of this 19-year-old young woman. These will be the loves of thousands and tens of thousands, who feel this land shaking in their veins. A holy and pure love, which cannot be replaced, which has no end. And hatred for the cruel, murdering oppressor. Bracha's last minutes will always stand before us...Whenever we remember her, waves of love and hate will roll over our hearts."

When the heat was really turned on, the British pulled out all the stops. At one point a car-bomb driven by an Arab, with three British soldiers inside ensuring safe passage through local checkpoints, parked in front of the *Post* newspaper building at 9 Havatzelet Street in Jerusalem and ripped through the paper's offices. Worse were the three British army vans, one police car escorting, which stopped one morning at the corner of Ben Yehuda and Ben Hillel Streets. Some one hundred innocent people lost their lives in that explosion. Such attacks were bloody, revolting and to a large extent pointless. The Jews of Eretz Israel in any case understood that the only way to stop the murder of innocents was to rid themselves of foreign rulers and provide for themselves.

An attempt to chronicle the underground war vs. the British would be a formidable task for even an experienced encyclopedist. A complete listing of the barest of the facts on all acts of sabotage, assault, assassination, appropriations, propaganda and assorted other forms of revolution would itself run dozens of pages. A thoughtful historian might suffice with a representative sampling of sorties, presenting the Lehi's actions of a few spring days chosen at random as a slice of the war waged in the 1940s:

The offices of the Haifa Shipping Agency (a British military agency handling the deportation of immigrants) were bombed, as was the military payments office in Haifa's Barclays Bank; the Tax Assessors Building in Haifa was blown up one afternoon and a machine-gun nest on its roof destroyed; that same night military vehicles and several army posts were attacked in Jerusalem; a command car was ambushed on the Haifa-Tel Aviv road one morning, two officers were killed and two wounded; the following night a barracks on Haifa's Allenby Street was attacked with grenades, three British soldiers were wounded in assaults in Jerusalem,

אני נפלתי בהגנה על העליה•
אמרו לי, כי על העליה ניתן את נפשנו•
אך הנה מגרשים מעפילים מחופי המולדת•••
ה י כ ן א ת ה ? ה י כ ן א ת ? •••
ברכה פולד

הוצאת הארגון הצבאי הלאומי בארץ-ישראל

שבט התש"ז

IZL broadside in memory of Bracha Fuld

the police and army compound in Sharona was machine-gunned and grenaded, guards were attacked in the Hatikva Quarter of Tel Aviv, and mines and booby traps took care of several armored vehicles in the area; the British Colonial Office in London was attacked; an automatic-weapons attack on Army Base 72 near Pardess Hanna killed 11 British soldiers and injured 18; a command car was ambushed near Ramat Gan; another car was hit outside Even Yehuda; another, the following day on the outskirts of Sharona; an army car was ambushed with grenades on the Tel Aviv-Jaffa road; seventy-five thousand lira worth of damage was done to the railway outside of Kalkilya when the tracks, locomotive and 17 wagons of oil were blown up; that evening, forty thousand lira in damages were inflicted on train and tracks near Bet Zefafa when an engine-car and six wagons were derailed and exploded; and the next day, another train was derailed just outside Be'er Yaacov.

One autumn day the young volunteers of the Stern Group pasted a notice on the walls and trees of Tel Aviv: "T. J. Wilkin (known as Wilkins), officer of the enemy's police force, hunter in the service of the Palestinian Gestapo, sworn enemy of all the Hebrew forces in the country and 'Jewish expert' of the secret police, was attacked and shot to death on Friday, the twelfth of Tishrei..." Wilkins' time had finally run out.

A cursory glance at the above list of almost two dozen acts of sabotage and mayhem perpetrated by the Lehi reveals not one directed at women, seniors riding buses, innocent people walking to work or children playing in schoolyards. The Lehi did not pretend to be fighting a war with kid gloves on. Innocent people were hurt. Two Jewish civilians were killed after the bombing of the Haifa Shipping Agency (when the British forced them to remove still undetonated explosives). But to specifically target women and children would have been unimaginable for any of the Hebrew forces.

The IZL under Menahem Begin's tutelage went even further in its attempts to wage a "clean" war. Warnings were more often than not phoned to buildings destined to be summarily demolished. Or, as in the railroad station, "Danger" signs were posted on mines to minimize any loss of life. An exception to this rule of thumb was made at the Goldschmidt House in Jerusalem.

Another cardinal rule was also broken at Goldschmidt. The attack occurred on a Sabbath. The IZL, respectful of Jewish tradition, almost never initiated operations on the day of rest. Yet after the *Arlosorov*'s refugees were deported and with the British readying gallows for captured Hebrew POWs, the Irgun leadership decided to hit the British. Hit by surprise, hit where it hurts and hit hard.

One might safely assume that Mr. Goldschmidt, when he designed the multistory structure on King George Street which to this day bears his name, never imagined that the office building/British Officers Club he raised would actually be a rubbly grave for 17 British soldiers.

The Officers Club was, at the height of the Underground's mobilization, one of the more well-guarded British haunts in Jerusalem. *Hit where it hurts*. Across the street was an army encampment, allowing the soldiers in the area to adopt an air of invincibility. *Hit by surprise*. This Saturday the club was jammed. *Hit hard*.

Earlier that week, twenty-five or thirty Irgunists had gathered in the Alliance School for Girls near Mahane Yehuda. Operations Commander Amihai Paglin drove in from Tel Aviv to personally brief the mission members. As he drew diagrams on a blackboard he informed the soldiers they had but three days to begin as well as complete all the necessary preparations.

Now they were ready. The Edison Room on Sukkat Shalom Street again served as starting point. One taxicab and one British vehicle, "borrowed" from Tel Aviv for the day, were waiting on Mesilat Yesharim Street near today's Morris Katz Gallery. Five men piled into the car and three into the cab which led the way. They drove slowly by the Officers Club but too many other vehicles blocked access. The eight tense men circled, made another pass and again aborted. On the third buzzing the way was clear. Dov Solomon gave the order to commence operations and enter. At the gate a British soldier asked for identification so they shot him. The assault team flew in, nestled the charge at the base of the columns supporting the structure and flew out. Move fast, they thought, keep moving. The timer was set for a mere 30 seconds. As they emerged into the street Cushi realized that when he'd picked up the explosives he'd let go of his pistol, which still lay where he'd placed it inside. Had it been crafted of solid gold a pistol would not have been worth more to an Irgunist than it already was. Cushi about-faced and announced he was going back in. His superior held on to him for dear life – Cushi's life, of course – and barely won the tug of war with the frantic, despondent Cushi.

The group ran via the Jeshurun Synagogue lot towards the Ratisbone Monastery complex. One or two scaled the fence; the force of the explosion a block away pushed them over the top. Behind Ratisbone they passed their ammunition and British uniforms to two waiting Irgunists who packed them in sacks and sunk them in a well, to be retrieved at some less-hectic date. The escaping unit fled through backyards and alleys to Ussishkin Street as Avshalom Haviv's unit continued to provide cover. "What a marvelous melody that firing was to us," says Solomon. Haviv's men pumped as many bullets as their guns would allow into the facades of the buildings adjacent to Goldschmidt. No one inside succeeded in so much as poking a head out.

One armored vehicle managed to get through the fire the Irgunists had set at the corner of Maalot Street to hinder would-be pursuers. Haviv shot the driver – impossibly enough through the eye slit of the armor. The car hit the nearest tree and overturned.

Seventeen British soldiers were killed that day in Jerusalem. Another thirty were wounded. The only Irgun casualty was a Bren-gun burn on Avshalom Haviv's hand. The United Nations responded to the gore and violence by advancing by five months its debate on Eretz Israel. The participants in the attack on Goldschmidt House are convinced that, following the course of events, this in turn advanced by five months the formation of the State of Israel.

To go astray in the morass of data is easy. This number of build-ings blown up, that number of police stations entered surreptitiously and relieved of all their guns, so many British wounded in one opera-tion and any number of Sternists or Irgunists captured in another. The heavily wooded forest of underground activity was, however, the sum of all its individual trees. Every operation was a premeditated endeavor rife with danger and bursting with the possibility of success or suc-cess' underground twin, death.

The British wading through the rubble of Jerusalem's Goldschmidt Building after the Irgun blew it up (Jabotinsky Institute photo)

The fighters who chewed their nails, paced nervously, or tried lamely to conceal the parade of butterflies in their stomachs before embarking on their missions bore no dog tags, flew no flag, wore no uniforms. For the most part they expected no more than a slab in a morgue if things went poorly, or perhaps a midnight funeral if a family member – who was often as not unaware that this "soldier" had even been "drafted," much less that he was participating at a particular hour in a specific assault – happened to merge in his mind the information that the lad had not returned home, with a radio report that an underground fighter had died.

One Lehi youth was Haim Applebaum, who shall henceforth be known as he was then to his brothers-in-arms, "Elimelech." Elimelech fought in and survived one of the Lehi's most spectacular military accomplishments, the destruction of the British Rail Works, which developed also, all-too-quickly and inescapably, into one of the Lehi's most costly operations. On June 17, 1946, Lehi assault teams were dispatched to inflict as much physical and financial damage as possible to the enemy's transportation network.

It was just another action, perhaps larger in scope and more fiery in results, among hundreds or thousands destined for the less-traveled historical road. The partakers in such an action – those who would walk away as well as those who would be carried away – could expect nothing other than that their names would never be known, their heroism never recorded, their adventure forgotten by all except themselves, and with the falling of the last leaf upon the tree, nothing would remain of that exceptional night, not even memories.

Surely this would have been the fate towards which that evening was dragged were it not for Elimelech's sentimental desire to record his thoughts in a diary, which has become the dowry he has bequeathed to history, a window through which future generations may peek into the machinery of a night underground:

Monday, 18 Sivan 5706. Evening. The sun is setting, the room darkening. The briefing has just ended. The purpose and operational plan of the action have been explained to the fighters. The aim tonight is to sabotage the railroad works in Emek Zvulun and to destroy the trains there. The group commanders know the terrain. For several days now lookouts have cased the site. Every man knows his task. Silence. Every man is armed and every soul ready.

7:00 P.M. A car is going from one mine-laying unit to

Haifa Rail Works, 1942 (Courtesy of Railroad Museum Archives, Haifa)

another distributing the payloads.

We know: The operation is difficult this time and quite daring. To the left of the workyards – a military airfield. Opposite – army warehouses and refineries filled with British and Arab Legion forces. Nearby – the Kiryat Haim police station with its Bren guns. Along the escape route – army posts. And there are also the patrolling armored police cars of Shfaram.

The operation's C.O. again checks each individual's equipment. Again the questions are asked; everyone knows his role. Soon we will depart. The car which will take us "there" is already parked outside. We are waiting for the darkness to thicken. We do not want local residents to detect the loading of a large group of ammunition-laden young men and women into the vehicle.

7:30. Our attack is scheduled to begin at 8:00. The C.O. gives us the password by which we will know who is with us and who against us. *Habal ba'oyev* (Sabotage the enemy). This will come in handy, for the theater of operations is large and we will be spread out. When we regroup for the retreat we must know who is approaching.

Unit after unit enters the truck as per our respective missions. First the saboteurs who will have to jump last. Their mission is but to detonate and destroy. Advancing before them will be the bridgehead and cover units whose job is to "clean" the territory of enemy troops. The saboteurs are therefore deepest inside, then the cover. Finally, last into the truck and therefore nearest the exit, the bridgehead dressed as British police with grenades and submachine guns. They are to penetrate the workyard gate and overcome its armed guards.

The truck moves. We are crowded inside. All watch each other. Only the blurry outlines of our friends' bodies are visible. Thoughts taunt us: Who among us will not return? This time we know some of us will fall. But the value of this evening's action is high: The financial damage will be great and this will be a continuation of our efforts to paralyze the country's railways, which serve to transport supplies, equipment and troops for the military authorities between their bases in Eretz Israel and the neighboring countries. We hug each other and wish each other luck. We are waved on at the Kfar Hasidim bridge, the road ahead is clear. We leave one unit of mine layers here. Their task is to guarantee that no one passes this bridge. We leave two more mining units at the refineries. Their job: blocking the Krayot road and the parallel military road. This job is not easy, for the road is heavily traveled. The refineries' spotlights search for any suspicious movement. Rolls of prickly barbed wire have been left by the army at the roadside for use during curfews or for roadblocks. Our mine layers will stretch this wire across the road. They will lay two rows of mines, checkerboard fashion, in front of the wire.

The truck drives on. "A little longer," someone sighs. A

little longer and we'll be there. A little longer and we'll be under fire. A few minutes more and the truck stops. We're there. About 150 feet from the workyards, the truck pulls under an awning which hides us as we set out and keeps the imminent attack from view.

The two-man strike force departs from behind the awning. They walk naturally and at a standard pace along the road leading to the gate. We stand beyond the awning and watch. We want to limit the casualties in this foray. We don't want to kill Arabs; the guards at the gate are Arab watchmen. "Who is there?" we hear the guards calling in the distance. "Friends," our two men respond. They hope to get close enough to order the guards to open up without resisting. Instead, the guards must suspect something. They open fire from behind sandbags.

Time becomes precious. We'd hoped to enter without a fight and lay the charges without alerting the army and police. Let the explosions alert them. No time can be wasted at the gate now. Alarms are probably being sounded in the surrounding bases. We open a direct attack. We keep behind the road's many eucalyptus trees. Submachine guns and a grenade force the guards to keep their heads down. Under cover of this fire one fighter ties two pounds of TNT to the gate, sets it and falls to the ground behind a tree. The explosion is heard a moment later. We charge. The guards abandon their position and run. They want to live.

Inside we split into squads. One cover team and two sabotage are sent to the workshops. Two cover teams are positioned to the workshops' left in opposite corners. Two teams speed towards the trains standing to the left. My wing – two cover teams and one sabotage – proceeds to the right, the cover teams to be posted in the two right corners. We run along a narrow alley, the workshops to our left and rows of freight cars and eucalyptus trees to our right. Almost immediately we find our path barricaded. A cover team is sent to dismantle the barricade while we remain behind the trains, but they are fired upon from inside these trains as they approach the barricade. We return fire. In the midst of the volleys we hear Ptachya: "He got me – Kill him!" Arye runs forward shouting "Okay," aims and fires. Suddenly we see him pitch forward, he's been hit. We lob a grenade into the train and send several more salvos towards it. The train is silenced. The barrier is removed, we press forward.

From the administrative offices – flares illuminate the area to expose us, and red flares are fired calling for assistance.

We are in position. The shooting on the left continues for another minute or two – then a deathly silence. We know: We now control the huge workyards in their entirety. The mines are laid, explosives put in one car after another, one piece of machinery after another. A few more minutes and a tremendous flame rises from the main workshop, casting light on the whole site, which is quickly shaken by an awesome explosion. Yes, the plan is being executed. Now the compressors. A series of explosions ensues, some stronger, some lighter. Occasionally there's a moment's pause between explosions, occasionally two or three are simultaneous. In one flame shooting upwards, announcing another explosion, I imagine I see the fighters destroying the cars and machinery: There is Z. fastening 50 pounds of TNT to a giant crane, now Y. plants a 60-pound charge under the bridge. Now he's activated it...

With the first detonation our sabotage team hurries to the workyard fence, made of steel poles connected by steel wires. We must cut an opening for the retreat. Two packs of TNT and the way is open. We assume posts behind the

265

eucalyptus to hold this exit on which the escape depends. The explosions are less frequent. My watch reads 8:30. We've already been here so long working on this job. We hear sporadic faraway explosions. Our mines. Have the reinforcements been caught in the trap? Or are they shooting them off from a safe distance? To avoid civilian casualties we left warning signs, so it shouldn't have been too difficult for them to spot the mines. We hear tank treads rubbing against the earth. They must have cleared the way. They're probably on the Krayot road looking for us. The retreat – and especially getting past that road – is going to be difficult, is what I'm thinking.

Short whistles. The signal to retreat. I respond with short whistles to reveal the location of the opening. We ready our guns and demand of those approaching the password, which they provide. Our forces. Unit after unit gathers. A head count. Two have fallen: Arye and Ptachya. But we are several short and cannot leave till we know what's happened to them. Are they wounded, unable to reach us? Have they, too, fallen? A detachment is sent to search. They head back to the workshops. We lie waiting. The detachment returns after ten minutes with the missing men. They hadn't heard the whistles, which were lost in the thunder of the explosions. It's as if a stone is lifted from our hearts. We exchange data. Yes, Arye and Ptachya are dead. Ptachya! In vain will his wife and few-month-old son wait for his return. He loved them so. He was a veteran, courageous fighter. "This time I came through safely – but in one battle or another I'll fall," he used to say. Actually, each of us believes that. That's war. Arye! This was his second expedition. An only son. Studied at the Technion. Wanted to be a construction engineer. Wanted to build. But he knew, he understood, that under these circumstances one cannot build. So he set out to destroy. To destroy oppression. Because he wanted to build his people's life, not bases for foreign occupiers...

266

We cannot take their bodies with us. We have another three wounded. So begins the retreat...I lead with two scouts, the others about sixty feet behind us. We cross the barbed wire, heading for Ir-Ganim. Every once in a while we drop to the ground as flares illuminate the sky. As darkness returns we resume. Every minute counts now. Though we walk quickly, we walk cautiously. The enemy may be lying in wait behind this hill. Or perhaps that mound. Eight hundred feet before the army warehouses we turn left onto a road skirted by two rows of eucalyptus in whose shadows we move towards the Krayot road.

Suddenly, the sound of tanks. A detail of soldiers searching for us. We assume defensive positions behind trees, machine guns and grenades at the ready. My heart pounds. Will the tankists discover us? We have no wish to engage in battle, not now, even if we would win; we cannot afford to get entangled now. Two soldiers with Brens are clearly visible. The desire to snipe at them is great. But we cannot. Fortunately, they don't spot us. Their traveling speed and the shadows of the trees protect us. Our hearts are relieved. We are up and running across the roadway. Now we are in another field. The Carmel spotlights are streaking across the area. We look back. The workyards are burning. One of the last explosions set the carpentry shops ablaze. Yes! We left behind only wreckage and destruction.

We reach the truck. From afar it appears a black block. Almost imperceptible in the shadow of a house. A few individuals are milling around. Two drivers and the mine layers. They've been waiting over an hour for us. Now we've come. We shake hands. "Success," one of us says. This appears to be the case. Apparently the hard work is behind us. Apparently half the retreat, the more difficult half, is also behind us. The wounded are sent from here to a first-aid station. They cannot be carried on our long, hard escape route. We wish them a speedy recovery and say our farewells.

Onto the truck. I am deep inside, by the driver's cabin. I must listen for the instructions of the operation's commanding officer who will be sitting next to the driver.

We're off. Slits are cut in the canvas covering the truck so we can see out. Our submachine guns are ready. The truck proceeds for several minutes. Around us, silence. "We've probably already gotten beyond the military ring surrounding the workyards." Suddenly the C.O. gives the "alert" signal. We remember: Now we are passing a small army base. The base's guards will almost certainly order us to halt and we'll exchange fire. Perhaps they won't be too serious an obstacle and we'll overcome them. Indeed, we hear two soldiers at the side of the road order: "Stop!" The truck passes and drives on. The soldiers fire a few rounds which we return.

We've seemingly gotten by, with an open road ahead. All of a sudden we feel ourselves veering left and crashing with a thud. We've slammed into the tanks which are blocking the road. Before we can figure out what's happened we're under fire from machine and submachine guns and rifles. We hear the C.O.: "Jump!" But the truck fills with the cries and choking of the injured. We shoot back, someone tosses a grenade. At the rear, some begin jumping out. The fire power directed at us increases. From three directions now. On the left from an open field, from behind and from in front. The troops are entrenched three rows deep in the field. I can no longer hear the C.O.

He's probably already jumped, it's easier from the driver's seat, I think to myself.

I try getting up to make my way to the exit but it's not easy. Someone is pressing against me, he lets lose a scream as I move. Wounded. My leg rubs against another body and he, too, gasps. I cannot see him, the darkness is total. I trip over him and fall with my hands in front of me. I feel them sink in a thick, warm liquid.

Blood! races through my mind. So much blood. I rise and again attempt to move forward. But with every movement of my leg I feel the living flesh underneath screaming in pain. I seem to be the only one left whole. Am I not injured? Is it possible? Again I'm immersed in blood. A bath of blood. Is no one else whole, other than me?

The shots have ceased. In the relative quiet are heard the coughs and cries of the wounded and the dying emanating from the truck and the road below. A melange of cries of pain and anger. Shouts and pleas. A shout: "My heart! They got me in the heart!"

Noah coughs an order: "Kill me, for the enemy has gotten me. Tell my brothers to continue in my place."

And then he sings "Soldiers without Names." The night's silence seems to echo in reply: Follow in my path, soldiers without names.

The spotlights are on us. Bodies are stacked upon bodies in the truck. Most are dead, some badly wounded. Most – with Tommy guns and pistols in their hands. Thus they fought, thus they fell. They are sunk in several inches of blood. The blood flows and drips to the road. There, more dead; blood mixes with blood. One body quakes – rigor mortis.

Here and there a lone shot is heard and shouts in English: "Hands up! This is a warning!"

The soldiers approach the dead and injured suspiciously. Is this a booby trap? A bayonet pokes a body, plunges in. No, the body does not move. A leg is raised, the corpse turned over. Yes. The stomach has been ripped open. A Bren has been emptied into it. The soldier smiles slightly. Victory.

The shouting has calmed. The enemy stares at us. Seeking, searching. They want to see the fear in our eyes. Our lips clench. The cries of pain are stifled. The first shock over

Haim Applebaum (Beit Yair photo)

the blow we've taken has receded. We are no longer beaten men. We are again proud Hebrew fighters, knowing their way, knowing the enemy, knowing the commands of war and the sacrifice it demands. The enemy will not hear another cry!

* * *

Eleven Lehi men and boys fell in the massacre outside Kfar Ata that night. Elimelech stood trial with the other survivors and was one of eighteen sentenced to death in August 1946. The defendants did not hear their death sentences pronounced; they were too busy singing Abraham Stern's songs. Only when they arrived back in their cells were they informed by their friends, who had heard the news on the radio, of their fate. The night before the Rail Works attack, Elimelech had shared his love with his wife, Hanna, a Lehi member who also participated in the attack the next day. From death row, Elimelech smuggled Hanna a message written in tiny letters on toilet paper. Not knowing she was pregnant with their child, Elimelech wrote: "I don't know how you would have managed alone with a baby. Still, I am sorry that it is not happening. We thought we had all the time in the world ahead of us, you remember?"

The death sentences were later commuted to life imprisonment. On May 4, 1947, two of the eighteen Lehi men who had fought at the Rail Works and who were now serving life terms were killed during the most staggering prison break of the Hebrew revolution: Over two hundred and fifty Jewish fighters and other inmates of Acre Prison,

New York Times report of Lehi attack at Rail Works, June 18, 1946

including many Arabs, were set free to the glory of world-wide headlines and the unendurable embarrassment of the supposedly in-control British. One of the two to fall on their way to freedom was Shimshon Vilner. The other was Elimelech. He was 21 years old.

Hanna had given birth to a girl six weeks earlier. Elimelech had never held his daughter, never even seen a photograph of her. Elimelech and Hanna's daughter took her first steps a little more than a year later, shortly after the establishment of the State of Israel; it was on the day her grandmother, Hanna's mother, who had been trying to teach her to walk, was killed in an Egyptian shelling of Tel Aviv.

Uzi the Red, in Blue

"Identity card!" demanded one of the two British soldiers who had stopped the imposing, muscular, red-headed young man.

"Oh," replied the redhead politely, putting his right hand in his pocket. "Please..."

Uzi the Red had vowed revenge. He was at the Rail Works that night. He'd lost some of his best friends. He'd vowed to avenge their blood. Not exactly an eye for an eye, but one for one. Eleven of his friends had died. Eleven English soldiers and policemen would die. Only then would Uzi's red-hot blood cool.

The soldiers did not know what was in Uzi's heart. They did not know what was in Uzi's pocket, either.

"Please..." replied Uzi. Then he pulled from his pocket a pistol and shot dead the man who'd demanded his identification papers. The second soldier fled with the speed of fright. Uzi looked at his victim. "That's for Ptachya," he said, and walked away. Ten more.

Uzi was 16 or so when he joined Lehi. He'd been a member of the socialist Hashomer Hatzair. His co-workers in the diamond factory on Mazah Street in Tel Aviv were in Betar. They argued as they polished. A fourth employee was in Lehi. One by one he recruited them

Dov Berman (Uzi) *(Beit Yair photo)*

for the Underground. Eventually Uzi joined his friends in Lehi. Uzi was a serious teenager, and courageous.

The Lehi members in Jerusalem had a joke: When the British see Uzi in blue, the air-raid siren goes off. Uzi color-coordinated his wardrobe; not tie with jacket or sox with handkerchief, but suit with murder. On days when he'd decided to avenge another of his dead comrades, he wore blue. One by one they fell, and each one had a name. "That's for Arye," he'd say, and walk away. Till the score was even.

One day Uzi was on a more prosaic mission. He and his friends helped themselves to the deposits at one of the Barclays branches in Tel Aviv. As he ran towards Ahad Haam Street, gun in hand, his eyes caught the eyes of an acquaintance staring at him. This acquaintance was no supporter of the Underground, and the eyes were full of hate.

The next day the British police broke into Uzi's house and arrested him. He was sent to Latrun. He vowed revenge.

That night, without getting permission from the Underground Command, without consulting experienced inmates, without asking for any assistance, Uzi shed his clothes. Clothing can get caught in barbed wire, and barbed wire surrounded the camp. Stripped to his underpants, Uzi opened negotiations with the barbed wire. A heavy rain made enough noise to drown that of the shaking fence. It also turned the ground into mud, which couldn't have made Uzi's late-night crawl any more pleasant. By dawn he'd reached the other side, naked, bloody and bruised. He hitched a ride with the first truck that passed, a Tenuva milk truck, telling the driver he'd been attacked by Arabs. The driver headed straight for the nearest address: the Latrun Detention Camp. Had Uzi had any strength left, he probably would have jumped, but he was too exhausted.

The driver had not bought Uzi's story. While he had not turned towards the camp to request medical assistance, neither was he returning Uzi to prison. His eyes were friendlier than the former friend who a day earlier had turned Uzi in. The Tenuva driver simply made a delivery of milk to the camp, then drove Uzi to Tel Aviv. Almost before anyone knew he'd been arrested, Uzi was back on the streets. He applied for permission to eliminate his informer, but the Underground Command was inundated with requests to "hit" Jews who'd allegedly turned on their countrymen and couldn't approve them all.

Time passed, till one day Uzi overheard a Lehi patrol reporting having come upon a Hagana outpost in south Tel Aviv, where they were threatened by this same informer, who'd waved his own gun at them to bolster his threat. Uzi could wait no longer.

As dusk fell, he set out for the Hagana position. He knew what he would do: Before shooting the informer, he'd say: "This is for being a British dog." This time, Uzi missed his revenge. He missed it by one half-hour. For just before he reached the Hagana men, a British unit found them. They lined the men up facing a wall and beat them, one by one. As he was leaving, a British sergeant, Plummer, pulled a pistol and, apparently at random, shot one of the Hagana men in the back. The British informer fell, dead. Uzi was too late.

Some say this story isn't true. They say Lehi fighters were not vigilantes engaged in vendettas of personal vengeance. After fifty years, there is no one who can, or will, confirm these events. Uzi the Red has no biographers. Outside of Lehi circles, he is unknown. Yet for some reason, among the Sternists, Uzi's name is spoken with awe.

Uzi, whose real name was Dov Berman, fell fighting for Jerusalem some months later, as he led a group of scouts near Ein Karem. The scouts were all killed.

These Will I Recall

Eleh Ezkara, "These will I recall." The night they died the two young boys sang, joked and sang some more. The rabbi who knew they were to die but not how, began the night depressed and concluded it smiling. The three voices shook the walls with song, then the rabbi left, then the boys shook the walls again – this time with a hand grenade placed between their hearts. On the morning of April 22, Meir Feinstein and Moshe Barazani lay dead.

That morning in the spring of 1947, the gallows that had been prepared for the two boys stood empty. Meir and Moshe had taken their own lives to prevent the British from hanging them, from executing Jews in Jerusalem. They had lived as fighters and were determined to die as fighters. As Meir wrote while on death row: "It is better to die with weapons in one's hand than with one's hands up."

Moshe Barazani had been working days to help support his parents and siblings. At night he'd been working for Lehi. He had been caught carrying a hand grenade, enough for him to be sentenced to hang. At his trial he sat, yarmulke on his head, reading from the Bible. His only statement to the court:

"The Hebrew nation sees in you an enemy, a foreign regime in its homeland. We, the Fighters for the Freedom of Israel, are fighting you to free the homeland. In this war I have fallen your prisoner, and you do not have the right to judge me. With hangings you will not frighten us, and to destroy us you will not succeed! My people, and all peoples oppressed by you, will fight your empire until its destruction."

Moshe was 20.

Meir had enlisted in the British army to fight the Germans. Afterwards he enlisted in the IZL. When he was sentenced to death for his role driving the getaway car in the Jerusalem railroad station attack, Meir responded thus:

"Officers of the invading army! A regime based on gallows – this is your idea for the Holy Land, the land predestined to serve as the lighthouse for mankind. Your vileness and folly lead you to believe that through such a regime you'll succeed in breaking the spirit of our people. But you'll soon realize your mistake; you'll discover that you are facing steel, steel that stood the test in the furnace of love and hatred: love for the homeland and hatred against a subjugating invader.

"Indeed, you are stricken by blindness. Are you really unaware whom you are going to encounter in this strife, which has no precedent in the history of nations? Do you really think that your gallows will frighten us? Do you mean to scare us, who have for years been hearing the clickety-clack of wheels carrying our brothers and parents and our finest people to the chambers of death? We – who have been repeatedly asking ourselves, why did fate treat us differently than the millions of our brothers? Why did we not share their days of fear and moments of agony?

"To this we have only one reply: We have remained alive not in order to live and hope in thraldom and repression for a new Treblinka. We have remained alive in order to make certain that life, freedom and honor will be our lot and the lot of our nation and the lot of our generations unborn. We have remained alive in order to make impossible a recurrence of what happened there and what is likely to happen under your rule of deceit, your regime of blood.

"We have learned our lesson, and paid for it dearly. But we have learned that there is a mode of life that is worse than death and there is a death that is greater than life. And if you fail to see this vision of a nation that has nothing to lose but the irons of slavery, but the 'hope' for a new Maidanek – then you are indeed stricken by blindness and doomed by Providence to share the fate of all those who have lifted arms against the Eternal People. Assyria, Babylon, Athens, Rome, Spain and Germany have tried before you, and you, too, will share their graves.

"This is what I wanted to tell you and your superiors, British officers. As for myself, I have nothing to add to what has been said by my friends. I regard myself as a prisoner of war and expect to be treated as such."

He was 19.

As Moshe and Meir sat in their cell, two or three yards from the gallows in the Jerusalem Central Prison, they decided: They would not go to the gallows, the British would not hang them. They would die the death of Samson, taking with them as many of the enemy as possible. They would blow themselves up, and blow up the gallows and any British in the room. They would die as fighters.

A request for grenades was smuggled to their fellow prisoners. Reluctantly, the weapons were manufactured inside the prison and sent to the death-row cell in hollowed-out oranges. The prisoners told the British that Moshe and Meir were "dying" for oranges, and every day a basket was brought full of fruit. As soon as the guards became accustomed to such procedure the grenades were included.

Moshe, Meir and the oranges waited.

The night before the scheduled hangings, the British called upon Rabbi Arye Levin to say the "Vidui" confession with the condemned. For the first time, Reb Arye refused to offer comfort. He told the British that the souls of these two were so pure they had nothing to confess, for there are none more righteous than martyrs for the sanctification of God and Israel. Privately, he was broken and asked, "Is a father to see the death of his children?"

Rabbi Jack Goldman was called. He went, but on entering the cell found himself speechless. The two boys, in a twist of fate, found themselves comforting him. At one point they asked for a rabbinical ruling: Is suicide permissible according to Jewish law, or is it a sin? The rabbi assumed they were referring to their refusal to appeal their sentences, as they had not recognized the right of a British court in Eretz Israel to judge them. Rabbi Goldman therefore answered that according to Jewish tradition, giving your life for the honor of Israel is considered heroic. Moshe asked the rabbi to tell the story of Rabbi Akiva's martyrdom.

The conversation turned to books, with the rabbi telling Meir he was familiar with a book written by his grandfather, a commentary on Shir Hashirim (the Song of Songs). Moshe exclaimed excitedly that his grandfather's brother had also written a book – but, he added dejectedly, Rabbi Goldman had probably never heard of it since it had been published in Baghdad.

Rabbi Goldman told Moshe he had read it but Moshe remained skeptical, assuming the rabbi was merely trying to console him. So Rabbi Goldman proved himself by relating a story from the book, a collection of Kabbalistic tales entitled *Minhat Yehuda*:

A soul had departed from this world and had gotten trapped in a pomegranate. The soul had not yet attained purification, but if the person who ate the pomegranate recited the proper blessing, then the soul would be able to continue on its way to heaven. The fruit was bought by an old man who recited the blessing and ate it at his Sabbath meal, thereby purifying the wandering soul and setting it on its course. Rabbi Goldman was, of course, unaware of the irony of his story, dealing with a soul saved by a fruit, when shortly the two boys were to die by a fruit.

The rabbi announced that instead of saying "Vidui," he would prefer "Adon Olam," since he did not feel the holy martyrs needed to say "Vidui." Moshe and Meir agreed to the rabbi's request, but on the condition they not say the prayer, but sing it. The prison walls reverberated with song.

As the singing and laughter quieted, the rabbi informed the doomed duo that he would return in the morning – they would not have to die alone, seeing only cruel and unfriendly faces. They tried and tried but could not deter the good rabbi from his intention of appearing at the hanging. Their plan underwent a last-minute change.

Unable to endanger the rabbi by blowing up the gallows with him there, they decided to show that as Jews they held their own fate, controlled their own lives. They would cheat the hangman, die by their own hands in their cell. If they would not die as Samson, at least they would die as at Masada.

Before the rabbi left the cell that night, one of the boys pulled out some sweet candies, gave them to the rabbi and said that as his fellow prisoners would doubtless be upset and unhappy the following morning, the rabbi should give them the candies so they would have something to sweeten their day. The other lad reached for a banana and handed it to the rabbi, asking that the next day, after their two souls had departed, the rabbi eat the fruit after reciting the blessing, in order to purify their souls so they might enter heaven.

The two boys found they could not wait long after the rabbi left. Meir put his right arm around Moshe, Moshe put his right arm around Meir. No differences mattered now: Meir an Ashkenazi, Moshe a Kurdish Jew; Meir a member of the Irgun, Moshe a member of Lehi. Now nothing separated them. Two Jews, two freedom fighters, two heroes – two young boys – hugged each other. Moshe placed the grenade between their hearts. With a cigarette, he lit the fuse.

The walls reverberated again.

Meir Feinstein and Moshe Barazani are buried side by side on the Mount of Olives in Jerusalem. Their *yahrzeit* is the second day of Iyar.

* * *

Eleh Ezkara. "These will I recall and my soul will I pour forth," begins the sacred Yom Kippur memorial to the ten martyrs burned, skinned, beheaded and mutilated by the Romans: "These will I recall and my soul will I pour forth, for the foreigner has eaten and beaten us, and in the time of our oppression, there was no compassion for the ten holy martyrs..."

279

Eleh Ezkara. When these are recalled, tears will pour forth, for the foreigner beat us back from our shores and then demanded more, in the time of unequaled oppression there was no compassion for the 13 holy martyrs who faced the hangman.

First in battle, first in death, first to rip the myth of *havlaga* and first to enter Hebrew myth, with no tears in his eyes and no fears in his soul, "A homeland is something for which one lives – or dies!" he cried; "the teacher of us all," Jabotinsky sighed, over Shlomo Ben Yosef.

No cries and no legend, no speeches and no fame were accorded the obeisant and silent Mordechai Schwartz, who fired first and sacrificed his life – and his name.

The "two Eliahus," Hakim and Bet Zuri, assassins in Egypt in the name of Lehi. Lord Moyne was the target, British minister of state, the man who shrugged off a German offer to free a million Jews: "But what would I do with a million Jews?" Shamir sent his two best shots, the judge accused them of shooting at Egyptian cops. "If you'll give me a rod I'll show you I never miss what I aim to hit," challenged Bet Zuri. Egyptian Arabs rallied en masse, but the British stood fast. "This is the finest suit I've ever worn," declared Hakim in the red robes of death. Bet Zuri with a High Priest's dignity, Hakim the epitome of a Prince of Israel, each hoping to be spared sight of his brother's death. The lot fell upon Hakim, he burst forth in song. Bet Zuri thanked his lawyers and kind Egyptian jailers, too: My debt to the British, others will pay. To his hangmen he turned: And now my friends, I'm ready.

But who can tell the story of Dov Gruner? His family almost finished by the Nazis, Gruner enlisted in the British army. His first employment in Eretz Israel: fixing the path to Ben Yosef's grave on the hill. A shame, a shame, he wrote to his girlfriend the day he reached the tomb, a shame he had to die, but on the necks of the Ben Yosefs a Jewish state will rise. Only the Lord above knows: Gruner's soul will one day ascend from Ben Yosef's gallows. A raid in Ramat Gan, his chin blown away, three months on death row with nothing to say. Just ask for your life, the British hinted they'd play; I ask you for nothing, was all he would say.

From Dov Gruner's last letter, written to Irgun Commander Menahem Begin: "Of course I want to live, who doesn't? But what pains me now that the end is near is mainly the awareness that I have not succeeded in achieving enough...I am writing this while awaiting the hangman...If I had my life to live anew I would choose the same path I have taken, regardless of the personal consequences...the only correct path is the path of the IZL..."

Yehiel Dov Dresner, Eliezer Kashani and Mordechai Alkoshi joined Gruner in his Jerusalem cell, the four were spirited one night to an Acre hell. The gallows was ready, *Hatikva* was sung, the prison was awakened, the fortress was shaken, the song was on hundreds of tongues.

Barazani and Feinstein would not be hanged, they prayed and they laughed and they sang, hugging each other and destiny, they rose heavenward in a burst of glory. The angels above must have wept bitterly: "Is this Your way and this its pay? The oppressor defiles Your people and puts You to shame, and Your children willingly die in Your name?" And a voice perhaps answered in Heavenly wrath: "This is My will, this the path."

Awaiting his sentence, Yaacov Weiss abandoned all pretense: When my fathers were kings writing Psalms in this land – he told the court – yours were swinging from trees in England. Sentenced to "hang by the neck till your soul leaves your body," Avshalom Haviv thanked God for the chance to suffer for nation and country: *Baruch ata Ha-shem e-lokeinu melech haolam shehecheyanu vekiyimanu vehigiyanu lazman hazeh.* Avshalom was 21 when Weiss, Meir Nakar and he took their final steps singing gallantly. The British were rushing, *Hatikva* too long, they hanged each youth in the midst of his song. Where one was cut off, his friend began, the song was not silenced till the last man was hanged. *Eleh Ezkara.*

281

HANGED BY THE BRITISH:
Shlomo Ben Yosef, aged 25

HANGED BY THE BRITISH:
Eliahu Hakim, aged 20

HANGED BY THE BRITISH:
Eliahu Bet Zuri, aged 23

HANGED BY THE BRITISH:
Dov Gruner, aged 34

HANGED BY THE BRITISH:
Eliezer Kashani, aged 24

HANGED BY THE BRITISH:
Mordechai Alkoshi, aged 22

HANGED BY THE BRITISH:
Yehiel Dresner, aged 24

DIED IN HIS CELL:
Moshe Barazani, aged 20

DIED IN HIS CELL:
Meir Feinstein, aged 19

HANGED BY THE BRITISH:
Avshalom Haviv, aged 21

HANGED BY THE BRITISH:
Meir Nakar, aged 21

HANGED BY THE BRITISH:
Yaacov Weiss, aged 23

283

The brief release issued by the British Foreign Office was years in the making, though not as many years as some of the Underground commanders had expected. The announcement was paid for in full and was most expensive. It cost lives, far too many Jewish lives and far too many British lives. The printed words were black and white but they had been inscribed in the warm scarlet ink shed by the most selfless and idealistic boys and girls of the Jewish nation. The British by their own admission finally realized that "84,000 soldiers...were not sufficient to preserve law and order when faced with a wave of terrorism committed by well-organized Jews armed with all the weapons of modern infantry...His Majesty's government has decided to remove its army from Eretz Israel and end its Mandate on May 15, 1948."

The Lehi fighters began convening at 7:00 A.M. Many found it unbearably difficult to give their true names and addresses when asked. They were on their way to Zahal – the Israel Defense Forces. By 11:00 A.M., all had gathered for the inspection. Eldad and Yellin-Mor (Yitzhak Shamir only recently escaped from his African prison and was in Europe on his way back to Eretz Israel) were ready to review the troops under their command for the first time since the revolution began. "Soldiers without names are we..." was sung. Eldad exhorted the no-longer nameless soldiers to "Remember Yair who created us in his clear wisdom, forged us in his steel soul, bore us with his holy blood..." Yellin-Mor read the Order of the Day: "All the roads of this war on which you journey will lead to Jerusalem. For its freedom you fight, and for its glory, for it is the heart of the homeland. Who rules in Jerusalem rules over the entire homeland...Only death will free us from service in the ranks!"

On 5 Iyar 5708, May 15, 1948, the British sailed from Eretz Israel and the Jewish state was born. On the sixth of Iyar, the Lehi Central Committee addressed its ranks:

"One chapter of the war has ended. The war has not. The British Mandate, that legal masquerade for foreign occupation, is null and void. The civilian regime of the enemy has disintegrated as an old carcass does and has been eliminated. The Empire's Commissioner has sailed off to his distant island and no other shall come in his stead...

"The State of Israel has risen and the government of Israel has been born by proclamation. The Hebrew flag flies openly and not secretively above the government buildings and on the poles of armed military camps. Taxes are collected by a Hebrew treasury. Pictures of ancient coins from the Hasmonean and Bar Kochba Revolts appear on Hebrew stamps.

"Fighters!

"Hold your heads high. Stand at attention. Honor the flag of our fighting movement. Its role was critical, your contribution great towards that which has been achieved. You are the first of the freedom fighters. Few responded to Yair's call. But the few brought about the great accomplishment...Our movement planted in the nation's heart new values, which turned the war of freedom into this generation's categorical imperative...

"Yair was first. Our movement was first. We cut with the scalpel of logic...We were a handful surrounded by hatred. We took pride in the hatred of the enemy, but our brother's animosity broke our hearts. In their eyes we were insane. Let us remember today those days. Not one house could be found in all of Greater Tel Aviv which would open its doors and give haven to a hunted fighter. And you – orchards were your rendezvous and public shelters your homes. You slid through the streets like shadows. Day was for you – night, and dark nights – day.

"...You were hungry always, savoring fruit left untended; a rare piece of bread was for you a royal feast. You trembled in the cold, the floor being your bed, and having no blanket...

"You, the persecuted, were the only free Hebrews among six hundred thousand...Weapons were the guarantors of your freedom. Each of you was a seed of total Hebrew freedom...The enemy saw in you an example of the new Hebrew, who knows not surrender as long as he lives...

"His eighty thousand troops were insufficient to maintain law and order in our homeland...The war of freedom forced them to leave the country and formed the basis for Hebrew independence...

"Your suffering and your deeds were great. Still, you remained ever modest, ever quiet...You are the nation's fighters, and this itself is your reward.

"With the national flag flying in every corner on Independence Day, let us remember the fallen.

"The memory of Yair will never leave us; the creator, an eagle in vision, smith in logic, pouring wisdom into the rhymes of his songs. From him we learned the laws of freedom and dedication and sacrifice and going to the limit...

"Let us visit in spirit the graves of the fighters scattered throughout the homeland and abroad. In Cairo and Tiberias, Haifa and Nahalat Itzhak, in Jerusalem the capital and places unknown. Those who were killed in homes and in streets and on gallows. Those who fell anonymously and only their Underground names remain. The best among us, the most precious...heroes to their last breaths. Splendid in their individuality, their singularity, each wrote a blazing page in the chronicles of the Freedom War. One day when their lives and heroism and deaths are recorded, they will wake to eternal life. Generations will quench their thirst for heroism from them...

"Fighters!"

"The war is not over yet.

"We will yet be called to many difficult battles. Many chapters lie ahead of us.

"In coming days, too, we will give all we have to free the homeland and to free Jerusalem...

"Today you are gathered round our glorious flag, which is soaked in blood and suffering. Raise it high. It will lead you on the road to the freedom of the entire homeland.

"And at chapter's end we will cry: *Hazak hazak venithazek*, 'From strength to strength we grow stronger!'

"Be strong and courageous, fighters, in the battles to come."

Chapter 9
The Road To Jerusalem

David still dances and Amos is burning in your eyes.
Professor Walter Kaufmann, to Eldad

The year: 1991. The four elderly men in the car are singing heart-
ily and obviously enjoying themselves: "In blood and fire Judea fell /
In blood and fire Judea will rise." At first only Shimon Barmatz in the
front passenger seat sings. His deep voice is hoarse with the years, and
he does not sing as loudly as he would perhaps like, but he imbues the
words with a contagious enthusiasm. Danny Bet Hamikdash, on the
far right in the rear, lends his clear and equally enthused voice. Next
to Danny sits a tenor, he has said almost nothing since they left Tel
Aviv, but he joins – initially hesitantly, soon gustily – the choir. Ezra
Yachin, driving, lets himself go as well. The past seems to live in this
car, at least for the duration of this song. Fifty years! There cannot be
many on the road today who recall these ballads.

They are returning to Jerusalem from Tel Aviv, where several hundred persons had gathered – most carrying gas masks, for the night
before last one of Saddam's missiles wrecked five hundred houses nearby
– to mark the forty-ninth anniversary of the death of Yair Stern. Prime
Minister Shamir was there, and Haim Dviri and dozens of others. Dviri
introduced a young friend to a limping Joseph Menkes: "You should

287

have seen him, a whirlwind storming the Burma Road in 1948!"

Danny Bet Hamikdash is easily the most popular of the former fighters and he was called from one to another to exchange greetings. "Over here, Har Habayit!" one old comrade called, using Danny's name of forty years ago. "Not Har Habayit" (Temple Mount), corrected Danny, "Bet Hamikdash" (Holy Temple). When the State of Israel was established in 1948, Danny paid a visit to Uri Zvi Greenberg. "Isn't it great," Danny exclaimed, "we have a state." "Yes," the poet replied, "but we do not have the Temple Mount and Old Jerusalem, which have remained outside our borders." Danny Shohami changed his name to Har Habayit to demonstrate the Jewish attachment to the Old City's Mount. Following the 1967 Six Day War, Danny paid another visit to Greenberg and declared triumphantly: "Now we have the Temple Mount!" "Yes," Israel's ever serious poet laureate answered, "but we do not have the Holy Temple." And Danny Har Habayit became Danny Bet Hamikdash.

Danny doesn't say "hello" or "good-bye," he says "It will be built." The words are accompanied by something resembling a fraternity handshake, in which both partners compress their five fingers to a point, touch – or wave if they are too far apart – and then kiss their own fingertips. When Jewish settlers were arrested in 1984 for retaliatory attacks on West Bank Arabs, Israeli newspapers reported that one man stood at the rear of the courtroom sending coded hand signals to the defendants. But of course they weren't coded hand signals, it was just Danny Bet Hamikdash saying hello.

At the cemetery, Danny scurried around informing everyone, "It won't help them," never quite specifying what "it" is or who "they" are, "It won't help them, nothing will, because the people of Israel are a good people!"

Danny went looking for the owner of the car. "Where's Elnakam [Avenging God]? Where's Elnakam?" referring to Ezra's *nom de guerre* of fifty years earlier.

Now in this car on the road to Jerusalem, Danny recalls an earlier visit to Stern's grave. "The first year after the British murdered him, in '43, we came at 2:00 A.M. so they wouldn't catch us. We stood by the grave singing Hebrew songs." Conversation turns to nights in Jerusalem, to changing street scenes and buildings and skylines. Barmatz offers a joke.

"Do you remember when they built the King David Hotel, I remember the building going up, one day the owner of the smaller Eretz Israel Hotel stood across the street watching this massive structure rise. 'Very nice,' he said, 'very nice, but where will they ever find enough bedbugs to fill a hotel this size!'"

As they laugh, Ezra lights up: "The owner of the Eretz Israel Hotel was..."

"Barmatz, that's right, my uncle. That's how I know the story."

"How can you remember the building of the King David," asks the tenor. "I can't."

"I guess I've a few years on you, my friend..."

"Can't be. I'm 65."

"Really, now, I've begun the 70s..."

"Ah, youth!" chirps Danny. "I'm 75."

There is some construction on the road ahead, and as tar is laid on one lane, traffic stops and they are redirected to another.

"Remember the roadblocks?" someone asks expressing, obviously, what all are thinking.

"Setting up roadblocks, yes..."

"Here's a story," Elnakam starts, suddenly energetic. "We were escaping; I had been shot in the stomach, this was after a shootout with the British, and now we were escaping. I hailed a cab and told the driver to find a doctor. Even as we drove off, roadblocks had already been set up, and we found ourselves in a long line of vehicles that were being searched. We watched the soldiers and observed the method: documents requested, drivers and passengers told to get out, then each car got a thorough going-over. Ordinarily I would have opted for a shootout – I'd start shooting, assuming all was lost anyway and whatever happened...happened. But here was this cabby with me and I figured I didn't have the right to risk his life just because I was in the Underground. So we approached the British with much uncertainty and even more trepidation. As we pulled up to the blockade they started yelling at us, really screaming, and at first I thought: Well, the gig's up, they must know who I am...but then it slowly dawned on me what they were shouting: 'F—ING JEWS, GET MOVING, GET OUT OF HERE, YOU F—ING JEWS ARE HOLDING EVERYTHING UP, GET OUT OF HERE ALREADY!' I've no idea why we weren't searched, but this was the second miracle that night as far as I was concerned, the first being that I was even alive.

"Now I needed a doctor; where could I direct the cabdriver?"

Everyone, all three former Sternists in the car, interrupts Ezra at this point. "Why didn't you go to Hepner?!" they all demand.

"No, no, I couldn't endanger Hepner, I didn't know who the driver was, I couldn't take a chance. So I said to him, 'Just take me to any doctor.' Then I remembered the name of a doctor from a sign on Agrippas Street. 'Take me to Doctor N., Agrippas Street,' I said, and he did. The driver practically carried me up the stairs and into N.'s apartment. I didn't know N. and he didn't know me. 'What happened?' inquired the already suspicious doctor. 'There was a gunfight with the British,' I began, but he cut me off. 'No, no, I do not have the proper equipment here, I cannot treat you, no, I am not set up here to help you, it cannot be done.' The cabdriver was ready to, in his words, bash the doctor's head with a wrench. 'He hasn't even seen your wound and already he knows he can't treat it!' When I wrote about this story years later I called him 'Dr. N.,' I didn't want him to sue me, since I don't know where the cabby is, or even who he is, and he's the only witness to the doctor's rude refusal to help. Some years ago I met a man who'd been operated on by this doctor; it was a botched job and the patient was in constant pain. So I guess it was a third miracle, that he didn't get his hands on me. The doctor died a few years ago."

The story continues, and of course Elnakam heals and lives to drive to Jerusalem this day 44 years later. But one thing leads to another and Ezra is now talking about his son.

"I tell you, Ariel was really broken for a while in the army. Really depressed. He went in full of plans, expecting to be a parachutist. When he was assigned to the slightly less prestigious but nonetheless elite Givati Brigade, he adjusted his sights and put everything into it. In the middle of the grueling course, several boys were pulled at random and transferred to a communications course. Ariel agreed to go with the proviso that he be allowed to participate in the cross-country Givati training run and the final swearing-in ceremony. While he was stuck in the technical communications course his buddies were exhausting themselves, and before he knew it, the training, the run and the ceremony were over and he hadn't been allowed to join in any of them.

"One day the wife of a Givati officer met me at a book-signing function and asked why I'd sent her husband a copy of my memoirs. I asked her name and thought for a few moments trying to remember, then made the association and explained that my son had served for a while under her husband and admired him. When she asked about Ariel I told her the whole story. The next week, Ariel was suddenly transferred to a Givati combat division where he was posted as communications man to the division commander. They were based in Lebanon and skirmished frequently with terrorists. Ariel was finally satisfied. He would telephone and say, 'Dad, you're going to hear something on the news soon; don't worry, I'm all right.'

"One night they were ambushed on patrol, the division commander was killed a few feet from Ariel – "

"Not Shmulik, you're not talking about that commander?!"

"Yes, Shmulik. A real hero. Another friend, Oz, was shot in the stomach, he lay in a hospital for days teetering between life and death

291

before he recuperated. A few months later he was miraculously back with his unit; his friends were training to take a hill and there was Oz suddenly out front leading the charge. Anyway, on this patrol, Ariel and another soldier were on the ground and as the earth began flying around them they ascertained the source of the bullets and charged the bushes where the terrorists were hiding, killing them. That night when Ariel called he said Shmulik had been killed, Oz was injured. I was so shocked I forgot to ask how he was, and all night I trembled remembering that I would never have told my father if I'd been injured, so as not to worry him.

"A few weeks later Ariel phoned and said there was some sort of ceremony on his base and I could come, but I shouldn't feel obligated since it wasn't that important. It turned out to be the Outstanding Soldier Awards, with every unit awarding one of its soldiers a certificate of excellence in his respective field. And there was Ariel receiving the award, not for excellence in communications; no, he was the only one in the Communications Corps to receive the award for outstanding bravery in combat."

"The children, the children," Danny and Barmatz and even the tenor sigh, all at once and then again individually, "the children make everything worthwhile."

As they pulled into Jerusalem, everyone was singing again.

* * *

The man who had perhaps started it all had died far from his beloved Eretz Israel and years before the creation of the Jewish state. Yet the forcibly exiled Vladimir Jabotinsky had been so sure of the future that he had ended his last will and testament with the clause that "I want to be buried wherever I die...and my body should be transferred to Eretz Israel only by order of that country's eventual Jewish government." In 1964 the government of Israel sent to New York for Jabotinsky's body. He was reinterred in Jerusalem opposite the tomb of Theodor Herzl.

The Egyptians returned the bodies of Eliahu Hakim and Eliahu Bet Zuri, the two Lehi boys hanged by the British in Cairo, to Israel in 1975. The funereal procession began from the Jerusalem Central Prison with Prime Minister Rabin paying homage. When, before the ceremony, the coffins were opened to identify the bodies, the coroners were shocked to find themselves staring straight into the undisturbed faces of the two Eliahus. The bodies were perfectly preserved, even to the unshaven shadows on their chins. One expert suggested this was a result of the hot, humid climate of their burial ground; another countered that humidity would only speed the decomposition of the corpses while the dryness of Egypt was undoubtedly responsible for the state of the bodies. Several more hypotheses were advanced but none satisfied all until a local rabbi remembered a Talmudic decree: The angel of death has no power over the martyrs of Israel.

Hakim and Bet Zuri were reburied on Mt. Herzl. They rest by the side of Joseph Lishansky and Naaman Belkind, two NILI members hanged by the Turks for aiding in the British capture of Eretz Israel during the First World War, and Moshe Marzuk and Shmuel Azar, two Egyptian Jews hanged for working with Israel in the 1950s.

Shlomo Ben Yosef, whose courage broke the spell of the gallows and whose manners and behavior on death row and with the noose around his neck – the politeness, consideration for others, insistence on cleanliness and composure, the singing and declarations on the threshold of the other world – were consciously imitated by those who followed him, rests in a woody hilltop grave on the Safed-Rosh Pina highway, not far from where he and his friends broke the official policy of *havlaga*. Those who pay their respects to Ben Yosef still climb the path carved and marked by Dov Gruner.

Gruner and his cellmates Alkoshi, Dresner and Kashani are buried in the cool mountain cemetery of Safed, not far from the hundreds-of-years-old grave of Rabbi Isaac Luria, the "Ari." Alkoshi, Dresner and Kashani were hanged for possession of a whip. They had

been sent to revenge the whipping of an under-18-year-old Irgunist by
the JCP authorities but were arrested before they had found any British officers to lash. Other Irgun teams had been more successful that
night but hadn't been caught; the British vented their spleen on these
three young men instead.

Avshalom Haviv, Meir Nakar and Yaacov Weiss, the last Jews
hanged by the British in Eretz Israel, lie together with Gruner and his
friends. Meir Nakar, the night before he, Haviv and Weiss helped the
hundreds escape from Acre, sat drinking coffee at his parents' home.
Georgie Levy, a feisty Iraqi Jew who had years earlier made aliya (all
the way from Baghdad by foot), offered to read the "mud," or ground
coffee, left in Meir's cup. "I see him falling," he said sadly, "and not
getting up. Your next mission will be your last." "Nonsense," replied
Meir.

Georgie turned up decades later as ticket taker at the Hall of Heroism Museum in the renovated former Jerusalem Central Prison. Both
the Acre and the Jerusalem prisons are today memorials to the fallen
fighters. In the 1980s Jerusalem's mayor Teddy Kollek had plans to
tear down the prison and erect there a new City Hall. Teddy's sketches
included the preservation only of the gallows, which was to stand in
his office lobby – perhaps as a tempting alternative for the overtaxed
residents of his city. National pride won out over the sprawling new
City Hall, which came to a stop several paces from the museum.

Barazani and Feinstein, who chose to take their own lives inside
the prison, rest today in the world's most sacred Jewish cemetery, on
the Mt. of Olives. Menahem Begin, Irgun Commander in Chief and
later prime minister of Israel, and his wife Aliza were interred at their
own request alongside Barazani and Feinstein.

Yitzhak Shamir, another underground chief-cum-prime minister,
recalls that while in prison "there was never a dull moment, we were
never bored," for after all, "I was always planning an escape." He succeeded twice and, with that kind of experience, naturally gravitated to

an illustrious if low-profile career in Israel's Mossad. Shamir eventually exchanged his cloak and dagger for the in many ways more dangerous arena of the Knesset and Prime Minister's Office. Eldad, who began his escape from Poland together with Begin and then headed the Stern Group with Yellin-Mor and Shamir, remained the most ideologically stalwart of the underground personalities. His 1950s journal *Sulam* featured headlines the likes of "The River of Desire and All Streets of Logic Lead to a Kingdom of Israel from the Euphrates to the Nile and a Temple of God on Mount Moriah." Yevin and Uri Zvi Greenberg were frequent contributors to the publication, which could still easily form the basis for a course entitled Revolutionary Zionism 101. Eldad meanwhile became professor of humanistic studies at the Technion, translated all of Nietzsche's writings into Hebrew, authored several books of his own, including the Biblical commentary *Hegionot Mikra*, and was at the time of his death in 1996 regarded as the doyen of Israeli nationalists. During a walk in Jerusalem a couple of years before, he had finally paused for breath, begging forgiveness of his younger companion. "I know what my problem is," he calmed his worried associate, "it's the *afikoman*, the Passover matzoh." Then he explained that he'd obviously eaten too many of them, having lived through "80 Passover holidays..."

Eldad once noted, in the philological exegesis he loved so much, that the Hebrew word for "progress" means, paradoxically, "towards the old" and, literally, "towards the east." Meaning, that the Jewish people's destiny is to return to Israel, and there to renew its days as of old.

Eldad's friend, and perhaps the only man more ideologically unmovable than he, Moshe Segal, continued to sound the shofar at the Western Wall till the year of his death. And he died, fatefully enough, on the anniversary of his appearance on the stage of history, the sacred day of Yom Kippur. He bit his lips in the hospital, refusing to display the pain he was in. Only once did he reveal some of what he

Dr. Israel Eldad (Courtesy of "Times of Israel")

was thinking when he confessed the frustration he felt at his imminent death: "There's still so much to do..." He was 81. His later years
had in fact been as active as his earlier ones, even as he lay in Shaare
Zedek Hospital.

In 1948 he had been a member of Dov Joseph's Jerusalem Committee. He was in charge of ensuring the distribution of food in the
city under siege. In the '50s he answered the government's call to "return to the land," and adopted an agricultural lifestyle in the Lubavitch
Kfar Habad. Segal founded the Beth Rivka school for girls and quickly
became secretary, or mayor, of the village. Hearing that Jerusalem had
been liberated in 1967, he phoned to see if he could visit but was ad-

vised to hold off until the bombing stopped. The next day he didn't bother phoning, just got a group of Lehi vets together and drove in. He stayed.

Moshe Segal passed the ruins of the thirteenth-century Ramban Synagogue, named for the acronym of the famous Rabbi Moshe ben Nachman (Nachmanides) who moved to Jerusalem and found only destroyed synagogues. The sage had sent to Shchem for a *minyan* so he would have someone to pray with. "And I was not Rabbi Moshe ben Nachman but 'Reb' Moshe ben Abraham, walking by the Ramban's synagogue and seeing all the ruin, all the mezuza holes in the doorposts of the once-Jewish homes, all the Arabs in those homes, and all the Jewish institutions and houses destroyed, and I decided I would do what the Ramban did. There are no Jews? All right, I'll stay. If Jerusalem is like a widow with no children – I'll be the child. How could I leave mother Jerusalem alone again?"

His wife remained in Kfar Habad till conditions improved. "Every Friday night I went with thousands of others to the Western Wall," recalled Segal. Everyone else left the Old City after the service. "I was one old Jew walking in the opposite direction." The Arab shopkeepers along Segal's route stood as he passed, in respect. Segal had no electricity in his "house," only the light of candles. "How lucky a Jew is to have Sabbath angels in his home. Otherwise to whom would I say Shabbat Shalom?" he smiled.

Some of Segal's anxious friends tried dissuading him from remaining alone in the hostile territory. When Segal refused to heed their warnings they appealed to the Lubavitcher Rebbe, hoping he would order Segal to less dangerous ground. It is a matter of life and death, they told the Rebbe. How do you know his life is in danger? the Rebbe asked, and they produced as evidence the fact that Segal slept with a pistol under his pillow. The Rebbe thought for a moment. Well, if he keeps a pistol under his pillow I guess he's safe enough, the Rebbe ruled.

Segal soon headed several organizations working to restore the holiness of the ancient Temple site. He opposed Israel's withdrawal from the Sinai desert and moved into the soon to be dismantled city of Yamit. When Israeli soldiers came to carry away the residents of what was then the Sinai's largest city, the almost 80-year-old Segal locked himself in a bunker with a coterie of much younger holdouts. They finally gave themselves up rather than physically fight with Jewish soldiers. Back in Jerusalem, Segal tried organizing a Jewish irredentist movement, in the tradition of Garibaldi's efforts to unite Italy a century earlier, to assert that though the Israeli government had relinquished the Sinai, the Jewish nation had not conceded its claim and would one day return to land rightfully its own.

The final year of his life Segal helped found the Temple Institute, dedicated to reconstructing the sacred vessels for use in the Temple service, and devoted almost all his time and energy to assisting David

Moshe Segal in 1984

Ben Shimol, an 18-year-old soldier whose girlfriend had been killed by Arab terrorists, along with two other friends of his, on a bus in Jerusalem. Ben Shimol volunteered at 17 for the army, was sent to Lebanon, watched the head of his commanding officer be blown off as they drove together, was himself injured, and while on leave saw the results of another heinous Arab attack on two innocent Israeli campers – a couple who'd been bound, gagged and shotgunned to death while on a walk near a Bethlehem monastery. Ben Shimol, in his words, "couldn't take it any more." Without knowing who Ben Yosef or Yehezkel Altman had been, without having read any of Jabotinsky's speeches, Ben Shimol went AWOL one morning and armed with a missile set out to break the government's policy of quietude and restraint in the face of consistent Arab terrorism. "I was sent to Lebanon to fight terrorists," wrote Ben Shimol, "while here at home they operate freely."

One of the judge's slept through part of the trial, and evidence in David's favor was ignored. David was sentenced to life in prison. David had not contested his conviction, only the sentence. He could not afford to pay a lawyer but received a letter from an attorney in Haifa volunteering his services: former Birion and Sternist Moshe Svorai, who had studied law long after receiving his own life sentence. Moshe Segal was the first public figure to adopt David's cause. Unlike most others, Segal not only protested the injustice done to David but wholeheartedly endorsed his reprisal action.

When Segal visited David in prison, David greeted the white-bearded old rabbinical figure by asking, "Who am I that you should come to see me?" while Reb Moshe responded by asking, "Who am I that I should have the privilege of sitting here with you?"

Eldad soon included David's plight in his newspaper column. Yoshke Eliav, upon hearing the radio broadcast of David's arrest, surprised those in the room by condemning the young soldier. The surprise evaporated when he explained his disgust: "This is no professional. How dare he let himself get caught, when it is his responsibility to continue with many more reprisal attacks!"

By 1993, 84 members of Israel's 120-seat parliament had signed a petition asking for presidential clemency. Arab members of Knesset, too, offered to sign, and support for David's cause spanned the entire political spectrum by the time he was released.

Segal was once asked to sum up his political outlook. He said he aspired to a "maximum of unity among Jews. But one must never concede a matter of principle," then added that "with an enemy one must never concede anything, even if it's not a matter of principle."

Tehomi, too, retained his legendary bearing to old age. He'd worked with the Free French in Lebanon during World War Two, sending agents to spy on German and Vichy officials in Beirut. As Rommel inched closer to Eretz Israel, Tehomi assembled a sabotage unit of Arabic-speaking Jews. He was arrested by the British and eventually left for America where he aided the Bergson group in its propaganda efforts for the Underground. After the war he dabbled in jewels in Hong Kong, Jerusalem and Santa Monica. Even at 88, all who managed to find Tehomi knew they were addressing a born commander, an exceptional man of charisma. Tehomi died in California in 1991, after a long illness.

Benjamin Zeroni is another fighter who has not changed much with the passage of time. He is still quick tempered and still accompanied by a dog. A visitor to his expansive villa in north Tel Aviv will most likely meet the dog first. As the stately door opens, the unrestrained attack dog jumps and sinks its teeth into rather sensitive parts of the visitor's body. Zeroni has trained him well.

Zeroni's "wild driver" in the Yazur attack in 1937 became a wild pilot two years later. Benjamin Kahane was in the first graduating class of Eretz Israel's first flying school, which was run by Betar. Kahane received his pilot's license from the British High Commissioner himself. In the 1956 Sinai Campaign, Israeli Air Force Colonel Kahane was killed piloting his Piper, after successfully fighting off four Egyptian MIGs. He was granted a posthumous purple heart by Chief of

Staff Moshe Dayan. Eilat's central park is named in Kahane's honor, as is the Eilat aquarium, which he founded shortly before he was killed.

Not long after the founding of Israel in 1948, an unemployed Haim Dviri sat in a Tel Aviv cafe chatting with a few of the fellas from Lehi. "It was one of the first times we spoke aloud. We were more accustomed to whispering," he says. A neighboring customer approached their table: "Excuse me, gentlemen, but I can tell from your conversation you are Lehi men...I was just asked to work getting land ready for

Haim Dviri, as he looked when exiled to Kenya in the 1940s

301

makeshift tent-cities for the new immigrants from Iraq, and I need someone who'll work like he did in the Underground – that is, from morning to night and then at night as if it were day." Dviri had been exiled for years in African detention camps and was anxious to work. Needless to say, considering Dviri's background, the sites he chose were developed regardless of the obstacles mayors, neighbors or bureaucrats put in his way. Dviri took to his work and rose steadily to a high position in the government's Ministry of Housing before departing for the private sector. He counted himself among the founding members of the Tehiya political party and, some sixty-odd years after his first Brit Habirionim rallies, Dviri was still marching. He attended all the big rallies in Jerusalem against any deals to turn the land of Eretz Israel over to the PLO.

Another man who in his eighties had lost none of his charm or commitment was Defender of Jerusalem Ben Zion Homsky. Incarcerated with Jabotinsky, Homsky once struck a fellow prisoner who broke ranks during a hunger fast. Jabo witnessed the blow and passed Homsky a postcard inscribed "To my loyal friend: In truth, never is there need to lose your temper." Homsky was deported by the British in 1927. His little son entertained himself on Jabo's lap during one of the great statesman's visits to the Homsky home in France. The son managed to wet both his own and Jabotinsky's pants. The elder Homskys were horrified but Jabo just laughed. "Don't worry," he said, "this boy will one day be an officer in the army of a Jewish state." Little Paul would later adopt the last name Kedar and serve as a colonel in the Israeli Air Force.

Homsky himself fought the Nazis and was taken prisoner in 1944. At war's end he hunted Nazis in Germany, then returned to Eretz Israel and assisted in keeping open the lines of communication between the Hagana, Irgun and Lehi. When war broke out in 1956 he volunteered but was turned down as too old. The restless 60 year old set up, on his own initiative, a roving library to supply injured soldiers with reading material. Twenty-five years later he hadn't yet taken a single day off.

Even after Yom Kippur, he went to work following the fast. Homsky's library by this time kept the entire army supplied with books and magazines in every language necessary and some that weren't. Over 80, Homsky was still doing nighttime guard duty in the Civil Guard.

Shortly after Esther Halevy pledged allegiance to the Irgun over a Bible and gun, she exchanged the gun for a shofar. Wanting to play it safe and get a head start, she rose early one Yom Kippur in the late 1930s and smuggled a shofar into the Western Wall area at 4 A.M. She spent the next 14 hours praying and pacing, then delivered the shofar to the Irgunist who blew it to signal the end of the fast. Following her Underground service and a stint in the Israeli War of Independence, Halevy pursued a career in education. In the 1990s, the municipality of Jerusalem named Halevy a city elder in recognition of her having endeared herself to 43 years worth of students. Today, in her eighties, Halevy continues to rise early and is usually one of the first to arrive for work at the Likud Party's Jerusalem headquarters, where she is the receptionist. Though dedicated to today's party, she says she misses the leadership of Menahem Begin.

Former Birion Avigdor Kipnis reports that Arye Bayevsky, the Russian who had issued off-color orders to shoot, later wrote articles and songs and for fun held up drug-running boats coming down the coast from Lebanon. He and a buccaneering friend would board the boats and at knifepoint demand "protection" money. Back on shore they would use the proceeds to throw parties for local unfortunates. Bayevsky was "drafted" by Yirmiyahu Halperin to assist him in training Jewish sailors and died of a sea-contracted illness in 1942. Captain Halperin, often called the Father of the Jewish Navy, commanded Betar's Maritime School in Italy and ran arms for the Allies with the Norwegian Navy in the Second World War.

Menachem Lewin was befriended after his arrest in 1939 by Hebrew University president Judah Magnes. "I disagree with everything you believe and I disagree with everything you do," Magnes told him, "but I salute the manner in which you fight for your beliefs." Magnes arranged for the incarcerated Lewin to receive chemistry books to keep up his studies and arranged a university stipend upon Lewin's release in 1942. In 1948 the Israeli Air Force asked Lewin to help set up a lab for the refining of oil. The Air Force had three planes and no fuel. Lewin's new laboratory evolved, eventually, into the Israel Aircraft Industries. Dr. Lewin later founded Israel's National Science Council, the Israel Fiber Institute, and in a fitting epitaph to the generosity of Judah Magnes, the Division of Polymer and Textile Chemistry at Hebrew University. Lewin has authored 25 books, holds 29 patents, and at the age of 84 continues to lecture half of every year at the Brooklyn Polytechnic Institute, edit international journals and chair international scientific conferences.

Joshua Cohen was, after many evasions, finally arrested in October 1944. The British seemed to have been as impressed by Cohen's legend as were Cohen's fellow Sternists. The police were so convinced of his daring that they imagined him acting the part of an Arab, hiding among his arch-enemies in an Arab village near Tulkarm. He was finally caught sitting in a Jerusalem café.

Though Cohen did not give up without a struggle, once in custody he did not maintain any pretenses. He admitted membership in the Stern Group, refused to divulge any data about the organization, and declared: "The Stern Group [members] definitely regard the British authorities as their enemy, mainly by virtue of the fact that the British are in occupation of this country; and the Group [members] regard their fight as a justified one..." Cohen went on to refer to establishment leaders who opposed the Underground as "quislings," endorse the death sentence passed on Wilkins and express the view that the entire Jewish community "sympathized with the efforts of the Stern Group to make Great Britain relinquish her hold on one of her Imperial possessions." The detective questioning Cohen reported that, like other Sternists, Cohen "would appear to border on insanity."

Within two months, Cohen was deported to Africa.

Upon his return to Eretz Israel – by then the State of Israel – Cohen rejoined the ranks and pulled the trigger on United Nations mediator Count Folke Bernadotte, who had come to Israel to ensure that Jerusalem would not be part of the Jewish state.

Joshua Cohen became one of the founders of Kibbutz Sde Boker in the Negev and helped arrange Ben Gurion's relocation there, at one point becoming Ben Gurion's bodyguard. Cohen fed and cared for the old man when no one else would. On the wall of Cohen's house was a picture of Hadrian, the Roman who crushed the Bar Kochba Revolt. To Hadrian's left hung a photo of Sir Alan Cunningham, the last British High Commissioner, saluting the British flag as it came down in Eretz Israel. "Look where you are and look where we are," Cohen would say. On a shelf above his bed he kept a prayer book lifted from a concentration camp. Our heroism was nothing compared to the heroism of Jews in that hell, he believed.

But the strangest transformation of all was undoubtedly that of Yoshke Eliav. Yoshke, "the Mad Bomber," bank robber and arms dealer par excellence, wanted or arrested in more countries than many people visit, his picture on the front page of England's *Daily Mail*, his bombs planted in the Colonial Office in London and over 70 of his letter bombs sent to British officials (for which he was arrested and jailed in Belgium), returned to Eretz Israel and headed...the Brink's armored car company responsible for guarding and transporting money to, from and inside local banks. At least two of the electronics experts with whom Yoshke worked in Jerusalem morphed into cabinet ministers: Haim Corfu, inventor of letter-bombs and exploding chocolates, served as Israel's minister of transportation for most of the 1980s, and Yaacov Meridor, inventor of exploding suitcases and later Commander in Chief of the Irgun, served as Menahem Begin's minister for economic development.

Rahamim Mizrahi, who sounded the shofar at the Western Wall

twice and who hoped to one day be prime minister of a Jewish state, was one of the first youths deported to Africa. He escaped from his detention camp, organized the successful escape of over fifty fellow prisoners, was arrested later with the other escapees, escaped a second time (while being led to court to stand trial for his first escape), was again caught, and managed to escape yet a third time from behind the barbed wires, together with Yaacov Meridor and several others. Apprehended before he could leave the African continent, Mizrahi was returned to Israel after the state's establishment and, pausing only long enough to marry his girlfriend, immediately joined the army. He was killed in the War of Independence, defending Jerusalem.

Abba Ahimeir continued his professorial duties, lecturing in the

Escape artists Rahamim Mizrahi (left) and former Commander in Chief of the Irgun, Yaacov Meridor, in detention in Africa, 1947

1940s on "Fundamental Issues in the History of Israel" to young Irgunists supposedly registered for first-aid training, a cover for the preparation of cadres of future combatants. Ahimeir pursued a literary and journalistic career till his death in 1962. Yehoshua Yevin continued his prodigious output, writing for the daily *Haboker* and retranslating, with others, the books of Herzl. In his later years he took the title of Israel's second "Bible champion," winning the national competition of Biblical scholarship in a nation of Bible scholars. In preparation for the contest Yevin's wife read the entire Bible, once, to the almost blind gentleman. Other than this one read-through he depended entirely on his earlier memories of the Holy Book, yet was still able to claim the prize. At Passover, too, he continued to lead the family seder, reciting the entire Hagada, word for word, from memory.

Uri Zvi Greenberg was awarded the prestigious Bialik Prize for his poetry – three times. He was elected to Israel's first Knesset in 1949 as the number two man on the Herut list, right after the party leader, Menahem Begin. In his first address to the plenum he said: "I must set, with your kind permission, the correct terms to be used in this

Dr. Y. H. Yevin

307

great institution: The nation's Jerusalem – lies between the walls and includes the Temple Mount. Outside the walls lie the outskirts of Jerusalem...A Hebrew Jerusalem saves the coastal plain, the state's honor, our bodies...Without her there's no redemption, all we build is nothing, and there's no road to true Israeli freedom."

Shortly before his death in the 1980s, Moshe Segal delivered a lecture in a school high above the Western Wall. He was so weak he literally had to be carried up the steps to the lecture hall. "Jewish history is so long," he opened, "and it is just beginning..." "'Your hands have established the Temple of God, and God will reign forever and

Poet Uri Zvi Greenberg, rifle in hand, with the Israeli troops on Temple Mount immediately after the liberation of Jerusalem in 1967

ever,'" Segal continued, quoting from the Bible. "Note that the first clause is the basis for the second: The establishment of the Temple is the basis, the foundation, of God's reign...The Temple Mount is within our grasp, theoretically under Israeli sovereignty...We could be free – yet we insist on remaining slaves. It is a form of *avoda zara* [idol worship] to look to other peoples for recognition. Freedom is not bestowed; it must be taken.

"Slaves want immediate gratification, they do not care about the future or the past. We cannot act in this manner. We cannot limit ourselves to our personal *teshuva* [repentance] or improvement and forget about all the rest. We have a responsibility to our people. We must heal the sick body which does not want to be free. We must stir our people to desire freedom; we are part of the sick body.

"When we will have full and real sovereignty over the Mount our sovereignty over all Israel will be different – as, for example, when the heart or brain is healed the whole body is healthier.

"Our destiny will be fulfilled, our purpose realized, when God will be one, and the Kingdom of Israel will be whole, and the Temple will be standing."

Yevin concluded his *Jerusalem Awaits* in 1931: "Outside, in the stillness of night, it didn't seem as if Jerusalem were sleeping, it seemed as if Jerusalem were waiting..."

She still is.

Index

311